THE DEAD THAT WALK

By the same author

Halliwell's Filmgoer's Companion
Halliwell's Film Guide
Halliwell's Hundred
Seats in All Parts: Half a Lifetime at the Movies

THE DEAD THAT WALK

Dracula, Frankenstein, the Mummy, and Other Favorite Movie Monsters

Leslie Halliwell

A Frederick Ungar Book

CONTINUUM • NEW YORK

1988

The Continuum Publishing Company
370 Lexington Avenue
New York, NY 10017

Copyright © 1986 by Leslie Halliwell

First published 1986 by Grafton Books,
a division of the Collins Publishing Group, London

Printed in the United States of America

Library of Congress Cataloging-in-Publication Data

Halliwell, Leslie.
  The dead that walk/Leslie Halliwell.
  p.   cm.
  Includes index.
  ISBN 0-8044-2300-8
  1. Horror films—History and criticism. 2. Monsters in motion
  pictures. 3. Death in motion pictures. I. Title.   II. Series:
  Halliwell, Leslie. Halliwell's moving pictures.
  PN1995.9.H6H35   1988
  791.43'09'0916—dc19   87-30062
                                                CIP

THIS BOOK IS DEDICATED
to Jimmie Beattie, in whose
company on a stormy night in 1944
I saw my first horror film
The Bride of Frankenstein.
It still seems the best.

CONTENTS

ACKNOWLEDGEMENTS

Although the aim of these essays is to take a reasonably comprehensive overview of the walking dead in motion pictures, and of the literary origins thereof, the chief burden of the story must concern the fantasies made at Universal Studios between 1930 and 1945, and by Hammer Films between 1956 and 1972. In respect of the former I am grateful for the help of Mr Don Gate of MCA TV, and in respect of the latter for that of Messrs Brian Lawrence and Roy Skeggs of the 'new' Hammer. Thanks, too, to the many previous writers on allied subjects, and to the stills department of the National Film Archive.

A still which expresses our theme. Una O'Connor, the archetypal frightened servant, is confronted in *The Bride of Frankenstein* by the monster she thought dead. But Boris Karloff is just a little singed around the temples, otherwise as bad as new. Note the asphalt-layer's boots to add height and clumsiness, and the shortened sleeves to add grotesqueness. The lowering skies add the final frisson of shivery horror; but there is also, as with all good horror films, a fine sense of comedy.

Introduction

A WORLD OF GODS AND MONSTERS

> A woman sits alone in her house. She knows, absolutely, that she is the only living being left on earth. The doorbell rings.

That is a very old candidate for the title of shortest short story, but it adequately illustrates one of our most fearful hopes, or hopeful fears: that the dead can return. It's a mental possibility that goes back, in all probability, to our prehistoric ancestors. The body stops, and can be put to no further use. It must be consigned to the scrap heap, like a broken cup or a clapped-out car. Yet the human mind is attuned to pleasant optimism, and a doubt still lingers. Surely a human body is not just a thing? It has an accumulation of experience, a personality, a few opinions, something extra that has been called a soul. It may well have educated itself into wisdom; very probably it has characteristics which have made it beloved; if it reached a fair age it will almost certainly have begotten dependants among whom its achievements command respect. Must all these admirable, interesting and unique facets be thrown away along with the carcass? Many of us have preferred to think otherwise, and the result has been a proliferation of religions preaching some sort of regeneration and rebirth, usually in an improved and purified spiritual form. Sometimes, however, higher thought is not involved, only a selfish continuance of the wicked pleasures of this life: 'If he can't take it with him,' ran the caption to a *New Yorker* cartoon, 'he's decided he ain't gonna go.' It is usually rich, powerful and corrupt people who have these fancies: mad doctors and millionaires. We have all seen them in the movies, cackling their impossible dreams and coming a cropper at the end. Probably we have all wished that just occasionally they might prove their points, and that is why we still cling to a number of primitive legends of death, despite the advance of physical science which tells us all too clearly what happens when our vital organs cease to function. Storytellers throughout history elaborated on these legends, because there was always a ready public for them; and it is on three such stories, as fancified and popularized in the movies, that this book will concentrate.

There are of course commentators who would include on this level of fancy the supposed resurrection of Jesus Christ from the tomb. Certainly the truth of that famous proposition cannot be demonstrated. It is the epitome of the desirable unprovable, and when confronted by questions and nagging doubts Christian teachers can only urge their followers to have faith. Faiths having become a little tarnished in the twentieth century, it has been asked why the truth could not have been made more evident. Why *did* Christ reappear after his apparent death only to a few disciples and acquaintances? Would it not have been more effective to tap Pontius Pilate on the shoulder while he was holding court, thereby establishing Christianity once and for all without the necessity for several centuries of achingly slow growth? The reason why the entire Roman and Jewish world was not astonished in this way may just be that the resurrection was a public relations exercise by the disciples; in other words, it never happened; it was wishful thinking. On the other hand the modern weavers of myth, especially in Hollywood, have often found that belief is stronger if absolute proof is lacking. They tell you the story with all possible emotional force, but they insert a disclaimer, a caveat, a loophole to satisfy the unbelievers (who on recognizing it may choose to ignore it after all). One remembers that when David O. Selznick was spinning a particularly tall tale of love and death called *Portrait of Jennie*, he persuaded the ace screenwriter Ben Hecht to compose one of his most artful introductions, which ran as follows:

> Since time began man has looked into the awesome reaches of infinity and asked the eternal questions: What is time? What is life? What is space? What is death? Through a hundred civilizations, philosophers and scientists have come with answers, but the bewilderment remains . . . Science tells us that nothing ever dies but only changes, that time does not pass but only curves around us, and that the past and the future are together at our side for ever. Out of the shadows of knowledge, and out of a painting that hung on a museum wall comes our story, the truth of which lies not on our screen but in your hearts.

That is indeed a choice morsel of Hollywoodiana which deserves to endure as long as *Citizen Kane*, for it exemplifies the mass entertainer's way of eating his cake and still having it, of providing what the public wants but giving no guarantees. The same Mr Hecht expressed a similar concept even more briefly when introducing *The Song of Bernadette*: 'To those who believe, no explanation is necessary. To those who do not believe, no explanation is possible.' And so our three fairy tales for grown-ups, all blessed by a literary heritage but reduced by familiarity to the level of comic strips and worse, may lodge more securely in your hearts than in your minds. But they do lodge, somewhere.

In this investigation we speak not of ghosts or poltergeists but of the survival of the body itself in some horrendous form. And we shall find that in every case the storyteller's moral, his justification, is his ability to point to the folly of human dabbling in matters which cannot be fully understood by the mind of man. This was the point of a chilling story written in 1902 by a storyteller named W. W. Jacobs, who usually confined his interest to nautical matters but came up surprisingly with a classic of the macabre in 'The Monkey's Paw'. It is a short enough story, but I will make it shorter still. It concerns a cosy middle-aged couple, the Whites, who seem to be on the wrong side of middle age. Their adored son Herbert lives at home with them, and works at Maw and Meggins. This happy trio one evening entertains an old acquaintance called Sergeant-Major Morris, back home from India after twenty-one years, and bearing in his pocket a fragment of ancient magic:

> His three listeners leaned forward eagerly. The visitor absent-mindedly put his empty glass to his lips and then set it down again. His host filled it for him.
>
> 'To look at,' said the sergeant-major, fumbling in his pocket, 'it's just an ordinary little paw, dried to a mummy.'
>
> He took something out of his pocket and proffered it. Mrs White drew back with a grimace, but her son, taking it, examined it curiously.
>
> 'And what is there special about it?' inquired Mr White as he took it from his son, and having examined it, placed it upon the table.
>
> 'It had a spell put on it by an old fakir,' said the sergeant-major, 'a very holy man. He wanted to show that fate ruled people's lives, and that those who interfered with it did so to their sorrow. He put a spell on it so that three separate men could each have three wishes from it.'
>
> His manner was so impressive that his hearers were conscious that their light laughter jarred somewhat.
>
> 'Well, why don't you have three, sir?' said Herbert White cleverly.
>
> The soldier regarded him in the way that middle age is wont to regard presumptuous youth. 'I have,' he said quietly, and his blotchy face whitened.
>
> 'And did you really have the three wishes granted?' asked Mrs White.
>
> 'I did,' said the sergeant-major, and his glass tapped against his strong teeth.
>
> 'And has anybody else wished?' persisted the old lady.
>
> 'The first man had his three wishes. Yes,' was the reply; 'I don't know what the first two were, but the third was for death. That's how I got the paw.'

The hint is not taken by the Whites, for whom greed is stronger than fear. The old man rescues the paw when the sergeant-major tries to burn it, and late that night, alone with his family, he somewhat shamefacedly wishes for two hundred pounds. Nothing happens at once, except that he feels the paw twist in his hands; and next morning Herbert goes to work as usual. It is at dinner time that the horror begins. A well-dressed stranger, sent from Maw and Meggins, calls on an awkward errand. There has been an accident; Herbert is badly hurt, very badly; in fact he is dead. He was . . . caught in the machinery.

> 'Caught in the machinery,' repeated Mr White, in a dazed fashion, 'yes.'
>
> He sat staring blankly out at the window, and taking his wife's hand between his own, pressed it as he had been wont to do in their old courting days nearly forty years before.
>
> 'He was the only one left to us,' he said, turning gently to the visitor. 'It is hard.'
>
> The other coughed, and rising, walked slowly to the window. 'The firm wished me to convey their sincere sympathy with you in your great loss,' he said, without looking round. 'I beg that you will understand I am only their servant and merely obeying orders.'
>
> There was no reply; the old woman's face was white, her eyes staring, and her breath inaudible; on the husband's face was a look such as his friend the sergeant might have carried into his first action.
>
> 'I was to say that Maw and Meggins disclaim all responsibility,' continued the other. 'They admit no liability at all, but in consideration of your son's services, they wish to present you with a certain sum as compensation.'

Mr White dropped his wife's hand, and rising to his feet, gazed with a look of horror at his visitor. His dry lips shaped the words, 'How much?'

'Two hundred pounds,' was the answer.

Unconscious of his wife's shriek, the old man smiled faintly, put out his hands like a sightless man, and dropped, a senseless heap, to the floor.

In the huge new cemetery, some two miles distant, the old people buried their dead, and came back to the house steeped in shadow and silence. It was all over so quickly that at first they could hardly realise it, and remained in a state of expectation as though of something else to happen – something else which was to lighten this load, too heavy for old hearts to bear.

But the days passed, and expectation gave place to resignation – the hopeless resignation of the old, sometimes miscalled apathy. Sometimes they hardly exchanged a word, for now they had nothing to talk about, and their days were long to weariness.

It was about a week after, that the old man, waking suddenly in the night, stretched out his hand and found himself alone. The room was in darkness, and the sound of subdued weeping came from the window. He raised himself in bed and listened.

'Come back,' he said tenderly. 'You will be cold.'

'It is colder for my son,' said the old woman, and wept afresh.

The sound of her sobs died away on his ears. The bed was warm, and his eyes heavy with sleep. He dozed fitfully, and then slept until a sudden wild cry from his wife awoke him with a start.

'*The paw!*' she cried wildly. 'The monkey's paw!'

He started up in alarm. 'Where? Where is it? What's the matter?'

She came stumbling across the room toward him. 'I want it,' she said quietly. 'You've not destroyed it?'

'It's in the parlour, on the bracket,' he replied, marvelling. 'Why?'

She cried and laughed together, and bending over, kissed his cheek.

'I only just thought of it,' she said hysterically. 'Why didn't I think of it before? Why didn't *you* think of it?'

'Think of what?' he questioned.

'The other two wishes,' she replied rapidly. 'We've only had one.'

'Was not that enough?' he demanded fiercely.

'No,' she cried triumphantly; 'we'll have one more. Go down and get it quickly, and wish our boy alive again.'

The man sat up in bed and flung the bedclothes from his quaking limbs. 'Good God, you are mad!' he cried, aghast.

'Get it,' she panted; 'get it quickly, and wish – Oh, my boy, my boy!'

Her husband struck a match and lit the candle. 'Get back to bed,' he said unsteadily. 'You don't know what you are saying.'

'We had the first wish granted,' said the old woman feverishly; 'why not the second?'

'A coincidence,' stammered the old man.

'Go and get it and wish,' cried his wife, quivering with excitement.

The old man turned and regarded her, and his voice shook. 'He has been dead ten days, and besides he – I would not tell you else, but – I could only recognise him by his clothing. If he was too terrible for you to see then, how now?'

'Bring him back,' cried the old woman, and dragged him toward the door. 'Do you think I fear the child I have nursed?'

He went down in the darkness, and felt his way to the parlour, and then to the mantelpiece. The talisman was in its place, and a horrible fear that the unspoken wish might bring his mutilated son before him ere he could escape from the room seized upon him, and he caught his breath as he found that he had lost the direction of the

W. W. Jacobs, author of 'The Monkey's Paw'. A 1910 portrait.

door. His brow cold with sweat, he felt his way round the table, and groped along the wall until he found himself in the small passage with the unwholesome thing in his hand.

Even his wife's face seemed changed as he entered the room. It was white and expectant, and to his fears seemed to have an unnatural look upon it. He was afraid of her.

'*Wish!*' she cried, in a strong voice.

'It is foolish and wicked,' he faltered.

'*Wish!*' repeated his wife.

He raised his hand. 'I wish my son alive again.'

The talisman fell to the floor, and he regarded it fearfully. Then he sank trembling into a chair as the old woman, with burning eyes, walked to the window and raised the blind.

He sat until he was chilled with the cold, glancing occasionally at the figure of the old woman peering through the window. The candle-end, which had burned below the rim of the china candlestick, was throwing pulsating shadows on the ceiling and walls, until, with a flicker larger than the rest, it expired. The old man, with an unspeakable sense of relief at the failure of the talisman, crept back to his bed, and a minute or two afterward the old woman came silently and apathetically beside him.

Neither spoke, but lay silently listening to the ticking of the clock. A stair creaked, and a squeaky mouse scurried noisily through the wall. The darkness was oppressive, and after lying for some time screwing up his courage, he took the box of matches, and striking one, went downstairs for a candle.

At the foot of the stairs the match went out, and he paused to strike another; and at the same moment a knock, so quiet and stealthy as to be scarcely audible, sounded on the front door.

The matches fell from his hand and spilled in the passage. He stood motionless, his breath suspended until the knock was repeated. Then he turned and fled swiftly back to his room, and closed the door behind him. A third knock sounded through the house.

'*What's that?*' cried the old woman, starting up.

'A rat,' said the old man in shaking tones – 'a rat. It passed me on the stairs.'

His wife sat up in bed listening. A loud knock resounded through the house.

'It's Herbert!' she screamed. 'It's Herbert!'

She ran to the door, but her husband was before her, and catching her by the arm, held her tightly.

'What are you going to do?' he whispered hoarsely.

'It's my boy; it's Herbert!' she cried, struggling mechanically. 'I forgot it was two miles away. What are you holding me for? Let go. I must open the door.'

'For God's sake don't let it in,' cried the old man, trembling.

'You're afraid of your own son,' she cried, struggling. 'Let me go. I'm coming, Herbert; I'm coming.'

There was another knock, and another. The old woman with a sudden wrench broke free and ran from the room. Her husband followed to the landing, and called after her appealingly as she hurried downstairs. He heard the chain rattle back and the bottom bolt drawn slowly and stiffly from the socket. Then the old woman's voice, strained and panting.

'The bolt,' she cried loudly. 'Come down. I can't reach it.'

But her husband was on his hands and knees groping wildly on the floor in search of the paw. If he could only find it before the thing outside got in. A perfect fusillade of knocks reverberated through the house, and he heard the scraping of a chair as his wife put it down in the passage against the door. He heard the creaking of the bolt as it came slowly back, and at the same moment he found the monkey's paw, and frantically breathed his third and last wish.

The knocking ceased suddenly, although the echoes of it were still in the house. He heard the chair drawn back, and the door opened. A cold wind rushed up the staircase, and a long loud wail of disappointment and misery from his wife gave him courage to run down to her side, and then to the gate beyond. The street lamp flickering opposite shone on a quiet and deserted road.

'The Monkey's Paw' is a fable of great universal power, based on a fear which must have been handed down through the centuries; there are situations not dissimilar in the *Arabian Nights*. The fact that the story is not much revived these days may have something to do with the fact that it was once so popular: radio productions of it were legion through the forties and fifties, though it never seemed to film satisfactorily, probably because it refrains from showing its monster. I suspect however that it fell into disuse because for the unpleasant times we live in it comes too close to the heart of the matter. How can the principle of resurrection apply to someone who has been blown up by terrorists or mutilated by atomic war? 'The Monkey's Paw' is a story which shocks the mind. Nevertheless, our little grey cells will recover, and our pleasant fantasies will continue.

Unpleasant ones, also. The Gothick thriller (the extra 'k' seems to suggest an imitation of medieval originals, but if they existed they are lost to us) was a literary creation, largely of the nineteenth century; but in the twentieth it has become the staple of that most popular of art forms, the cinema. By courtesy of television and video the cinema has now penetrated all our living rooms, so that even those who would never have chosen to see a horror film can now scarcely fail to be aware of at least a few examples of the species. Meanwhile the short horror story has become the province of intellectuals, thanks to such scholarly practitioners as M. R. James, who can chill with a single word. His description of a ghost which 'ran very low' iced my spine in 'Martin's Close', and in 'The Tractate Middoth' he was almost as sparing in his account of a personage clearly long dead who is met by the hero among the more remote shelves of the Cambridge University Library:

> . . . there was my parson again, back to me, looking at the books on the shelf I wanted. His hat was on the table, and he had a bald head. I waited a second or two looking at him rather particularly. I tell you, he had a very nasty bald head. It looked to me dry, and it looked dusty, and the streaks of hair across it were much less like hair than cobwebs. Well, I made a bit of a noise on purpose, coughed and moved my feet. He turned round and let me see his face – which I hadn't seen before. I tell you again, I'm not mistaken. Though for one reason or another I didn't take in the lower part of his face, I did see the upper part; and it was perfectly dry, and the eyes were very deep-sunk; and over them, from the eyebrows to the cheekbone, there were *cobwebs* – thick. Now that closed me up, as they say, and I can't tell you anything more.

The audience's delight in having its flesh made to creep in this way is a happy circumstance for the film producers who over the last sixty years and more have made so much capital out of the fears of mankind, turning an age of galloping cynics into one filled with credulous fantasists who take E.T. and Indiana Jones and C3Po for their hero figures but are really more fascinated by the larger-than-life villains, and especially by the mysterious and magical killers of such claptrap as *Halloween* and *The Fog* and *The Amityville Horror*. But, no matter how many new concepts are added to the remoter galleries in the cinema's chamber of horrors, affection and admiration still vividly linger for the original three mythic figures exemplifying various forms of the walking dead: Dracula, the Mummy, and the Frankenstein monster. These living corpses, having transfixed two or three more naïve generations, are now accepted, in the age of doing one's own thing, as amiable eccentrics who have a perfect right to their peculiarities. They may have been dead to begin with, but the public does not insist that they lie down; and so this is the story of how they originally came to exist on the printed page, of how the cinema taught them to walk if not talk, and of how, having once been reanimated in the public imagination, they refused to die again. The Swedish Film Institute reported in 1985 that the key words in the titles of films shown in its country's cinemas have shown an interesting change of emphasis. In the 1930s the chief come-ons were LOVE, NIGHT, WOMAN, MAN, GIRL and ADVENTURE. By the end of the seventies, the top ten supposedly evocative words were, in this order, SEX, DEATH, LOVE (which, the Swedes note, is often used by porn films as meaning physical love), MAN, DEVIL, CHASE, BLOOD, LIFE, WILD and REVENGE. Curiously enough, every one of these elements is present in the first of the legends we shall explore, that of the vampire count of Transylvania.

Vampire stories date back to the Middle Ages and earlier: it seems that blood has always exerted a curious fascination over the mind of man. 'The life of the flesh is in the blood,' says Leviticus. The shedding of blood was always a feature of ritual sacrifice. Christ's blood is still drunk (by proxy) at communion services around the world; and in some parts of our continents cannibalism is still practised. In South America, of course, there is also a bloodsucking vampire bat, but this seems to have been named after the supernatural human form rather than vice versa. The word derives from an old Magyar concept meaning a reanimated corpse which lives by drawing blood from sleeping persons, and whatever sophisticated gloss critics may recently have put upon it, this is the essence of our research. ('Dracula', by the way, means son of the dragon, and was apparently a nickname given to the historical character Vlad Drakul, the Impaler, of whom more later; he was a spiller of blood rather than a sucker of it.) Some legends affirm that a vampire is the result of copulation between a witch and the Devil; be that as it may, our predecessors have accepted lore to the effect that the victims of vampires become vampires in their turn. Creatures of darkness, they cannot abide the light of day. By some accounts they can transform themselves into animals, or into mist; they shrink away from running water, from Christian symbols, and, for some mysterious reason, from garlic and wolfbane; they have foul breath and hairy palms; they cast neither shadows nor mirror reflections. If the vampire strays from home he must take with him a coffin containing earth of his homeland, and woe betide him if he does not return to it ere the first rays of dawn strike his pale flesh and wither it away to dust. Byron knew all about these weird creatures:

> But first on earth, as vampire sent,
> Thy corpse shall from the tomb be rent,
> Then ghastly haunt thy native place
> And suck the blood of all thy race.

Since vampire stories frequently turn on the revenge motif, they clearly include manifold possibilities for suspense and horror, while the fact that the victim is usually female, and the blood sucked from the neck, adds a macabre romantic touch that has undoubtedly been responsible for turning a morbid literary fancy into a stimulus for literally hundreds of commercially successful and increasingly

THE GOLEM (1920). Paul Wegener as the clay man of Jewish legend in a film which did much a decade later to stimulate Hollywood's interest in horror themes. Compare the monster's boots with those of Boris Karloff in the frontispiece; the meeting with the little girl was paralleled in the 1931 *Frankenstein* (see page 119).

sex-oriented feature films between 1922 and the present day. The flow of blood shows no sign of being stopped: 1985 was but a few days old when Icelandic TV, of all possible creators, offered its viewers a play set at night in Reykjavik's television station, with a mad young nightwatchman dressing up as a caped and fanged Dracula. The count seemed quite at home in these hitherto unfamiliar northern surroundings.

Frankenstein is also a name which has struck terror into generations of filmgoers: quite improperly, for the menace comes not from the man but from his ugly giant creation, known either as the creature or the monster. The more scientific theme here is what we would now call spare-part surgery: life being reconstituted by the assembly of the best parts from several dead bodies. The apparent immortality of the resulting monster is quite *un*scientific, but it was there by implication in Mary Shelley's novel of 1816, long before Hollywood got its hands on the property. For a hundred-odd years after the novel was published, the whole concept was taken to be the merest fantasy; in this age of heart and lung transplants, nobody can be quite so sure.

Mummies have struck awe into the minds of men ever since the first revelation by archaeologists of the curious funeral practices of the ancient Eygptians. Edgar Allan Poe, naturally in view of his prevailing melancholy, was obsessed by the idea of the infinite preservation of the body, and around the turn of the century such authors as Gautier and Conan Doyle were toying ingeniously with this aspect of the living dead, their reanimated corpses being driven by obsession rather than by all those centuries of acquired wisdom. But it was the events associated with the excavation of Tutankhamun's tomb in 1922 that gave a fresh and sinister impetus to the myth, an impetus on which Hollywood was not slow to capitalize.

The recycling of these and similar themes in film terms was begun by the Germans during their national depression after losing the First World War: powerful fantasy figures from Europe's past admirably suited the creative mood, especially if they could return from the dead (like Germany); so a whole world of Gothick romance was created, with Fritz Lang's *Die Nibelungen* in the vanguard. For our purposes the most interesting figures in this group are the Golem, and Cesare the somnambulist in *The Cabinet of Dr Caligari*; both are in a sense dead before the action begins, and both were amiably plundered by Hollywood ten years later. In this Californian lotus land, not far from the waters of the blue Pacific, it turned out to be the least artistic or imaginative of the major studios which picked up the European myths, squeezed them dry, and reduced them gradually to the lowest popular box-office level. Universal since its inception in 1915 had been run by a diminutive but hard-headed German called Carl Laemmle, who was content to churn out westerns and crime stories for the bottom end of the action market. In *The Phantom of the Opera* and *The Hunchback of Notre Dame* he had had two unexpected successes with grotesque themes; both had starred Lon Chaney, who was in great demand by other studios and who died in 1930 just as he was considering a return to Universal to play the title role in a property called *Dracula*, which had come Laemmle's way along with other successful Broadway plays. By a happy coincidence, however, certain other talents came to Laemmle's notice at around the same time, talents which revelled in the macabre and were

THE CABINET OF DR CALIGARI (Germany 1919). It is never made clear that Cesare (Conrad Veidt, right) is supposed to have been revived from the dead, but he lives in an upright box from which he emerges at the bidding of a mad scientist (Werner Krauss). The scene in which he kidnaps a virginal heroine, her white clothes trailing behind her, is also repeated in *Frankenstein* (see page 120).

admirably suited to it. They included actors Boris Karloff and Bela Lugosi; director James Whale; writers John Balderston, Garrett Fort and later R. C. Sherriff; make-up artist Jack Pierce; art director Charles D. Hall; and Laemmle's own son Carl Laemmle Jnr, a 22-year-old who masterminded the series and became known, like a character in *The Pickwick Papers*, as 'the boy who wants to make your flesh creep'. Another useful asset was the expensive exterior set of a German town, built for Universal's most prestigious production *All Quiet on the Western Front* (and still standing 55 years later, the oldest set in Hollywood); there was obvious economic sense in generating films which by their period European settings could make regular use of it.

It transpired that the enthusiasm for horrors was not confined to goggle-eyed American teenagers. Despite the frequent disapproval of Authority, all the world lapped up Universal's charnel-house fantasies, and when in 1936 the original *Dracula* and *Frankenstein* were reissued on a double bill, the response was so overwhelming that the genre promptly got a second wind which lasted till the end of the forties. Yet when World War II broke out, the British censor banned cinematic horrors for the duration, a quite irrational act since it is during the dark days of war, with violent death all around and the likelihood of personal tragedy, that people need to be uplifted by the suggestion of supernatural forces pulling the strings, even by the suggestion of continued life in some form for those who have died in action. The film censor could not prevent, but must surely have remarked on, the astonishing popularity throughout the war years of a radio series called *Appointment with Fear*, its scary stories of ghosts and long-leggedy beasties brought to the nation by a sepulchral-toned 'Man in Black'.

Universal's original gallery of ghouls had of course admitted new members, some of them merely honorary. *The Mummy* first stalked in 1932. *The Invisible Man* appeared – and disappeared – in 1933, but he was a mere scientific dabbler, not even dead until the end of the film, when he came back to visibility if not to life. *The Old Dark House*, from the same director, could produce no sequels: it was a parable of post-war attitudes from the pen of J. B. Priestley, with Karloff's bearded butler as the beast in all of us, and God symbolized by a frail old man upstairs who has abdicated his responsibilities. Karloff and Lugosi together appeared to diminishing returns in *The Black Room*, *The Raven* and *The Invisible Ray*, without ever striking a contagious spark. Other studios were invading Universal's preserves with titles like *The Walking Dead*, *Dr X* and *Mystery of the Wax Museum*: the Laemmles required another self-propagating graveyard image in order to make their superiority in the field self-evident. In 1933 they thought they had it when they read the reviews of a Guy Endore novel called *Werewolf of Paris*, based on another European legend bearing a distinct resemblance to vampirism. Unfortunately they abandoned the novel's convoluted plotline and substituted an inferior one of their own, not to mention an unsympathetic hero; but they worked for seven years to correct that mistake, and when *The Wolf Man* emerged in 1941 it was the studio's top box office hit of the year, starting Lon Chaney Jnr on a successful series career as the hairy hero. But the wolf man was not by definition one of the undead, and became so only by Universal box-office fiat.

From time to time another major Hollywood studio might dubiously set foot inside the graveyard, and in the sixties and seventies there poured from foreign-speaking countries a deluge of horrific exploitation pieces which seldom reached the major outlets. But it was Universal, even in the days of Hammer and later of parodies like *The Munsters*, which constantly gave the genre its forward thrust, and if even today you take Universal's studio tour – which ranks as the number one tourist attraction in Southern California – you are likely to find yourself hosted by one of the famous monsters. Familiarity has made them friends of everybody's family, handing out smiles and thrills and a vague expectation that with a little bit of luck all our mundane lives can be redirected by supernatural forces. Laurence Olivier's was: as late as 1979 he was playing Van Helsing to Frank Langella's Dracula in an umpteenth version which failed because it tried to be too clever. In myth it is the original pure form which contains the power; variations, however ingenious, are generally doomed to disappointment.

In this book we trace, separately, three myths of the undead. In each essay the literary sources come first; next their treatment by Universal; then the variations by Hammer. Finally I have mentioned some of the cinematic additions to the myth since Hammer shut up shop in the early seventies; but no reporter could hope to enumerate all of them, for although horror is still big business around the world, some of the more local experiments in the genre, like Dracula himself, do not travel well over water.

Christopher Lee, as Hammer's incarnation of a 'sexy Dracula', here adds another nubile victim to a list which is already long.

Chapter 1
THE DREAD OF DRACULA

'Rich, immortal, irresistible, and nearly omnipotent,' writes Les Daniels, 'Dracula is the embodiment of an unleashed *id*, sleeping all day and spending his nights creeping into bedrooms. The sexual side of his ungentlemanly behaviour undoubtedly titillated Victorian readers; this is particularly evident in the incident of his first English victim Lucy Westenra, who keeps three suitors at arm's length while Dracula is turning her into a lustful fiend like himself. The highly-charged scene in which her frustrated admirers converge on her coffin to hammer a stake into her has overtones of a symbolic rape.'★

Well, myths can be interpreted in any number of ways. What's certain is that without Bram Stoker and the publication in 1897 of his sensational novel, the legend of the human vampire might not even have survived into the twentieth century. Never until then a professional writer, Stoker may have become interested in the Dracula image as a part worthy of his admired mentor and employer Sir Henry Irving, whose manager Stoker was for 25 years. Indeed, the role of the count would seem to have fitted Irving's declamatory style of acting, but it is unlikely that he ever thought of playing it, or even, after noting the book's instant notoriety, that Stoker ever suggested such a thing. Stoker may have been joking when he told the press that what inspired him to create *Dracula* was a nightmare brought about by a surfeit of dressed crab; he probably knew very well what he was up to, offering a fresh banquet of sensation to a public which clearly thrived on such things. The adventures of altruistic Dr Jekyll and evil Mr Hyde, also allegedly based on a bad dream, had been avidly followed on their publication in 1886, and Hyde had emerged the clear favourite with the groundlings. The detective processes in Stoker's fantasy, and the figure of the wise avenger Van Helsing, must have guaranteed the readership of the Sherlock Holmes devotees, who were already in full flourish. Indeed, in a 1978 pastiche called *The Adventure of the Sanguinary Count*, Dr Watson suggests (through his spokesman Loren D. Estleman) that without his friend Holmes's uncredited assistance Van Helsing might have had a harder time tracking down and staking his adversary:

★ In *Living with Fear* (Da Capo Press, 1975).

Dracula swung about with the speed of a panther caught between two marksmen. His expression when he saw me with his hostage was savage.

'Run, Watson, run!' In three leaps Sherlock Holmes succeeded in thrusting himself between the Count and the *Baltimore*. It was the bravest deed I have ever witnessed, my friend placing himself in the fiend's path and brandishing his revolver, as if it could be of any use against so impregnable a foe, that I might escape. I was so caught up in this spectacle that I did not give a thought to the welfare either of my wife or myself, and instead of running I remained rooted before the entrance to the captain's cabin. Dracula laughed.

'Fire your pitiable weapon, Sherlock Holmes,' he taunted. 'See what good it will do you against a man who commanded armies hundreds of years before you were born.'

Holmes fired, once, twice, thrice. He kept squeezing the trigger until the hammer clicked against an empty cylinder. When the smoke cleared the vampire was still standing. His laugh was hideous. He swept Holmes aside, as at the slaughterhouse, with an indifferent arm and began climbing up the side of the vessel, upon which I was standing, in the manner of a lizard scaling a craggy rock.

'Run, Watson!' Holmes cried again, scrambling to his feet. 'As you value your life, flee!'

At last, with the fiend less than two yards away, the import of my friend's words struck home. I was on the point of leaping over the side, Mary and all, when I locked glances with Dracula – and froze.

'Mind his eyes! Their gaze is death!'

Dracula's undertones of sexual decadence, and the theme of a man keeping his youth by supernatural means, had much in common with Oscar Wilde's *The Picture of Dorian Gray*, published in 1890; while the lust for blood and the preference for women as victims must have further whetted the voracious appetites of readers of such dubious pornobiographies as *My Secret Life*, by 'Walter', which proliferated in the nineties. *Dracula* fits snugly into an age when the male was dominant in society and minds were alert to the fantastic possibilities of science but had not abandoned their long-held faith in other worlds than ours, an age when gaslight was a useful reality but the motor car was still being ridiculed. Even the famous pea-souper fogs of London would provide the Count with just the right cover for his nefarious wanderings, while the mists arising from our dewy countryside must have reminded him affectingly of his native Transylvania. The busy travelling from place to place in the book would appeal to a time when the Grand Tour was being replaced by Cook's Tours. Setting aside his unusual personal proclivities, the Count could have passed for a typical late Victorian upper-class Londoner, a clubbable man and, in his black suit and cape, a fashionable figure. The scheming and evil husband in Patrick Hamilton's much later Victorian thriller *Gaslight* would have warmed to him.

Dracula is a long novel, four times the length of *Dr Jekyll and My Hyde*, and like the latter it is written in the form of letters and diary extracts. This renders its startling events sufficiently plausible for Stoker's purpose, though a more direct method would surely have resulted in a tighter narrative. Originally it was to have been even longer, starting at an earlier point in the unlikely journey of the apprentice estate agent, Jonathan Harker, from Exeter to Transylvania in order to go over the details of a London house with the mysterious nobleman who proposes to buy it. (One deleted chapter, a preliminary episode containing a warning of what is to come, was later published as a separate story, 'Dracula's Guest'.) The novel as we have it begins with Harker at Bistritz, and since by common consent the early chapters, depicting his first meeting with a man whom he realizes only gradually must be a vampire, are the most atmospheric as well as the best written, here are some excerpts to give the flavour, beginning with Harker's account of his first hours at Dracula's castle after being picked up at the Borgo Pass by a calash whose mysterious driver, later revealed to be Count Dracula himself, gives him a nightmare journey before depositing him at the castle gateway.

I heard a heavy step approaching behind the great door, and saw through the chinks the gleam of a coming light. Then there was the sound of rattling chains and the clanking of massive bolts drawn back. A key was turned with the loud grating noise of long disuse, and the great door swung back.

Within, stood a tall old man, clean shaven save for a long white moustache, and clad in black from head to foot, without a single speck of colour about him anywhere. He held in his hand an antique silver lamp, in which the flame burned without chimney or globe of any kind, throwing long quivering shadows as it flickered in the draught of the open door. The old man motioned me in with his right hand with a courtly gesture, saying in excellent English, but with a strange intonation:—

'Welcome to my house! Enter freely and of your own will!' He made no motion of stepping to meet me, but stood like a statue, as though his gesture of welcome had fixed him into stone. The instant, however, that I had stepped over the threshold, he moved impulsively forward, and holding out his hand grasped mine with a strength which made me wince, an effect which was not lessened by the fact that it seemed as cold as ice – more like the hand of a dead than a living man. Again he said:—

'Welcome to my house. Come freely. Go safely; and leave something of the happiness you bring!' The strength of the handshake was so much akin to that which I had noticed in the driver, whose face I had not seen, that for a moment I doubted if it were not the same person to whom I was speaking; so to make sure, I said interrogatively:—

'Count Dracula?' He bowed in a courtly way as he replied:—

'I am Dracula; and I bid you welcome, Mr Harker, to my house. Come in; the night air is chill, and you must need to eat and rest.' As he was speaking he put the lamp on a bracket on the wall, and stepping out, took my luggage; he had carried it in before I could forestall him. I protested but he insisted:—

'Nay, sir, you are my guest. It is late, and my people are not available. Let me see to your comfort myself.' He insisted on carrying my traps along the passage, and then up a great winding stair, and along another great passage, on whose stone floor our steps rang heavily. At the end of this he threw open a heavy door, and I rejoiced to see within a well-lit room in which a table was spread for supper, and on whose mighty hearth a great fire of logs flamed and flared.

The Count halted, putting down my bags, closed the door, and crossing the room, opened another door, which led into a small octagonal room lit by a single lamp, and seemingly without a window of any sort. Passing through this, he opened another door, and motioned me to enter. It was a welcome sight; for here was a great bedroom well lighted and warmed with another log fire, which sent a hollow roar up the wide chimney. The Count himself left my luggage inside and withdrew, saying, before he closed the door:—

'You will need, after your journey, to refresh yourself by making your toilet. I trust you will find all you wish. When you are ready come into the other room, where you will find your supper prepared.' . . .

The Count himself came forward and took off the cover of a dish, and I fell to at once on an excellent roast chicken. This, with some cheese and a salad and a bottle of old Tokay, of which I had two glasses, was my supper. During the time I was eating it the Count asked me many questions as to my journey, and I told him by degrees all I had experienced.

By this time I had finished my supper, and by my host's desire had drawn up a chair by the fire and begun to smoke a cigar which he offered me, at the same time excusing himself that he did not smoke. I had now an opportunity of observing him, and found him of a very marked physiognomy.

His face was a strong – a very strong – aquiline, with high bridge of the thin nose and peculiarly arched nostrils; with lofty domed forehead, and hair growing scantily round the temples, but profusely elsewhere. His eyebrows were very massive, almost meeting over the nose, and with bushy hair that seemed to curl in its own profusion. The mouth, so far as I could see it under the heavy moustache, was fixed and rather cruel-looking, with peculiarly sharp white teeth; these protruded over the lips, whose remarkable ruddiness showed astonishing vitality in a man of his years. For the rest, his ears were pale and at the tops extremely pointed; the chin was broad and strong, and the cheeks firm though thin. The general effect was one of extraordinary pallor.

Hitherto I had noticed the backs of his hands as they lay on his knees in the firelight, and they had seemed rather white and fine; but seeing them now close to me, I could not but notice that they were rather coarse – broad, with squat fingers. Strange to say, there were hairs in the centre of the palm. The nails were long and fine, and cut to a sharp point. As the Count leaned over me and his hands touched me, I could not repress a shudder. It may have been that his breath was rank, but a horrible feeling of nausea came over me, which, do what I would, I could not conceal. The Count, evidently noticing it, drew back; and with a grim sort of smile, which showed more than he had yet done his protuberant teeth, sat himself down again on his own side of the fireplace. We were both silent for a while; and as I looked towards the window I saw the first dim streak of the coming dawn. There seemed a strange stillness over everything; but as I listened I heard as if from down below in the valley the howling of many wolves. The Count's eyes gleamed, and he said:—

'Listen to them – the children of the night. What music they make!' Seeing, I suppose, some expression in my face strange to him, he added:—

'Ah, sir, you dwellers in the city cannot enter into the feelings of the hunter.' Then he rose and said:—

'But you must be tired. Your bedroom is all ready, and to-morrow you shall sleep as late as you will. I have to be away till the afternoon; so sleep well and dream well!' and, with a courteous bow, he opened for me himself the door to the octagonal room, and I entered my bedroom . . .

I am all in a sea of wonders. I doubt; I fear; I think strange things which I dare not confess to my own soul. God keep me, if only for the sake of those dear to me!

7 May. – It is again early morning, but I have rested and enjoyed the last twenty-four hours. I slept till late in the day, and awoke of my own accord. When I had dressed myself I went into the room where we had supped, and found a cold breakfast laid out, with coffee kept hot by the pot being placed on the hearth. There was a card on the table, on which was written:—

'I have to be absent for a while. Do not wait for me. – D.' So I set to and enjoyed a hearty meal. When I had done, I looked for a bell, so that I might let the servants know I had finished; but I could not find one. There are certainly odd deficiencies in the house, considering the extraordinary evidences of wealth which are round me. The table service is of gold, and so beautifully wrought that it must be of immense value. The curtains and upholstery of the chairs and sofas and the hangings of my bed are of the costliest and most beautiful fabrics, and must have been of fabulous value when they were made, for they are centuries old, though in excellent order. I saw something like them in Hampton Court, but there they were worn and frayed and moth-eaten. But still in none of the rooms is there a mirror. There is not even a toilet glass on my table, and I had to get the little shaving glass from my bag before I could either shave or brush my hair. I have not yet seen a servant anywhere, or heard a sound near the castle except the howling of wolves. When I had finished my meal – I do not know whether to call it breakfast or dinner, for it was between five and six o'clock when I had it – I looked about for something to read, for I did not like to go about the castle until I had asked the Count's permission. There was absolutely nothing in the room, book, newspaper, or even writing materials; so I opened another door in the room and found a sort of library. The door opposite mine I tried, but found it locked.

In the library I found, to my great delight, a vast number of English books, whole shelves full of them, and bound volumes of magazines and newspapers. A table in the centre was littered with English magazines and newspapers, though none of them were of very recent date. The books were of the most varied kind – history, geography, politics, political economy, botany, geology, law – all relating to England and English life and customs and manners. There were even such books of reference as the London Directory, the 'Red' and 'Blue' books, Whitaker's Almanack, the Army and Navy Lists, and – it somehow gladdened my heart to see it – the Law List.

Whilst I was looking at the books, the door opened, and the Count entered. He saluted me in a hearty way, and hoped that I had had a good night's rest.

They converse of Transylvanian legend and tradition, and of Dracula's proposed purchase of an estate in England. It is a cosy evening, but early next day the real horror begins, while Harker is making his toilet:

I had hung my shaving glass by the window, and was just beginning to shave. Suddenly I felt a hand on my shoulder, and heard the Count's voice saying to me, 'Good-morning.' I started, for it amazed me that I had not seen him, since the reflection of the glass covered the whole room behind me. In starting I had cut myself slightly, but did not notice it at the moment. Having answered the Count's salutation, I turned to the glass again to see how I had been mistaken. This time there could be no error, for the man was close to me, and I could see him over my shoulder. But there was no reflection of him in the mirror! The whole room behind me was displayed; but there was no sign of a man in it, except myself. This was startling, and, coming on the top of so many strange things, was beginning to increase that vague feeling of uneasiness which I always have when the Count is near; but at the instant I saw that the cut had bled a little, and the blood was trickling over my chin. I laid down the razor, turning as I did so half round to look for some sticking plaster. When the Count saw my face, his eyes blazed with a sort of demoniac fury, and he suddenly made a grab at my throat. I drew away, and his hand touched the string of beads which held the crucifix. It made an instant change in him, for the fury passed so quickly that I could hardly believe that it was ever there.

'Take care,' he said, 'take care how you cut yourself. It is more dangerous than you think in this country.' Then seizing the shaving glass, he went on: 'And this is the wretched thing that has done the mischief. It is a foul bauble of man's vanity. Away with it!' and opening the heavy window with one wrench of his terrible hand, he flung out the glass, which was shattered into a thousand pieces on the stones of the courtyard far below. Then he withdrew without a word. It is very annoying, for I do not see how I am to shave, unless in my watch-case or the bottom of the shaving-pot, which is fortunately of metal.

When I went into the dining-room, breakfast was prepared; but I could not find the

Count anywhere. So I breakfasted alone. It is strange that as yet I have not seen the Count eat or drink. He must be a very peculiar man! After breakfast I did a little exploring in the castle. I went out on the stairs and found a room looking towards the south. The view was magnificent, and from where I stood there was every opportunity of seeing it. The castle is on the very edge of a terrible precipice. A stone falling from the window would fall a thousand feet without touching anything! As far as the eye can reach is a sea of green tree-tops, with occasionally a deep rift where there is a chasm. Here and there are silver threads where the rivers wind in deep gorges through the forests.

But I am not in heart to describe beauty, for when I had seen the view I explored further; doors, doors, doors everywhere, and all locked and bolted. In no place save from the windows in the castle walls is there an available exit.

The castle is a veritable prison, and I am a prisoner!

That evening the Count returns, and continues his impersonation of a genial host, even giving Harker a somewhat excited account of his heritage:

'We Szekelys have a right to be proud, for in our veins flows the blood of many brave races who fought as the lion fights, for lordship! . . . When, after the battle of Mohacs, we thrust off the Hungarian yoke, we of the Dracula blood were among the leaders, for our spirit would not brook that we were not free!'

Harker has by now surmised that he and his host (plus three deathly ladies, presumably the Count's mistresses, who materialize when they are thirsty for blood) are alone in the castle, and Dracula knows that he has surmised it, which is why he issues a grim little warning:

'Let me advise you, my dear young friend – nay, let me warn you with all seriousness, that should you leave these rooms you will not by any chance go to sleep in any other part of the castle. It is old, and has many memories, and there are bad dreams for those who sleep unwisely. Be warned! Should sleep now or ever overcome you, or be like to do, then haste to your own chamber or to these rooms, for your rest will then be safe. But if you be not careful in this respect, then' – He finished his speech in a gruesome way, for he motioned with his hands as if he were washing them. I quite understood; my only doubt was as to whether any dream could be more terrible than the unnatural, horrible net of gloom and mystery which seemed closing round me.

Later. – I endorse the last words written, but this time there is no doubt in question. I shall not fear to sleep in any place where he is not. I have placed the crucifix over the head of my bed – I imagine that my rest is thus freer from dreams; and there it shall remain.

When he left me I went to my room. After a little while, not hearing any sound, I came out and went up the stone stair to where I could look out towards the south. There was some sense of freedom in the vast expanse, inaccessible though it was to me, as compared with the narrow darkness of the courtyard. Looking out on this, I felt that I was indeed in prison, and I seemed to want a breath of fresh air, though it were of the night. I am beginning to feel this nocturnal existence tell on me. It is destroying my nerve. I start at my own shadow, and am full of all sorts of horrible imaginings. God knows that there is ground for any terrible fear in this accursed place! I looked out over the beautiful expanse, bathed in soft yellow moonlight till it was almost as light as day. In the soft light the distant hills became melted, and the shadows in the valleys and gorges of velvety blackness. The mere beauty seemed to cheer me; there was peace and comfort in every breath I drew. As I leaned from the window my eye was caught by something moving a storey below me, and somewhat to my left, where I imagined, from the lie of the rooms, that the windows of the Count's own room would look out. The window at which I stood was tall and deep, stone-mullioned, and though weather-worn, was still complete; but it was evidently many a day since the case had been there. I drew back behind the stonework, and looked carefully out.

What I saw was the Count's head coming out from the window. I did not see the face, but I knew the man by the neck and the movement of his back and arms. In any case I could not mistake the hands which I had had so many opportunities of studying. I was at first interested and somewhat amused, for it is wonderful how small a matter will interest and amuse a man when he is a prisoner. But my very feelings changed to repulsion and terror when I saw the whole man slowly emerge from the window and begin to crawl down the castle wall over that dreadful abyss, *face down*, with his cloak spreading out around him like great wings. At first I could not believe my eyes. I thought it was some trick of the moonlight, some weird effect of shadow; but I kept looking, and it could be no delusion. I saw the fingers and toes grasp the corners of the stones, worn clear of the mortar by the stress of years, and by thus using every projection and inequality move downwards with considerable speed, just as a lizard moves along a wall.

What manner of man is this, or what manner of creature is it in the semblance of man? I feel the dread of this horrible place overpowering me; I am in fear – in awful fear – and there is no escape for me; I am encompassed about with terrors that I dare not think of . . .

It has never been clear to me why Dracula, who has the ability to transform himself into a flying bat, should choose this singularly clumsy way of progressing from one room to another in his own castle. Nor can I understand what holds his cloak up, or whether he carries his shoes in his fangs. The sight nevertheless is sufficient, especially when repeated, to strike Harker into a state of abject terror; but he is not too far gone to resist the blandishments of Dracula's mistresses (who make do with a baby kidnapped by their master) or to continue his search of the labyrinthine old castle for a path to freedom. What he eventually finds is his host, sleeping off the excesses of the previous night, in a coffin-like box in the old chapel:

> The great box was in the same place, close against the wall, but the lid was laid on it, not fastened down, but with the nails ready in their places to be hammered home. I knew I must search the body for the key, so I raised the lid, and laid it back against the wall; and then I saw something which filled my very soul with horror. There lay the Count, but looking as if his youth had been half renewed, for the white hair and moustache were changed to dark iron-grey; the cheeks were fuller, and the white skin seemed ruby-red underneath; the mouth was redder than ever, for on the lips were gouts of fresh blood, which trickled from the corners of the mouth and ran over the chin and neck. Even the deep, burning eyes seemed set amongst swollen flesh, for the lids and pouches underneath were bloated. It seemed as if the whole awful creature were simply gorged with blood; he lay like a filthy leech, exhausted with his repletion. I shuddered as I bent over to touch him, and every sense in me revolted at the contact; but I had to search, or I was lost. The coming night might see my own body a banquet in a similar way to those horrid three. I felt all over the body, but no sign could I find of the key. Then I stopped and looked at the Count. There was a mocking smile on the bloated face which seemed to drive me mad. This was the being I was helping to

transfer to London, where, perhaps, for centuries to come he might, amongst its teeming millions, satiate his lust for blood, and create a new and ever-widening circle of semi-demons to batten on the helpless. The very thought drove me mad. A terrible desire came upon me to rid the world of such a monster. There was no lethal weapon at hand, but I seized a shovel which the workmen had been using to fill the cases, and lifting it high struck, with the edge downward, at the hateful face. But as I did so the head turned, and the eyes fell full upon me, with all their blaze of basilisk horror. The sight seemed to paralyse me, and the shovel turned in my hand and glanced from the face, merely making a deep gash above the forehead. The shovel fell from my hand across the box, and as I pulled it away the flange of the blade caught the edge of the lid, which fell over again, and hid the horrid thing from my sight. The last glimpse I had was of the bloated face, blood-stained and fixed with a grin of malice which would have held its own in the nethermost hell.

We leave Jonathan desperately contemplating his escape; and at this point the book almost takes leave of Dracula himself. Having been announced and described in such detail, the Count appears only minimally in the rest of the story, nine-tenths of which is set in England: he sees the new country, where he is unknown, as a fertile ground for his ghastly maraudings. Sometimes he is experienced only as a shadow, a fear, or an animal into which he has miraculously transformed himself. The constant threat of his reappearance is just about enough to strike terror into the hearts of characters and readers alike, but one's final impression is that a fabulous creation has been stretched too thin. Having started his tale with a metaphorical thunderstorm, Stoker is content for the rest with occasional distant flashes of lightning, as though having once set the world about its ears he wished to tantalize his readers with the mere possibility that he could turn the trick again. In fact he does not; after a few graveyard stakings and a transcontinental chase the book ends somewhat lamely, almost depriving its readers of the climax they expected.

It would be foolish to read too much into a piece of arrant blood and thunder, but quite likely one of Stoker's main aims was less to terrify than to unsettle the smug society in which he lived, to undermine the hypocrisy which covered women's legs with crinolines and table legs with frills. He may have wished to question the official certainties of organized religion (there are no priests in *Dracula*), or to explore the horrid realities of the vast urban graveyards with their Gothic monuments and their prim assumption of an idyllic life to come. If so, he struck a chord in the minds not only of his own generation but of that ninety years after, which finds man surrounded as never before by the horrors of the real world and aware of the need to escape into a fantasy one. If first encountered today, *Dracula* would seem a comparatively mild example of the way the comic strip has been admitted into so-called adult entertainment, cunningly depicting the female sex as both victim and monster. The blood-lusting count might, however, be thought a more interesting and provocative figure than the inane monsters of *Star Wars, Gremlins* and *Poltergeist*, and the excitement of his destruction might seem healthier than the bland optimism of *E. T.* and *Close Encounters of the Third Kind*. In 1985 the world's most commercially successful film was *Rambo, First Blood II*, a violent account of an avenger who blasts his way into Vietnam and with skill, cunning and ruthlessness conducts an orgy of killing in the name of justice. His creator described him as 'a one-man war machine that can't be turned off'. In the broadest sense, is Rambo, all sweat and pectorals, any less distasteful, any less of a scourge, than the Transylvanian count driven to kill by a family curse? Which is the more proper villain for the twentieth century? A half-naked savage with a machine gun or a master magician with fangs? Which is the more obscene in a century which found real vampires in one John George Haigh, who in 1949 murdered women for their money, drank their blood, and disposed of their bodies in a bath of acid; and in Steven Sabin, a 19-year-old who in 1985 was charged with stabbing an elderly woman as a sacrifice to Satan? (He was described as having 'an intense urge to bite the necks of young boys and to drink their blood'.)

The immense success of *Dracula*, all the more terrifying for its prosaic setting in English country houses haunted by a supernatural predator, sparked off an interest in Stoker's source material. The Balkan countries had of course a history of robber barons who were hated in life for their cruelty. Vlad the Impaler is the one most often cited, but a runner-up is Countess Elisabeth Bathori (1560–1614) who in an attempt to preserve her own youth is said to have drunk the blood of 600 virgins. The evil perpetrated by such people became legendary to the extent that it was deemed supernatural and bred its own fantasies; but an interest in the ghostly macabre can be traced back as far in literary history as anyone cares to go. Certainly to Chaucer, and the Faust legends of the Middle Ages, when the devil was a frequent character in miracle and morality plays. With ease, also, to the ancient Romans and Greeks. But *Dracula* is the culmination of a more recent cycle of 'Gothick' romances, that extra 'k' perhaps signifying that they were mocking older styles. The book itself quotes Bürger's 'Lenore' and Goethe's *Die Braut von Korinth*, but the English trend can probably be said to have begun in 1765 with Horace Walpole's *The Castle of Otranto*. Walpole, son of Britain's first Prime Minister, was a dandified eccentric who inoculated himself with fantasy as a defence against morbidity, much as we now inoculate ourselves against the 'flu. He even built himself a so-called Gothick castle by the Thames at Strawberry Hill, and stocked it with relics of the picturesque past. (It stands today, as a teachers' training college.) His highly idiosyncratic novel resulted from a nightmare of a 'gigantic hand in armour', and concerns the villainous Manfred, who goes somewhat mad at the death of his son on his wedding day and makes superhuman efforts to perpetuate the family line, locking up the while his insane wife. The events take place within a sinister fortress, and there are magical happenings such as a portrait walking out of its frame, and the giant armour which started it all.

Walpole was imitated to a degree by William Beckford in his *Vathek*, published in 1786. This told of a Middle Eastern potentate who sold his soul to the devil and was tormented for his increasing list of crimes by visions of reptiles with human faces, and skulls from which hair was growing. Just as Walpole drew his inspiration from Strawberry Hill, so Beckford imagined his grisly events as taking place within his family pile, Fonthill Manor in Wiltshire, a lofty and complex building with many vistas to stir the morbid imagination.

Next, an apparently staid housewife called Ann Radcliffe began to publish fantasy novels which probably sprang from the repression of her own feminine

Eighteenth-century originators of Gothick horror: Horace Walpole, and 'Monk' Lewis (right).

instincts (as did those of the Brontës half a century later). The longest and best known of them, *The Mysteries of Udolpho*, appeared in 1794 and is well nigh unreadable today, largely because the author insisted on inserting quite arbitrarily whatever irrelevant matter, in the way of poems and prose descriptions, she had to hand. Her main story concerns a double-dyed villain called Montoni, who locks up in his gloomy Alpine castle not only his wife but his wealthy niece, with obvious designs on both inheritances. Mrs Radcliffe shunned the supernatural, explaining away as best she could all the macabre twists and turns of her

interminable story, which is remarkably reminiscent of today's teleserials *Dallas* and *Dynasty*. Not so Matthew Lewis, who wrote *The Monk*, published in 1796, and was henceforth known as 'Monk' Lewis. His hero is a Capuchin called Ambrosio, who falls victim to the wiles of wanton Matilda. She, disguised as a boy, has entered his monastery and taken vows; through events which lead him into great depravity he eventually kills the temptress and is himself condemned to death, escaping from burning on earth only by allowing the devil to whisk him away into eternal damnation.

In 1816 Samuel Taylor Coleridge produced a fine, though drug-induced and therefore unfinished, narrative poem called *Christabel*. He employed a similar combination of ruinous castle, diabolic characters and revenge, with a spot of lesbianism thrown in for good measure in the shape of the wicked Geraldine, who simply turns up one night behind an oak tree, and must be given hospitality since she 'scarce can speak for weariness'. She is however a dangerous guest, warning off the benevolent spirit of Christabel's mother:

> Off, wand'ring mother! Peak and pine . . .
> Off, woman, off! This hour is mine!

The two girls share a bedroom, and Christabel has no suspicions:

> Her gentle limbs did she undress,
> And lay down in her loveliness.

Geraldine says she must pray first, but it will be an odd kind of prayer:

> Beneath the lamp the lady bowed
> And slowly rolled her eyes around;
> Then drawing in her breath aloud,
> Like one that shuddered, she unbound
> The cincture from beneath her breast:
> Her silken robe and inner vest
> Dropt to her feet, and full in view,
> Behold! her bosom and half her side
> Are lean and old and foul of hue.
> A sight to dream of, not to tell –
> And she must sleep with Christabel!

By 1803 Jane Austen had completed her *Northanger Abbey*, which chastises those who perpetrate the absurdities of these morbid romances, and reveals their horrors as the thinnest of thin air. In 1818 Thomas Love Peacock followed with his similarly shafted satire *Nightmare Abbey*. By this time, however, the genre had gathered fresh wind as the result of sexually-charged exchanges in 1816, during a wet Swiss summer, between an odd group of English people on holiday. Their temporary home, the Villa Diodati above Lake Geneva, was eerie enough in itself; an expedition to the nearby castle of Chillon suggested medieval fancies; the weather was sufficiently appalling to induce gloom. Kept indoors a good deal, they passed the time reading German Gothick romances, having doubtless devoured all the available English ones. There seems to have been a bet as to which of them could write the best ghost story, and since the travellers included the psychologically unstable poets Shelley and Byron, much might have been expected to result. In fact the two poets failed to finish their assignments, and the most important and influential contribution came from Shelley's wife-to-be, a girl of 19, who produced a novel of which we shall hear more in the next chapter, its title was *Frankenstein*. But the fourth contributor also finished a short novel, and although there was gossip about its having been written by Byron himself, the poet later disclaimed the honour and assured literary London that it was entirely the work of his physician and jealous friend John Polidori. (See pages 108, 109.)

The Vampyre, a slight and indisputably naïve work, took the book world by storm. Its hero, or villain, was almost a parody of Byron himself, handsome, pale-faced and catnip to the ladies; this suggests that the tale was written in a spirit of affectionate mockery. Lord Ruthven is a mysterious and evil nobleman, followed everywhere by misery and misfortune. He overpowers a young Englishman named Aubrey, who witnesses his vampiric crimes but is sworn to secrecy. Ruthven apparently dies, but the corpse disappears, and the nobleman later reappears in society to marry Aubrey's sister. Because of his vow of silence Aubrey is unable to intervene.

Incredibly, this absurd and insufficient story became immensely popular throughout Europe and was not only dramatized (by Dumas *fils* among others) but turned into an opera. In 1852 Dion Boucicault wrote and starred in an amended and extended version in which the action was transferred to the time of Charles II and the vampire was a sinister black-clad figure with piercing eyes and no hair; he is revived from death by the moon but eventually shot with a charmed bullet which puts an end to him. (The moon and the bullet later appear in the mythology of werewolves; plagiarism is not a crime in these circles.)

In 1820 *Melmoth the Wanderer* produced fresh sensations. Its author, an Irish clergyman called Robert Maturin, conceived a wild seeker after forbidden knowledge who made the usual pact with the devil but tried ever more desperately as his time for repayment approached to find some other mortal willing to exchange destinies with him. The novel becomes a series of strange tales, in which the central character moves like a man demented through a series of graveyard images.

In early Victorian times an obsession with the darker side of life seemed natural, for life was short, and death a frequent visitor. The Lake Poets had induced a love for ominous country scenes with wind blowing through the trees and storms on the horizon, and the advent of the industrial revolution seemed only to increase man's reluctance to part with his old cosy world of superstition and legend. If the 'romantic revival' had a single motif it was surely an ivy-covered ruin, and in such properties the devil must be considered a natural inhabitant. The Brontës, who seldom write of towns and seem obsessed with madness and death, upheld this tradition in a romantic way: Rochester and Heathcliff are both Satanic figures to begin with, though heroes by the end of the novels in which they appear. They would no doubt have found much to admire, or at least to enthral them, in the stories of the American Edgar Allan Poe, whose morbid preoccupations, combined with his drinking, led to his death on the streets of Baltimore in 1849. His legacy, apart from some poems, is a single volume of macabre stories, two or three tinged with detection but most of them based on his morbid fear of death and bodily decay. The first few sentences of 'The Fall of the House of Usher' may serve as a model of the language desirable for the writing of the Gothick romance:

> During the whole of a dull, dark and soundless day in the autumn of the year, when the clouds hung oppressively low in the heavens, I had been passing alone, on horseback, through a singularly dreary stretch of country; and at length found myself, as the shades of evening drew on, within view of the melancholy House of Usher. I know not how it was – but, with my first glimpse of the building, a sense of insufferable gloom pervaded my spirit. I say insufferable; for the feeling was

unrelieved by any of that half-pleasurable, because poetic, sentiment, with which the mind usually receives even the sternest natural images of the desolate or terrible. I looked upon the scene before me – upon the mere house, and the simple landscape features of the domain – upon the bleak walls – upon the vacant eye-like windows – upon a few rank sedges – and upon a few rank trunks of decayed trees – with an utter depression of soul which I can compare to no earthly sensation more properly than to the after-dream of the reveller upon opium – the bitter lapse into everyday life – the hideous dropping-off of the veil. There was an iciness, a sinking, a sickening of the heart – an unredeemed dreariness of thought which no goading of the imagination could torture into aught of the sublime.

Poe's range of subjects is limited but remarkable:

'The Fall of the House of Usher'	the dead revived
'The Pit and the Pendulum'	torture
'The Premature Burial'	burial alive
'The Tell-Tale Heart'	a murderer's conscience
'The Masque of the Red Death'	plague
'The Facts in the Case of M. Valdemar'	dissolution of the body
'Ligeia'	the dead revived
'The Black Cat'	murder
'The Cask of Amontillado'	burial alive

His avoidance of the vampire theme may be taken as an oversight; but back in England, in 1872, there appeared the first fully-fledged modern work in the true vein, J. Sheridan Le Fanu's 'Carmilla', which included in its morbid romantic theme not only the lust for blood, but lesbianism. It merits a full description later in this essay, when we deal with the distaff side of the vampire family; but already immensely popular among the just-literate classes was a lengthy part-work called *Varney the Vampire*, published in 1853 under the name of one Thomas Prest. Its literary status may be judged from the following excerpt:

There can be no mistake. The figure is there, still feeling for an entrance, and clattering against the glass with its long nails . . . A small pane of glass is broken, and the form from without introduces a long gaunt hand, which seems utterly destitute of flesh. The fastening is removed, and one half of the window, which opens like folding doors, is swung wide open on its hinges . . .

The figure turns half round, and the light falls upon the face. It is perfectly white – perfectly bloodless. The eyes look like polished tin; the lips are drawn back, and the principal feature next to those dreadful eyes is the teeth – the fearful-looking teeth – projecting like those of some wild animal, hideously, glaringly white, and fang-like. It approaches the bed with a strange, gliding movement . . .

With a sudden rush that could not be foreseen – with a strange howling cry that was enough to awaken terror in every breast, the figure seized the long tresses of her hair, and twining them round his bony hands he held her to the bed. Then she screamed . . . Shriek followed shriek in rapid succession . . . Her beautiful rounded limbs quivered with the agony of her soul . . . With a plunge he seizes her neck in his fang-like teeth – a gush of blood, and a hideous sucking noise follows. The girl has swooned, and the vampire is at his hideous repast.

It reads like a stage direction for Bela Lugosi, but we are still eighty years from that influential performance, and more than forty from Bram Stoker's surfeit of dressed crab. There seems little doubt however that they both read *Varney the Vampire*.

Despite such excesses, by the mid-1860s the public appetite for violence was being channelled, following Poe's tentative lead, into the detective story. Dickens had of course, on occasion, introduced into his novels elements of mystery, and even of the supernatural: *A Christmas Carol*, when encountered for the first time, can be seen as a true Gothick extravaganza. But it was Wilkie Collins who, having in 1860's *The Woman in White* produced a muted and more sensible variant on the Udolpho school, published in *The Moonstone* (1868) the first real detective novel, with a story which still works. Its elements (country house, stolen jewels, mysterious foreigners seeking revenge) are repeated in many Sherlock Holmes stories; which brings us on neatly to the nineties, a decade of fertile imagination from which Dracula sprang more or less full-clothed.

As to what really caused Bram Stoker, an overworked administrator for the most famous actor-manager of his day, to conceive such a character, we have little enough to go on. Most of the book is far superior to anything else he ever wrote – the much later *Lair of the White Worm* is unreadably stilted – so perhaps it did come, as he claimed, in a flash of inspiration and indigestion. Certainly he had never been to Transylvania, which he so aptly described by the use of guide books, just as Jules Verne had described Iceland for his *Journey to the Centre of the Earth*. Stoker's primal sources include 'Carmilla', to which he is indebted for the inscription in 'Dracula's Guest' relating to Countess Dolingen; but he must have been equally aware of all the references cited in the last dozen paragraphs, back probably to the Saxons who drove wooden stakes through certain bodies in order to keep them in the grave where they belonged, and buried honest folks at crossroads so that the shape of the cross would protect them from vampires and other evil beings. He must also have read the well-known English stories of semi-authenticated fact, such as that of the Croglin Hall Vampire. Croglin Hall was a lonely property in Cumberland, and in 1874 a new family, the Cranswells, moved in. They included two boys and their sister Amelia, and it was she who was first troubled at night by scratching at her bedroom window and the sight of two small yellow lights, like the eyes of an animal . . . Awakened by her shrieks, the brothers reached her room in time to see a tall figure bounding away across the lawn, while their sister lay on the carpet with blood streaming from her throat. A second attack followed months later, and this time the monster was shot at and tracked to the local churchyard, where it disappeared into a large vault. Inside, the brothers found a long thin corpse with sharp teeth, and a bullet in its leg. It was exorcized and burned . . .

Finally, Stoker had a close acquaintance in one Arminius Vambery, a silver-tongued international traveller who hailed from Budapest. Vambery was a member of Stoker's club, and by all accounts told many a tall postprandial tale in the flickering candlelight. One of these doubtless concerned the aforementioned Vlad Drakul, the fifteenth-century sadist who had ruled Wallachia with an iron fist. The Impaler was clearly referred to in a contemporary manuscript as a vampire, no doubt a metaphorical reference to his spilling of human blood with no supernatural motive. But Stoker wanted a supernatural villain, such a monster as had never before existed in literature, and with Vambery's help he succeeded admirably. Let us quote from the novel Professor Van Helsing's account, in his rather irritating broken English, of the capabilities of the true vampire:

'There are such beings as vampires; some of us have evidence that they exist. Even had we not the proof of our own unhappy experience, the teachings and the records of the past give proof enough for sane peoples. I admit that at the first I was sceptic. Were it not that through long years I have train myself to keep an open mind, I could not have believe until such time as that fact thunder on my ear. "See! see! I prove; I prove." Alas! Had I known at the first what now I know – nay, had I even guess at him – one so precious life had been spared to many of us who did love her. But that is gone; and we must so work, that other poor souls perish not, whilst we can save. The *nosferatu* do not die like the bee when he sting once. He is only stronger; and being stronger, have yet more power to work evil. This vampire which is amongst us is of himself so strong in person as twenty men; he is of cunning more than mortal, for his cunning be the growth of ages; he have still the aids of necromancy, which is, as his etymology imply, the divination by the dead, and all the dead that he can come nigh to are for him at command; he is brute, and more than brute: he is devil in callous, and the heart of him is not; he can, within limitations, appear at will when, and where, and in any of the forms that are to him; he can, within his range, direct the elements: the storm, the fog, the thunder; he can command all the meaner things: the rat, and the owl, and the bat – the moth, and the fox, and the wolf; he can grow and become small; and he can at times vanish and come unknown. How then are we to begin our strife to destroy him? How shall we find his where; and having found it, how can we destroy? My friends, this is much; it is a terrible task that we undertake, and there may be consequence to make the brave shudder. For if we fail in this our fight he must surely win: and then where end we? . . .

'Now let us see how far the general powers arrayed against us are restrict, and how the individual cannot. In fine, let us consider the limitations of the vampire in general, and of this one in particular.

'All we have to go upon are traditions and superstitions. These do not at the first appear much, when the matter is one of life and death – nay of more than either life or death. Yet must we be satisfied; in the first place because we have to be – no other means is at our control – and secondly, because, after all, these things – tradition and superstition – are everything. Does not the belief in vampires rest for others – though not, alas! for us – on them? A year ago which of us would have received such a possibility, in the midst of our scientific, sceptical, matter-of-fact nineteenth century? We even scouted a belief that we saw justified under our very eyes. Take it, then, that the vampire, and the belief in his limitations and his cure, rest for the moment on the same base. For, let me tell you, he is known everywhere that men have been. In old Greece, in old Rome; he flourish in Germany all over, in France, in India, even in the Chersonese; and in China, so far from us in all ways, there even is he, and the peoples fear him at this day. He have follow the wake of the berserker Icelander, the devil-begotten Hun, the Slav, the Saxon, the Magyar. So far, then, we have all we may act upon; and let me tell you that very much of the beliefs are justified by what we have seen in our own so unhappy experience. The vampire live on, and cannot die by mere passing of the time; he can flourish when that he can fatten on the blood of the living. Even more, we have seen amongst us that he can even grow younger; that his vital faculties grow strenuous, and seem as though they refresh themselves when his special pabulum is plenty. But he cannot flourish without this diet; he eat not as others. Even friend Jonathan,★ who lived with him for weeks, did never see him to

★ Jonathan has by now made his way back to England, more than slightly shaken by his Transylvanian encounter.

eat, never! He throws no shadow; he make in the mirror no reflect, as again Jonathan observe. He has the strength of many in his hand – witness again Jonathan when he shut the door against the wolfs, and when he help him from the diligence too. He can transform himself to wolf, as we gather from the ship arrival in Whitby, when he tear open the dog; he can be as bat, as Madam Mina saw him on the window at Whitby, and as friend John saw him fly from this so near house, and as my friend Quincey saw him at the window of Miss Lucy. He can come in mist which he create – that noble ship's captain proved him of this; but, from what we know, the distance he can make this mist is limited, and it can only be round himself. He come on moonlight rays as elemental dust – as again Jonathan saw those sisters in the castle of Dracula. He become so small – we ourselves saw Miss Lucy, ere she was at peace, slip through a hairbreadth space at the tomb door. He can, when once he find his way, come out from anything or into anything, no matter how close it be bound or even fused up with fire – solder you call it. He can see in the dark – no small power this, in a world which is one half shut from the light. Ah, but hear me through. He can do all these things, yet he is not free. Nay; he is even more prisoner than the slave of the galley, than the madman in his cell. He cannot go where he lists; he who is not of nature has yet to obey some of nature's laws – why we know not. He may not enter anywhere at the first, unless there be some one of the household who bid him to come; though afterwards he can come as he please. His power ceases, as does that of all evil things, at the coming of the day. Only at certain times can he have limited freedom. If he be not at the place whither he is bound, he can only change himself at noon or at exact sunrise or sunset. These things are we told, and in this record of ours we have proof by inference. Thus, whereas he can do as he will within his limit, when he have his earth-home, his coffin-home, his hell-home, the place unhallowed, as we saw when he went to the grave of the suicide at Whitby; still at other time he can only change when the time come. It is said, too, that he can only pass running water at the slack or the flood of the tide. Then there are things which so afflict him that he has no power, as the garlic that we know of, and as for things sacred, as this symbol, my crucifix, that was amongst us even now when we resolve, to them he is nothing, but in their presence he take his place far off and silent with respect. There are others, too, which I shall tell you of, lest in our seeking we may need them. The branch of wild rose on his coffin keep him that he move not from it; a sacred bullet fired into the coffin kill him so that he be true dead; and as for the stake through him, we know already of its peace; or the cut-off head that giveth rest. We have seen it with our eyes.

'Thus when we find the habitation of this man-that-was, we can confine him to his coffin and destroy him, if we obey what we know. But he is clever. I have asked my friend Arminius, of Buda-Pesth University, to make his record*; and, from all the means that are, he tell me of what he has been. He must, indeed, have been that Voivode Dracula who won his name against the Turk, over the great river on the very frontier of Turkey-land. If it be so, then was he no common man; for in that time, and for centuries after, he was spoken of as the cleverest and the most cunning, as well as the bravest of the sons of the "land beyond the forest". That mighty brain and that iron resolution went with him to his grave, and are even now arrayed against us. The Draculas were, says Arminius, a great and noble race, though now and again were scions who were held by their coevals to have had dealings with the Evil One. They learned his secrets in the Scholomance, amongst the mountains over Lake Herman-stadt, where the devil claims the tenth scholar as his due. In the records are such words as "stregoica" – witch, "ordog", and "pokol" – Satan and hell; and in one manuscript this very Dracula is spoken of as "wampyr", which we all understand too well. There have been from the loins of this very one great men and good women, and their

---

* This apparently fictional reference is Stoker's way of thanking his friend Arminius. Note also, by the way, that Stoker gave to the shrewd and knowledgeable Van Helsing the Christian name of himself and his father – Abraham.

graves make sacred the earth where alone this foulness can dwell. For it is not the least of its terrors that this evil thing is rooted deep in all good; in soil barren of holy memories it cannot rest.'

The public of the day lapped up *Dracula*, and the critics scarcely demurred:

The Bookman: Since Wilkie Collins left us we have had no tale of mystery so liberal in manner and so closely woven . . . but the audacity and horror of *Dracula* are Mr Stoker's own . . . A summary of the book would shock and disgust, but we must own that, though here and there in the course of the tale we hurried over things with repulsion, we read nearly the whole with rapt attention . . .

Daily Mail: In seeking a parallel to this weird, powerful and horrible story, our minds revert to such tales as *The Mysteries of Udolpho, Frankenstein, Wuthering Heights,*

The Fall of the House of Usher, and *Marjery of Quelher.* But *Dracula* is even more appalling in its gloomy fascination than any of these.

The Lady: Its fascination is so great that it is impossible to lay it aside . . .

Liverpool Daily Post: Much loving and happy human nature, much heroism, much faithfulness, much dauntless hope, so that as one phantasmal ghastliness follows another in horrid swift succession, the reader is always accompanied by images of devotion and friendliness.

Pall Mall Gazette: It is horrid and creepy to the last degree. It is also excellent . . .

Only *The Athenaeum* kept its nose in the air: 'Highly sensational, but wanting in the constructive art as well as in the higher literary sense . . . Still, Mr Stoker has got together a number of horrid details, and his object, assuming it to be ghastliness, is fairly well fulfilled.'

The book was dramatized within days of its first appearance in the bookshops. The 'play' took the form of a four-hour reading at the Lyceum, undertaken as a protection against copyright infringement. Ironically, when the story was first filmed it was twenty-five years later in a pirate version called *Nosferatu*, made in Germany by the great director F. W. Murnau. Stoker's estate sued at once, and won its case; the negative was supposed to have been destroyed. But luckily for posterity, prints had been hidden in several archives, and even today the 1922 silent, despite variations of detail, can evoke much of the horrid power of the book. This is the plot summary given in Siegfried Kracauer's *From Caligari to Hitler*, still the best account of German films between the wars:

A real estate agent in Bremen sends his recently married clerk to see Nosferatu who, living far away in the Carpathian woods, wants to settle some business matter. The clerk's travel across these woods – macabre with mists, shying horses, wolves and eerie birds – proves but an innocent prelude to the adventures awaiting him in Nosferatu's castle. The day after his arrival he wanders, in search of his host, through abandoned rooms and cellars, and eventually finds Nosferatu lying in a sarcophagus – like a corpse with eyes wide open and a ghastly face. Nosferatu is a vampire, and vampires sleep by day. By night the monster approaches the sleeping clerk to suck his blood. At this very moment Nina, the clerk's wife, awakens in Bremen with the name of her husband on her lips, whereupon Nosferatu withdraws from his victim. After the clerk's escape, the vampire, who comes to appear more and more as an incarnation of pestilence, leaves his castle to haunt the world. Wherever he emerges, rats swarm out and people fall dead. He goes aboard a sailing ship: the crew dies, and

NOSFERATU (1922). The mysterious Max Schreck (Schreck means terror) was made up as the very personification of evil from beyond the grave. His prominent fang-like tooth, his pointed ears, his all-white eyeballs added up to one of the screen's nastiest monsters: you could almost smell the bad breath. Even his shadow was made to elongate and contract in the most sinister fashion.

the ship continues cutting the waves on its own. Finally Nosferatu makes his entrance in Bremen and there meets Nina. Instead of fleeing the vampire's presence Nina, her arms extended, welcomes him into her room. As she does so a supreme miracle occurs: the sun breaks through, and the vampire dissolves into thin air.

Clearly the variations devised by scriptwriter Henrik Galeen are designed to further the poetic principle that love conquers all and that evil cannot defeat those who meet it fearlessly. But the aspects which make the film memorable are its brilliant visual composition and its highlighting of the details of horror: glinting eyes, low arches, long pointed fingers, rats, shadows. Above all, an actor called Max Schreck, who seems shrunken almost into a mummy, makes Nosferatu a loathsome walking corpse with rotted teeth and pointed ears, enough to give anybody a nightmare. The critic Béla Bálasz wrote that it was as though 'a chilly wind from doomsday' passed through the scenes, and the feeling was accentuated by all manner of camera tricks, including missing frames which caused jerkiness, scenes shot in negative, and fast motion for Nosferatu's coach. It all added up to a worthy fellow for the morbid masterpieces of post-war Germany: *The Cabinet of Dr Caligari*, *The Golem*, *Warning Shadows*, *Waxworks*, *The Student of Prague*, *Pandora's Box*, *Siegfried* and *Metropolis*.

Two years after *Nosferatu*, a British actor-manager called Hamilton Deane gave to the world the first authentic stage presentation of the Dracula story. It was a project he had mooted for years, to general ridicule; Grand Guignol was thought to be all very well for Paris, but entirely beneath London sensibilities. Finally, it was almost by accident, because some other project fell through, that Deane's company included *Dracula* in its repertoire at the Grand Theatre, Derby. Deane had intended to play the Count, but found himself needed for the much longer role of Van Helsing; and when gradually his other plays were abandoned, and he took *Dracula* on tour in a run that lasted for years (bolstered by the well-publicized attendance at each performance of a Red Cross nurse), the Count came to be played by a 23-year-old actor called Raymond Huntley, for the next fifty years a pillar of English stage and screen. Against all odds the play was even a hit in sophisticated London, and the Americans were quick to buy it up for Broadway, where, after considerable rewriting by John Balderston, the role of the sinister nobleman was filled by an unknown Hungarian actor named Bela Lugosi Blasko. Having broken several records in England, *Dracula* became the most successful modern play on tour in America, and that despite a general consensus that it was both stilted and silly. Somehow the audiences who came along in this belief never felt quite the same way when they left, having been mesmerized by the sense of danger to the cosy Victorian atmosphere, and by the few but choice trick effects: flying bats, puffs of smoke, and a chaise-longue which in the wink of an eye replaced the dormant Dracula with a skeleton. In 1939, when Hamilton Deane revived the play in London, he took over the Dracula role; and it seemed especially fitting not only that in mid-run he was forced to transfer to Stoker's old theatre the Lyceum, but that one evening a fully-caped Bela Lugosi, in England for a film thriller called *Dark Eyes of London*, came on stage to wish the show well. The two Draculas embraced each other to hysterical audience enthusiasm.

But we anticipate, for the most fateful day in the post-publication history of

Dracula had dawned in Hollywood in 1930, when the first sound film version was directed by Tod Browning. It was almost by accident that it was made at all: Universal Studios had picked up the rights along with several other hit Broadway plays of the previous season.

The 1930 *Dracula* has not maintained its original impact. That it is watchable at all is most probably due to the strange tricks which Bela Lugosi performs with the English language, and to the absurd exaggerations that pass for acting with him and Dwight Frye. It is the Hollywood equivalent of a Tod Slaughter melodrama, but even more stagily presented. Tod Browning had some sort of reputation as Lon Chaney Snr's favourite director, but this may have been merely because he did not interfere when the star felt like showing off. Certainly in *Dracula* he shows no command of pace, or editing, or composition, or camera movement, and only because the story itself was so odd can the film have fascinated those early talkie audiences as it did; even for *aficionados* Browning's handling makes it hard to follow. The almost total absence of music doesn't help, and a sense of strain is evident in the attempt to turn Dracula's few appearances and scant dialogue into a star part.

The shiver show (as *Variety* described it) begins well, if jerkily. Universal's backlot hill stands in adequately enough for the mountains of Transylvania, with the help of some glass drawings that look more like the Troll Mountains of Norway. The basic theme is stated as directly as one could wish, just as soon as the superstitious peasants in their national costume hear that the dapper traveller from England (Renfield in this version) proposes to be at the Borgo Pass at midnight in order to be met by a carriage from Count Dracula's castle: 'But Dracula and his wives, they take the form of wolves and bats. They leave their coffins at night and they take the blood of the living!'

Just to underline the point, the film cuts helpfully to a cellar where coffin lids open to permit the nightly exercise of three shrouded ladies and the Count himself, who seems to have a good deal more get-up-and-go than they do. Not all the occupants of the crypt are vampires, for rats and (oddly) armadilloes scuttle in and out of other broken coffins from which bony hands protrude as though in a final posthumous twitch.

Renfield gets his wish, and is hastily deposited at the pass by a frightened coachman who bolts without waiting for a tip. The driver of the waiting carriage silently motions Renfield to board, and there follows a nightmare journey at top speed through the darkness. When Renfield looks out, he can't seem to see the coachman, but a large bat flies above the horses as though guiding them. As the coach finally draws to a halt Renfield leaps out to berate the driver –

What do you mean by going at this – ?

– but there is nobody. He is in the castle courtyard, and a huge creaking door admits him to a ruinous interior with a vast staircase down which his impeccably dressed host is descending, with the immortal words of greeting:

I am Dracula. Welcome to my house.

DRACULA (1930). 'Welcome to my house!' urges Bela Lugosi, the screen's first official Count
Dracula. But few would willingly accept the invitation: the smile is not persuasive, and the
maids are clearly on holiday.

Can he possibly have been also the coachman? Renfield can't decide. The
nobleman motions his guest to follow him, and immediately steps through – or so
it seems – a spider's web twenty feet across. Perhaps realizing his error, he waits
with a wry smile while his guest puts a nervous stick through the web: 'The spider
spinning his web for the unwary fly. The blood is the life, Mr Renfield.'

   As in the book, the English visitor has come to assure the Count that preparations are well advanced for his purchase of a residential property in England. The Count nods his approval: 'I am taking with me only three – ah – boxes . . . I have chartered a ship to take us to England . . . we shall be leaving tomorrow evening . . .' The sentiments are simple enough, but not when enunciated by an actor who makes five syllables out of every one he comes across. We have already heard Dracula's famous line on hearing the wolves howling outside:

Children of the night. What music they make!

And now he directs his guest's attention to a rare old wine, nodding approvingly at its reception but taking none for himself: 'I never drink . . . wine.'

The Count's true nature is revealed to the audience when Renfield pricks his finger and the Count's gaze is riveted by the drop of blood which emerges. Only a cross on a chain round Renfield's neck saves the visitor at this moment. But Renfield very shortly finds himself not merely alone but dizzy from the wine, fighting off a huge bat which hovers at the window. When he sinks to the carpet, no doubt drugged by the wine, the three female vampires instantly enter the scene, like tigresses at the kill. The Count, however, stalks in to warn them off, with an expression as the scene fades out which seems to say: this man is mine. *

The pace slows considerably after that. Following the discreet fade to black, a few shots cover the voyage of the *Demeter*, with the vampirized Renfield, now mad as a hatter, letting the Count out of his coffin in the hold: 'Master, the sun has gone! I'll be loyal, master . . . you'll see that I get lives? Not human lives, but small ones, with blood in them . . .'

The boat turns up at Whitby with a crew of dead men aboard. Nobody blames Dracula, who arrives unnoticed as a dog; only the hysterically shrieking Renfield is in view, and he is promptly carted off to Dr Seward's asylum. Dracula has introduced himself to Dr Seward at the opera. Living in a house sombrely called Carfax, he is to be the doctor's neighbour. When told that the old house needs work, he smiles curiously: 'I shall do very little repairing . . . It reminds me of the broken battlements of my own castle in Transylvania . . .' This rather unusual interval conversation turns to darker matters: 'To die . . . to be really dead . . . that must be glorious. There are far worse things awaiting man than death . . .'

'I think he's fascinating,' says Lucy Westenra in the bedroom afterwards: she is clearly to be the Count's first victim. Mina Seward, her friend and hostess, demurs: 'Oh, I suppose he's all right, but give me something a little more normal.' Meanwhile Renfield is causing his keeper at the asylum some difficulty:

– Flies? Flies? Who wants to eat flies?
– You do, you loonie!
– Not when I can get nice fat *spiders*!

Several local people die mysteriously, drained of blood, and Lucy is one of them, but she reappears in her shroud by night, rather unexpectedly tempting small

* How he gets over the problem of the cross is left to our imagination.

DRACULA (1930). The Count goes to the opera, and the dress extras look ready to form a
musical chorus.

children with chocolates. Mina sees her once: 'She came out of the shadows. I
started to speak to her. Then I remembered she was dead.'

So far the Count has had it all his own way. It is time for his antagonist to
appear. Van Helsing, a consultant brought in by Dr Seward, is played by Edward
Van Sloan, and has a splendid first line:

> Gentlemen, we are dealing with the undead.

He interviews Mina, who has survived one of Dracula's nocturnal attacks: 'It
seemed that the whole room was filled with mist. There were two red eyes . . . a
white livid face . . . he came down out of the mist towards me . . .'

Unfortunately the descriptions are more vivid than what the audience sees.
Even Dracula's nightly awakenings in the Carfax crypt disappoint: it was this film
which set the standard for his too reticent assumption of full power. The coffin
opens slightly; a hand emerges, groping; the camera moves away; we hear the lid
slam shut; we track back, and Dracula is standing erect, flexing himself. Okay,
getting out of the coffin was bound to be clumsy, but the constant avoidance of it
quickly becomes a laughing matter. On a similar point, even when we see him
attack, he shows no fangs; and when Van Helsing examines Mina's neck, we
never see the famous marks, we only hear them described. 'What can have caused
them, professor?' some one asks; and at that very moment the servant announces:
'Count Dracula.'

DRACULA (1930). The evil Count does not get things his own way while Professor Van Helsing (Edward Van Sloan) is around, and he may be making a rude Transylvanian gesture.

The count, not knowing that he is already under suspicion, has chosen this time to socialize; always in evening dress even when the others are casual. But he is not to be trifled with. Van Helsing realizes that the guest probably casts no reflection, and tricks him into looking into a box with a mirror lid. The Count hurls it to the ground and retreats a few steps, hissing; then he recovers his poise, and smiles half-apologetically at the assembled company: 'I dislike mirrors. Van Helsing will explain.'

He is about to take his leave when he can't resist adding:

DRACULA (1930). Beastly Bela carries off the delectable Helen Chandler to his crypt. She doesn't seem to mind too much.

> For one who has not lived even a single lifetime, you are a wise man, Van Helsing . . .
> But you are too late. My blood now flows through her veins.
> – But I know how to save her soul.

The famous garlic does not come into use in this film, but Van Helsing strews Mina's room liberally with wolfbane. Her fiancé fails to heed the warning signals, and takes her out on to the balcony, where she eyes his throat evilly: 'I love the night. It's the only time I feel really alive.'

The climax approaches. Van Helsing prepares his stakes, but the Count abducts Mina. They are tracked down to the crypt of Carfax Abbey, where, since dawn approaches, the Count has withdrawn to the safety of his coffin. Mina is rescued, while Van Helsing, offscreen, drives his stake home. A short gurgle is the last we hear of Dracula, and the film ends on a lovers' clinch.★

Twenty-odd years later, Hammer would demonstrate how to treat the story in a more full-blooded way; but for the audiences of 1931, this was horror; and without this now stiff and unfrightening film, there would have been no other Universal monsters and no family sagas of their dark doings. As it was, within a year the genuinely classical *Frankenstein* was unleashed to strike true terror into the hearts of the world, and from then on there was no turning back.

★ In the original prints of *Dracula*, after the end title, his Van Helsing persona murmured: 'Just a moment, ladies and gentlemen . . . When you go home tonight, and the lights have been turned out, and you are afraid to look behind the curtains, and you dread to see a face appear at the window . . . why, just pull yourself together and remember that, after all . . . *there ARE such things!*'

Meanwhile, back at Universal, *Dracula* had become the top money-making film of the year, and by rights its star, Bela Lugosi, ought to have gone on to bigger and better things. Alas, his accent, his somewhat limited acting ability and his lack of foresight were all against him. Offered the role of the monster in *Frankenstein* – early posters for the film even bear his name – he turned it down because he would have no dialogue, and elected instead to make nothing in particular of the role of Dr Mirakle in a flat and ill-scripted version of *Murders in the Rue Morgue*. He seems never even to have been considered for any of Universal's later monsters – the mummy, the invisible man, the werewolf – and that was probably clear thinking on the part of the front office, for Lugosi's screen personality suggested evil from the outset, whereas all those roles required at least an initial sympathy if not tragic stature. It seems surprising, though, that no effort was made to weave him into the fabric of *Dracula's Daughter*, which emerged in 1936 and sadly lacked a name except for fans of Otto Kruger. Since Universal's battery of writers had already shown the Frankenstein monster safe and well after his apparently fatal adventure in the blazing windmill, it can surely not have been beyond their imaginative powers to resurrect the Count. Instead, they played perfectly fair by starting the new film where the old one left off, in the cellars of Carfax Abbey, with Van Helsing hammering a stake – off-screen – into Dracula's chest. (The indomitable Edward Van Sloan was even retained to play Van Helsing again.) We are given a glimpse of the staked vampire, who has neither withered into his real age nor crumbled into dust: he lies almost intact in his coffin, elegant in his dinner jacket and cloak, but played by a wax dummy which bears no resemblance to Lugosi. The young romantic characters in the original story seem to have vanished into thin air; at any rate none of them come forward to support their loyal friend when a comic relief policeman noses into the scene and promptly arrests Van Helsing for murder:

HAWKINS: Who is 'e in there?
VAN HELSING: His name was Count Dracula.
HAWKINS: 'Ow long 'as 'e been dead?
VAN HELSING: About five hundred years.
HAWKINS: Albert – 'and me them 'andcuffs!
VAN HELSING: That won't be necessary, constable.
HAWKINS: So *you* say. One bloke a-welterin' in 'is blood with a stake driven through 'is 'eart. A gentleman lying 'ere with 'is neck broke – by the way, who 'is 'e?
VAN HELSING: A poor harmless imbecile who ate spiders and flies . . .

While the pros and cons of Van Helsing's case are being argued out with the naturally incredulous local judiciary, a pale-faced and black-cloaked lady appears to claim the Count's body. A picture of elegant melancholy, she claims to be the daughter of Count Dracula, and nobody seems disposed either to argue with her or to hold the body as necessary evidence in the Van Helsing case. With the help of her servant Sandor, who looks even more vampiric than she does, she cremates the Count's body on a rough pyre in a forest glade. DD, as we may call her, holds a crucifix over the corpse but is forced to turn her own head away from it, intoning the while a remarkable prayer:

DRACULA'S DAUGHTER (1936). Halliwell Hobbes as the investigating police sergeant may well be mystified if he has seen the previous picture, for the corpse in the coffin looks nothing like Bela Lugosi, nor does it show any obvious sign of having been staked. However, Gloria Holden as Dracula's daughter seems to accept it without hesitation; at any rate she cremates it in a convenient glade.

Unto Adoni and Aseroth, into the keeping of the lords of the flame and lower pits, I consign this body to be for ever more consumed in this purging fire. Let all baleful spirits that threaten the souls of men be banished by the sprinkling of this salt. Be thou exorcised, o Dracula, and thy body, long undead, find destruction throughout eternity in the name of thy dark unholy master. In the name of the all-holiest and through this cross be thy evil spirit cast out till the end of time.

Van Helsing calls in a former pupil to plead his case. Dr Jeffrey Garth is something of a playboy, and though initially sceptical, when he meets DD at a swank party he begins to suspect that she may be who Van Helsing says she is, despite her alias of Marya Zeleska. The dark lady admits soulfully to many problems, one of which is that she wishes to be rid of an old family curse. One senses that in her view an affair with the dashing Garth might help, but back in her London studio flat (hurriedly rented, one presumes) poor DD discovers her evil side to be uppermost, and sends out Sandor to procure a young female subject for her to paint. The suggestion of lesbian love in the ensuing sequence is quite remarkable for a Hollywood film of the mid-thirties; perhaps the Hays Office was lulled by the suggestion that the production was based on a literary classic, i.e. 'Carmilla' (of which more later). Nan Grey gives a sensitive cameo performance as the innocent victim of DD's love, lust, and requirement for fresh blood. Nervous at her unfamiliar surroundings, she becomes frightened when DD advances upon her, and as she screams the camera swings away to focus on a primitive wall-mask. Found dying in the street, she is put under hypnosis by Garth and is just able to reveal that she was abducted by someone called Sandor. As she dies, Garth learns that DD has kidnapped his own attractive secretary Janet, perhaps as a victim, perhaps as a hostage. Van Helsing is still musing:

> How can a vampire have a daughter? I thought they were only legends, but now I must begin to doubt. One says that her mother became Dracula's victim while she was carrying the child, so that it was born neither human nor vampire. There are other different tales. But this is what it means for you, friend Jeffrey: the Countess will return to Castle Dracula. She must think of that as her home.

Seems logical, if only in a Hollywood way. Taking the hint, Garth loses no time in renting a plane and flying to the Carpathians, so that the finale of this brief film can take place in the cobwebby castle set which so amply created the right mood for the first two reels of its predecessor. Janet is still safe, but Sandor is aggrieved because DD wants to make Garth her own instead of him. So when Garth arrives he shoots an arrow at him . . . and DD bravely steps forward to take it in the chest. Since it has a wooden shaft, this solves her problems once and for all, and Janet recovers sufficiently to contemplate the corpse and say how beautiful she was. Van Helsing, who has brought up the rearguard, nods sagely: 'She was beautiful when she died . . . a hundred years ago.'

Dracula's Daughter is a neat if rather doleful little film, but despite careful attention it has the look of a support. The central character casts no reflection in a mirror, but apart from that she is more tragic than frightening, and her activities build up to no big suspense scenes. In fact, what we are invited to enjoy is less a

DRACULA'S DAUGHTER (1936). Irving Pichel, a popular heavy before he became an efficient director, pleads with the Countess to make him immortal like her. But in the tradition of the best fairy stories she has other things on her mind, like falling in love with a mortal.

feast of horror than a number of mildly interesting hors d'oeuvres. The script is carefully balanced but never finds its batwings; and it remains hard to explain why DD refuses for so long to grant Sandor's wish to become a vampire too, since one presumes that the briefest bout of fang-flashing would have made him happy, and therefore loyal, for all eternity.

In 1936 and 1937 a double bill revival of *Frankenstein* and *Dracula* played all over the world, and Universal executives were astounded when they came to tot up the enormous receipts. So in 1939 a big budget was expended on *Son of Frankenstein*, a few scenes of which were shot in colour before taste and a sudden economy drive dictated otherwise. Its great success meant that similar largesse would have been poured over the Dracula myth but for the outbreak of the Second World War, which had several effects relevant to the horror cycle. First of all it cut off the enthusiastic middle-European market for the duration. Then the British Board of Film Censors directed that all horror films must be either banned or have their teeth drawn, on the grounds that the world now had enough real horrors without adding imaginary ones. (In fact the opposite is true: amid the innumerable deaths which are an inevitable consequence of war, audiences lovingly cling to legends which suggest the existence of a world beyond.) At home, Americans found it difficult enough to comprehend what was happening in the real Europe, while the imaginary one, natural habitat of the legendary monsters, seemed more and more remote. Quality of production no longer paid off; instead there was an insatiable public appetite for cheap, brisk entertainment on the comic-strip level, with plenty of mindless action and not too much regard for logic or probability. The monsters had a place here, but the new young generation of filmgoers refused to take them seriously, requiring only that they should provide a few easily forgotten thrills, compatible with the consumption of popcorn and Pepsi-Cola.

The next Dracula film, *Son of Dracula*, was a hybrid, caught between these trends. Released in 1943, it had a low budget, but was the work of Europeans, the Siodmak brothers. It was fast moving, with a story set in America for easy assimilation by the juvenile audience, and the vampire performed magic tricks which would have been thought absurd in the earlier stories, yet it achieved a unique sombreness from its Louisiana bayou setting and its characterization of the heroine as a melancholic depressive who longs above all to become one of the

SON OF DRACULA (1943). Lon Chaney Jnr tried hard to justify his publicity tag as 'the screen's master character actor', but he still looked like an American tourist in Transylvania.

undead. Miscasting, however, was a central flaw. By this time, following his success in *Of Mice and Men, The Wolf Man* and *The Ghost of Frankenstein* (of which more later), the hulking Lon Chaney Jnr had to be allowed a crack at every horror character in the canon. His Dracula, however, was not repeated. No actor was more American or less ethereal than Chaney, and despite his quite valiant efforts in this movie he could never convince as a mystery man from middle Europe, not even with grey-streaked temples and a newly devised special effect which by use of cartoon animation for the intermediate shots allowed man to change into bat before our very eyes. He also changed quite convincingly into white mist; but for some reason he was allowed to cast a reflection in a mirror. Perhaps it was thought that the very idea of so bulky an actor not doing so would be a little rich for the audience's blood.

The story of *Son of Dracula* was sufficiently strange and shapely. We are introduced to the gloomy heiress Katherine, who while travelling in Europe has met an elegant nobleman called Count Alucard (spell it backwards) and invited him to stay for a while at the old plantation. She's a moody girl prone to odd ideas, and it's with some reluctance that her friends go to meet the unknown guest at the railroad depot. He isn't on the train; but in some mystification they bring back several boxes of earth and a coffin-like trunk, all marked with his name. Katherine meanwhile gets her fortune told by an old gypsy who lives in the middle of the bayou, but all she learns is the uncomfortable news that she will marry a corpse and live in a grave. Katherine does not seem too put out by this information, but a huge bat, apparently disgruntled by it, flies in and attacks the old crone, who promptly dies of fright. That evening, the cloaked count arrives silently from nowhere at the mansion where a party is being held, supposedly in his honour. His first ungrateful move is to cause Katherine's father to die in a fire, making the lady very rich indeed. Later still, she is lured back to the swamp where the count makes an improbably regal entrance, standing on his own coffin as it floats through the bayou. Totally in Alucard's power, Katherine consents to marry him before a justice of the peace, but when her erstwhile lover Frank finds out, he takes a gun to the damned interloper. Unfortunately the bullets entirely fail to injure the count, but kill Katherine who is standing behind him. The hysterical Frank confesses his crime, but when the police investigate they find Katherine, now Countess Alucard, apparently alive and as well as can be expected. Enter Professor Laszlo, clearly yet another pupil of our old friend Van Helsing. He knows all about vampire lore, and spots the count's real identity, within a relative or two, at once:

> Broadly speaking, a vampire is an earth-bound spirit whose body comes to life at night and scours the countryside satisfying a ravenous appetite for the blood of the living . . . My own homeland in the Carpathian Hills where Count Dracula lived is sad testimony to the truth of this. What was once a happy productive region is today a barren waste – villages depopulated – the land abandoned . . . Alucard is undoubtedly a vampire, probably a descendant of Count Dracula.

While all this ancient lore is being explained for the audience's benefit, Alucard seeps under the door in a cloud of mist, and makes his position clear:

SON OF DRACULA (1943). 'Who's doing what to whom?' might be the caption for this tense situation. It's the old eternal triangle: Louise Allbritton pretends love for Dracula so that she can pass on the secret of immortality to her true love, Robert Paige. The Count is understandably miffed at being used as a patsy.

> You are right, Professor. I am here because this is a young and virile race – not dry and decadent like ours. You have what I want – what I need – what I must have!

The Count is easily sent packing when Laszlo brandishes a cross ('It would take too long to explain why they fear it') but next, Katherine is found, during daylight hours, apparently dead in a coffin in the family crypt, and Frank is imprisoned for her murder. Awakened and presumably full of blood, she appears to him by night and explains the real situation:

> Count Alucard is immortal. Through him I achieved immortality. Through me you will do the same – and we will spend eternity together. I have already taken the first step while you were sleeping . . .

Now that she has her eternal life, she goes on to say, she wants her husband disposed of so that she can wed her true love. Frank, in the grip of romantic frenzy, escapes from jail, finds Alucard's coffin and sets it ablaze. The vampire appears, naturally enraged, and the two men have a remarkably physical fight, one which the American groundlings might be expected to appreciate. Frank seems to have had it when, in the nick of time, dawn breaks, and the vampire tumbles into a watery grave, the flesh dissolving from his bones as he does so. (It was the first time this particular trick had been performed, and audiences were fascinated.) Without his support Katherine dies too, and a sadder but wiser Frank is left setting light to a funeral pyre.

Within its limits reasonably logical, and unusually plotted to say the least, *Son of Dracula* seems only to have been made at the wrong time. In America it was virtually ignored; in Britain the censor, very curiously, did not see fit even to award it the 'H' for horror certificate (though it has some very unpleasant moments) and it was uncomfortably released as support to a woebegone historical romance about Dolly Madison, *Magnificent Doll*. I imagine it gave one or two schoolboys bad dreams for all that.

Less than two years later, and with no explanation for his resurrection, the original count was back under the Universal banner. Audiences were presumably expected to forget that he was last seen cremated on a forest pyre: he merely turned up, impeccably outfitted, somewhere in period Europe, victim of a perplexing physical predicament from which on certain conditions he might be freed by Boris Karloff. But he was no longer the solo star of the show. In 1943 the studio had noted the box office success of their rather cheeky pairing of two trademarked monsters in *Frankenstein Meets the Wolf Man*. Surely, thought the moguls, this must be the way to the future: individually the ghouls have worn out their welcome by now, but billed in all-star horrors they still have value at the box office. It proved a sure way to a satisfactory bank balance, but since from now on Universal's horrors would be presented somewhat tongue-in-cheek, it was thought unnecessary to provide them with logical or even watertight scripts. The billing was all that mattered: providing the audience saw five monsters, it would be satisfied. The first of these ghoulish reunions was prepared in 1944 under the title *Chamber of Horrors*, but this was changed during pre-production to *The Devil's Brood*. It finally hit the screen as *House of Frankenstein*, though no member of the Frankenstein family appeared in it, and Dracula figured in a story separate from the rest, occupying only the first three reels. Boris Karloff had either grown weary of playing the Frankenstein monster, or was simply too old; but he was lured back to Universal, after considerable Broadway success in *Arsenic and Old Lace*, as Dr Niemann, a murderous physician who with the aid of a manic hunchback breaks jail during a thunderstorm, murders the owner of a travelling circus of horrors, and assumes his identity. One of the exhibits of which he thus finds himself master is an upended coffin containing a skeleton with a wooden stake through the spot where its heart ought to be. No prizes were awarded for guessing the identity of the bones, especially when the script explained that they had been 'borrowed' from their resting place near Castle Dracula, and that the coffin contained a supply of the old count's homeland earth. After a performance during which he has recognized an old enemy in the audience, Dr Niemann almost abstractedly removes the stake, and finds to his surprise that flesh promptly grows upon the bones, assuming within a few seconds the caped and top-hatted form of the bloodthirsty count. The actor finding himself thus restored to life is the suitably emaciated John Carradine, who relishes his introductory dialogue with Karloff:

HOUSE OF FRANKENSTEIN (1944). The stake which you see embedded in the skeleton of Dracula has this time had an untraditional effect, but the removal of it produces not only John Carradine but an immaculate set of evening clothes. Boris Karloff and J. Carrol Naish are the showmen.

DRACULA: Drop that stake from your hand. Drop it.
NIEMANN (*looking away to avoid being hypnotised*): If you move, I'll send your soul back to the limbo of eternal waiting. Do as I ask and I will serve you. I will protect the earth in which you lie, so that before sunrise, your coffin will always be ready for you.
DRACULA: For that, I will do whatever you wish.

With his long face, grey hair and moustache, Carradine looked more like the Bram Stoker description of Dracula than Lugosi ever had, and certainly he gave a suave enough performance; but in this film Dracula's presence was required only as an aperitif to the reviving of the wolf man and the Frankenstein monster, and he is confined to a short sequence during which, under threat of the stake being replaced, he carries out for Niemann a scheme of revenge. Things do not go entirely smoothly, and after a frenzied carriage chase he is left struggling to reach his coffin before daylight. He fails, of course. A nice touch is the slipping of his ring, as he himself turns to bone again, from the finger of the innocent girl who had been cast under his spell.

Since the Dracula section of *House of Frankenstein* was by far the best, it came as no surprise that within a few months *House of Dracula* was circulating among the double bills. It was a misnomer: the house in question, allegedly the old Frankenstein place though now situated by a cliff-edge, quite clearly belongs to genial Dr Edelmann, a most benevolent gentleman engaged on research into the world's ills. The involvement here of the Frankenstein monster will be noted later; so far as Dracula is concerned the role is again a fairly brief one, though it does have more bearing than last time on the main plot. Once more the role is essayed by Mr Carradine. He turns up very early on in bat form, then makes himself presentable and knocks at the front door. Though later events suggest that we are in the same region as *House of Frankenstein*, Edelmann does not recognize his visitor, nor does the latter ever explain how he escaped from his previous predicament (or even who looks after his immaculate laundry). His hair is now white, and while spying out the land he introduces himself as Baron Latos; but once in the cellar with Edelmann he points to his crested coffin which has been smuggled in by presumably supernatural means, and admits his true identity. He is bored with bloodsucking, it seems, and begs the doctor to release him from his cursed supernatural existence. Edelmann is the irritating type who likes a scientific explanation for everything, and on taking a sample of the Count's blood he discovers parasites which in his view have caused the tendency to vampirism. All that is required, he suggests, is a series of blood transfusions. If good blood – his own, why not? – is pumped into the Count, it will contain antibodies capable of polishing off the parasites. Dracula sighs somewhat disbelievingly, but has nothing to lose. All goes well until, halfway through the series of transfusions, the Count falls for the doctor's glamorous assistant, and decides that he will stay undead after all if she can be persuaded to be his Transylvanian bride. To this end he stops the flow of blood while the doctor is asleep, under self-hypnosis, and for good measure causes some Dracula blood to flow into Edelmann. Realizing what has happened, Edelmann saves his assistant's neck by driving the Count away with a handy crucifix. Next day he traces the coffin and exposes the contents to the sun, with predictable results. But for Edelmann himself it is too late: Dracula's blood has done its work, and before he can set up more transfusions he turns into a kind of Dr Edelmann and Mr Hyde, murdering the local village folk with many a nasty hee-hee.

House of Dracula is vintage comic strip, a fairy tale not even for grown-ups; but the sheer outrageousness of its plot-line, of which the above comprises about half, makes one wish that it had been produced by talents with an eye for satire. Alas, it contains not a single intentionally funny line, just a score of *un*intentionally funny ones.

So far as Universal was concerned, Dracula seemed to have come to the end of the road. He was out for the count, just one of a gallery of second-hand monsters which now played cameo roles in silly plots featuring newer and less interesting characters. Yet during the forties the old Count made two major reappearances in the person of Bela Lugosi, who for some reason was not asked to play in any of the 'serious' Dracula sequels, though he was kept fairly busy in other Universal thrillers. While *House of Frankenstein* was still in the planning stage he had himself been starring at Columbia in *The Return of the Vampire*, a curious but not unrewarding one-off. He played Armand Tesla, but had Universal not held the literary copyrights concerned the film might well have been called *Dracula Meets the Wolf Man*, for Tesla hails from Transylvania, sleeps in a crypt, and has an assistant who sprouts hair at every full moon. Destroyed in London during the

LONDON AFTER MIDNIGHT (1927). An apparently lost film of which only tantalizing stills remain, with Lon Chaney Sr looking more like a shark than a vampire. Polly Moran is the terrified housekeeper.

First World War, Tesla is staked and buried; but his grave is accidentally uncovered during the 1941 blitz, and two kindly air raid wardens remove the stake, which they take to be an unfortunate result of the recent bombing, before reburying him. The vampire then claws his way out of the earth bent on revenge. The non-monstrous characters are of the titled class, and the plot development strongly resembles that of the play version of the original *Dracula*; but for an unpretentious Columbia 'B' the movie works pretty well and leads to a chilling finish (made inexplicable by the British censor) when the vampire is once more caught out in the sun and his facial features seem to melt from the bone like wax.

Lugosi had played a vampire of sorts for MGM in a rather unsatisfactory 1935 thriller called *Mark of the Vampire*, a remake of a lost Lon Chaney silent, *London After Midnight*. The film boasts a few frissons, but Lugosi has no dialogue and is disappointingly revealed at the end as an actor hired to lend atmosphere to a ghoulish evening of 'hunt the murderer'.* Nor was Humphrey Bogart any luckier in 1939's *The Return of Dr X*, a catchpenny 'B' in which, with pallid face and white-streaked hair, he played a modern urban bloodsucker and looked most unhappy in the role.

Lugosi's 1948 return to the Dracula role at Universal was surprisingly satisfactory, though no project can at first have seemed less promising. The title *Abbott and Costello Meet Frankenstein* is yet another misnomer, for the Baron is one of the few horror characters they *don't* meet. They meet his monster, and they meet the Wolf Man, and for a moment at the end there's an encounter with an invisible gentleman, but the chief villain of this well-regulated little horror comedy, which plays rather like a British pantomime with the audience shouting 'He's behind you!', is the old Transylvanian bloodsucker himself. The script had once, rather half-heartedly, been conceived as a straight thriller called *The Brain of Frankenstein*, but when Abbott and Costello were set to burlesque it, a thorough change of style seemed in order. Lugosi therefore bares no fangs, and seems to connive with the audience in getting a few laughs at the comedians' expense. In pursuit of his nefarious designs he does change into a bat more than once, but even then he is able to kid his old role while outwardly presenting it with the utmost seriousness. Sixty-six years old, and suffering from drug addiction, Lugosi looks a little careworn for a successful vampire, but thick make-up takes care of most of the problems, and at least on this outing he doesn't have to romance anybody. He does have under his hypnotic spell a glamorous scientist called Sandra, who seems to have been conducting some rather nasty experiments, and there's a splendid moment when he tells her to look into his eyes and we see a flapping bat in each pupil. Their dialogue together is succinct:

---

* Lugosi's female associate in this film cuts a memorable figure. She was Carroll Borland and, forty years later, remembering her one film role, she explained in an introduction to his biography how delighted she had been to spend evenings with Bela Lugosi, dining and dancing at the Hollywood Roosevelt Hotel and watching heads turn everywhere in the room. She explains too that in the film's original script there was a suggestion of incest between father and daughter vampire; that naturally had to be eliminated. Producers for many years were very wary of ascribing unhealthy motives to female characters: *Dracula's Daughter*, as we have seen, was lucky to get through. In 1946's *Devil Bat's Daughter* crooks managed to convince the daughter of a mad scientist who wasn't a vampire that she nevertheless was; but it was all explained away as a hypnotic dream. The world was not ready.

THE RETURN OF DR X (1939). Humphrey Bogart gave positively his worst performance – quite possibly the worst performance by any major star – in this lethargic potboiler about a modern vampire. The hairstyle seems to have been borrowed from a skunk. Wayne Morris and Dennis Morgan represent the forces of good: Lya Lys is the recumbent victim.

– Have you mastered Dr Frankenstein's notebook?
– Let me get my hand on a scalpel again and you shall see.
– This time the monster must have no will of his own, no fiendish intellect to oppose his master.
– There, my dear count, I believe I have exceeded your fondest wishes. The new brain I have chosen for the monster is so simple, so pliable, he will obey you like a trained dog.

For most of the running time Lugosi is simply a suave stock villain in a black cloak. His very best moment comes when, having approved Sandra's dumb subject for a transplant, he pats the unsuspecting Costello on the head and murmurs: 'What we need today is young blood . . . and brains . . .'

Bud and Lou play baggage checkers in Florida. Accused by the owner of the wax museum of losing the contents of two crates, they go looking for them: and that's the plot. The crates, of course, contained the dormant figures of Dracula and the Frankenstein monster, finding their way into the country under the alias of wax figures. The first unpacking in the chamber of horrors is a 'look behind you' sequence of the first order, with Bud always out of the room when anything happens:

– I'm going out to get the other crate.
– I've got just two words to say to you.
– What's that?
– Hurry back.

Lou sees Dracula's coffin open and the Count's hand move, but when he shrieks
for his partner the latter is sceptical:

– You're all excited reading this card. 'Dracula can change himself at will into a
vampire bat' – that's a lot of phony-baloney to fool McDougal's customers. Listen, *I*
know there's no such person as Dracula. *You* know there's no such person as Dracula.
– But does *Dracula* know it?

There follows much effective business with a candle which moves as Dracula's
coffin opens and shuts. Finally the count contrives to leave his coffin, hypnotize
Lou, and bring the monster to life by applying an electric current to its neck
electrodes. The giant creature rises stiffly to its feet and starts back in fright as it
notices the dumbfounded Costello. Dracula is parental in his concern for the great
brute: 'Don't be afraid,' he tells the monster; 'he won't hurt you!'
    The extracts we hear from Dr Frankenstein's notebook are far from impressive,
e.g.: 'All my research is based on the premise that all things, including thoughts,
are material.' But they are sufficient, it seems, for Sandra to bring the monster
back to crackling life on the night when all the other principals are off to a
masquerade ball. 'Ah, you young people,' nods the count approvingly, 'making
the most of life . . . while it lasts.'
    When, trussed up and ready for the operation, Lou discovers the Count's game
plan, he is less than impressed, and tells the monster so: 'Frankly, Franky, it's a
bad idea. I've had this brain for more than thirty years and it hasn't worked right
yet.' Events lead to a fracas in the castle with all the monsters activated and the two
comedians running down the drive with Frankenstein's creation in full pursuit.
They meet the still angry owner of the chamber of horrors, and Lou stops for a
word:

– Do you still want your exhibits?
– Of course I do.
– Well, here comes one of 'em now.

The entire object of the picture is to raise laughs and a few screams, which it did
most effectively when I first saw it, with a full house, in Cambridge in 1949. (It
then had the even less apposite British title *Abbott and Costello Meet the Ghosts*, but
all the same I had to queue for two hours to get in.) It still holds the third highest
audience share achieved by a movie on British television. But one of its chief
pleasures always was that it re-established the Dracula character as a force to be
reckoned with, one which can be routed by two buffoons without becoming a total
laughing stock. In fact, so far from closing the book on Universal's monsters, this
unpretentious farce gave them all fresh life, for they met Abbott and Costello one
by one, with varying results. At least this kept the images warm until a little studio

by the banks of the Thames was ready to take them over and revitalize them for the hardened appetites of the fifties.

A small British company called Hammer, after its founder Will Hammer, had been in existence since the thirties, usually on or near the breadline. During the war it disappeared altogether, but in 1948 it was reactivated as the production arm of Exclusive, a busy little independent distributor slowly raising its sights from the fleapit level. The first post-war Hammer productions were fairly dire: *Who killed Van Loon?*, *Dr Morelle and the Missing Heiress* and *The Black Widow* are still spoken of in awe by those who had to endure them as second features at their local ABCs. Many of the early films were based on radio characters (*Meet Simon Cherry*, *The Adventures of PC 49*, *Dick Barton at Bay*) or they were adapted from BBC radio thriller serials (*Celia*, *The Man in Black*, *The Lady Craved Excitement*). Either way, something in the adaptation always managed to kill the original interest, and Hammer moved on (with slightly improved results) to a number of original crime thrillers, always with an imported American star to assist transatlantic release: Robert Preston in *Cloudburst*, Richard Carlson in *Whispering Smith Hits London*, George Brent in *The Last Page*. Some of these films are tolerable today; others are not, despite their emphasis on guns, girls and gangsters. But it was a television serial in 1953 which pointed the way to Hammer's successful future. The serial was *The Quatermass Experiment*. A mixture of highbrow science fiction and horror, it had kept a huge national audience glued to its armchairs over six consecutive Wednesdays, and when two years later Hammer chose to film it (very economically) they did so with sufficient crude skill to make it a box-office sensation. It was a small step from this little shocker, with its horrified hero slowly turning into a carnivorous cactus, to a genuine monster movie. In *X the Unknown* Hammer made one further experiment in the genre; then in 1956 they calculatedly remade the Frankenstein story in colour, their intention being to concentrate on sex and gore in a way which had never been possible for Universal in the black-and-white days of the thirties and forties. It was a gamble whether the cinema audience was ready for another bout of fearsome fables, but the gamble paid off handsomely for Sir James Carreras (and for Peter Cushing, who played Frankenstein), and over the next ten years Hammer's supply of horror movies barely kept up with the demand for them. At first, for copyright reasons, the Universal monster make-ups could not be copied, but soon the two companies got together for their common good and the Hammer product began to have the streamlined look of the old Universals, though with a shallower pool of acting and technical talent, and a much more gruesome style.

Dracula was the second Hammer horror subject in colour. I remember attending a pre-production press conference at which Sir James Carreras announced that he was going to make a *sexy Dracula*, which had Peter Cushing looking rather worried. 'Not you, Peter,' said Sir James: 'We'll leave that to Chris Lee. *You* can be a sexy Sherlock Holmes in *The Hound of the Baskervilles!*★ Sex was certainly the difference in Christopher Lee's Dracula portrayal as against Lugosi's, who had

★ In fact Sir James compromised and left the sexiness, in his view, to the hungry hound; to everybody I knew it was just a big dog.

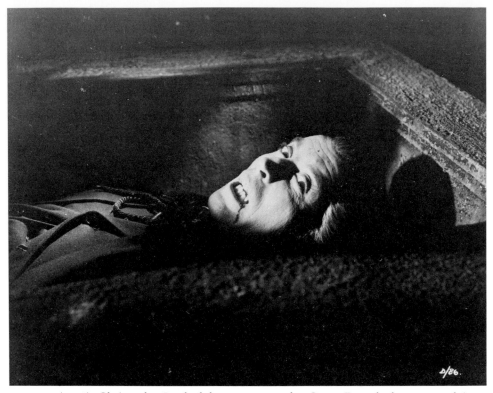

DRACULA (1958). Christopher Lee had the presence to play Count Dracula, but not much in reserve. His appearances therefore tended to be brief and violent: he became a star with very few lines of dialogue.

never suggested such a thing: blood was all he was really after. Christopher Lee, with his imposing stature, trim guardsman's figure and hungry eyes, conveyed an appreciation of both commodities, and although he never showed much in the way of acting talent he had undoubted star appeal of a rather cold variety. His shock appearance towards the beginning of *Dracula*, with bloodshot eyeballs and dripping red fangs, knocked the stuffing out of everyone who experienced it, and the vivid staking which followed soon after must have taken aback all those who remembered the reticence with which Lugosi was staked offscreen. Then, the Count's female victims all sported low-cut dresses and push-up bras, and they sighed in ecstasy when his sharp-pointed fangs finally penetrated their throats after much preliminary nuzzling. Lee was never allowed much dialogue, less even than Lugosi, and as the series went on his role sometimes amounted to a cameo appearance, perhaps because he had too tough an agent and was paid by the day. But the fact was that he was never an interesting adversary: he looked good, but one felt neither history, tradition, nor even bad breeding behind his performances.

Despite these reservations, the 1958 *Dracula* (*Horror of Dracula* in the US) still survives as an entertainment, and recalls for those who were present the atmosphere of the first West End press show, where journalists and executives realized that they were in the presence of a new, vivid, modern type of horror film with rich artificial décor, scepticism about the supernatural and (as it then seemed) no subtlety whatever. Its eighty-three minutes, tightly edited, passed in a whirl of nightmarish sensation, nightmarish, that is, by comparison with anything which had gone before. A great deal of care had been expended on making Bram Stoker's story more geographically concise: there was now no water to be crossed, all the incidents taking place in a vaguely defined middle Europe whose various locations were easily reached by horse-carriage. With the natural exception of the Count and his female disciples, the acting soft-pedalled the histrionics. Peter Cushing, keeping Frankenstein's worried frown but losing his fanaticism, was a natural Van Helsing, concerned for Dracula's victims but obsessed by his own plans to thwart the monster. John Van Eyssen played Jonathan Harker, now from the start an undercover agent of ace vampire staker Van Helsing, and the first observed victim of Dracula after having the exposition pretty well to himself. Insect-eating Renfield was eliminated altogether. The result was true to the spirit rather than the letter of the book. Gone was the stagebound feel of the first Dracula film: in its place was constant movement, with the Count first chasing his victims and then being chased in his turn. But a place was found to pause for comic relief: like the porter in *Macbeth*, George Benson got a few laughs as a bemused customs guard.

This was the new storyline, imbued by Terence Fisher with a short-lived vitality which caused critics to credit him with more style than he normally possessed. Jonathan Harker goes to Castle Dracula (arriving rather oddly in bright sunshine) as the Count's new librarian. His host, who appears at nightfall, is suave and cordial, but a strange woman bites Harker in the neck and although Dracula viciously banishes her from the room it is clear that Harker will become a vampire. He stakes the woman as she lies in her coffin, and she turns into an incredibly old hag, but he has failed to notice that night has again fallen: Dracula overpowers him hypnotically and puts him under his spell. Back at base, Van Helsing soon discovers that his colleague has turned vampire, and reluctantly stakes him. An enraged and revengeful Dracula then arrives in town to corrupt Harker's fiancée Lucy, who dies and returns as a vampire, and her brother's wife Mina. Prompt action deflects the vampire's further foul intentions and Van Helsing tracks him back to his castle, where after a savage fight he is trapped by a crucifix in the rays of dawn's early light, and decomposes into dust which blows away in the morning breeze.

The publicity tag line for *Dracula* was 'The Terrifying Lover Who Died Yet Lived!' It was apt enough: love, terror and death were the principal ingredients, with magic taking a back seat until that fascinating decomposition scene. Van Helsing even laughs away the myths about a vampire's ability to change into animals: the vampire, he says, is simply an evil man who has discovered that the secret of eternal life is sex and blood. (The whole thrust of the plot is the Count's needs for a mistress to replace the one who was staked.) Alas, the first fully fledged example of the Hammer technique displayed the company's limitations as well as its virtues. Increasing budgets had led to more imposing décor, but one could not get a quart into the pint pot of Bray, and audiences became bored with the lush yet styleless sets, like a Woolworth's view of baroque, and with the one convenient exterior location which suggested Transylvania. This was Black Park, near Pinewood, a secluded public playground whose lake, trees and boulders, already familiar from scores of other movies, rapidly became hilariously recognizable whenever Dracula's funereal carriage was driven back and forth along the foreshore, which was roughly twice per film. The explicit gore of the Hammer versions, while attracting many teenagers who had no appreciation of subtlety, became boring from over-use, and certainly alienated many fans of the older, tamer, wittier films. There were constant allegations that Hammer made its films in three versions, a modest one for Britain, a bolder one for America, and one with no holds barred for the Far East. This has been denied as often as it has been claimed, and one feels that had the shock sequences really existed they would have been profitably advertised on reissue as censorship gradually became more lax.

A rapid sequel was inevitable, but Dracula's dust had carelessly been allowed to blow away, and Hammer had not yet grown impudent enough to devise a reassembly from that particular predicament. A plot line was therefore cooked up under the title *Disciple of Dracula*. ('He made a school of innocent girls the prey to his fiendish desires!') The required sexual emphasis changed this to *The Brides of Dracula*, which was still a fair representation of the story, and the film certainly gave satisfaction. In fact, if Peter Bryan and Jimmy Sangster's original script had been directed by James Whale or Jacques Tourneur instead of by the competent journeyman Terence Fisher, it might have made far and away the most interesting Dracula of them all. *The Brides of Dracula* starts and proceeds somewhat obliquely. One is never quite sure to begin with what the precise thrust of the plot is going to be, and much of it is expressed in action rather than dialogue; the nominal heroine for once very nearly becomes a victim, and Van Helsing, when he makes his belated appearance, is a confident but by no means an infallible avenger. From this point, however, with a single pause for another Macbeth-like piece of comic relief, he is in constant battle with the evil which surrounds him. The so-called horror moments in this movie are few and far between, but they are held together by genuine suspense, which holds even through a hiatus at the halfway mark when the plot changes gear and prepares itself for the final bout of bloodletting. Altogether this is a film which inhabits a world of its own, despite the pantomimish Hammer chorus of rhubarbing villagers and the inevitable parade of nubile young females.

The scene is an undefined middle Europe in 1890, several years before Bram Stoker even thought of Dracula. Marianne is our heroine, a self-possessed Parisienne en route to a new teaching post at a school for young ladies in Badstein. Stranded when her coach unaccountably leaves a rest stop without her, she is offered hospitality, with apparently kindly intent, by the autocratic Baroness Meinster, who as played by Martita Hunt (Miss Havisham in *Great Expectations*) is awesome even without make-up. We may well guess that a vampire lurks in the baroness's half-derelict castle, but we remain unsure of the lady's motives. Does she procure victims for the monster? And why? It certainly seems sinister that she always has two places laid at her lonely dinner table, in case of visitors. Yet she eats nothing herself. 'I am not hungry . . . yet.' And do we not recognize her coachman as the fellow who encouraged Marianne's transport to depart without

THE BRIDES OF DRACULA (1960). David Peel, here seen (with Yvonne Monlaur) getting the worst of it, was a rather splendid Dracula. Oddly enough he was billed way down the cast list and made no further screen appearances. Some say he became an estate agent.

her? Even more oddly, how comes the girl's luggage to be waiting for her in the room to which she is shortly led?

Whatever the plan, it goes sadly wrong for the baroness. Marianne espies in an inner courtyard a handsome, sad young man. Full of self-pity, the baroness explains that he is her son, who is feeble-minded and has ruined the last many years of his mother's life. She had in fact let it be known that he had died; it seemed more convenient that way. Marianne is offended by the adjective, and the baroness rises to retire, having perhaps deliberately set the girl in sympathy with her son. 'I shall not be breakfasting with you,' she announces, adding ambivalently: 'I have found that I sleep better in the hours of daylight.' Marianne can't sleep either, and in the middle of the night she steals down to make the acquaintance of the young baron, a pale young fellow who spins a convincing yarn about having been imprisoned by his mother so that she can take over his estates: she has even shackled his ankle by a gold chain. Marianne, outraged by this, steals the key from the room of the baroness, who seems to be sleeping rather well after all; but needless to say, just as soon as the baron is free, an evil smile creeps across his face and he reveals a truly nasty nature.

Early next morning, before dawn, Marianne finds the baroness dead in her chair, with blood still dripping from two telltale marks on her throat: the baron has vampirized his own mother. The castle now rings with the mad laughter of the baron's old servant Greta: 'You've set free a vampire,' she cackles. Running in terror from the spot, Marianne stumbles in the forest upon the nocturnal funeral of a young girl, the baron's first victim, and is mistaken by the mourners for another vampire. She is saved from their fury by the sudden terrifying appearance of the baron, but he, though now replete with blood, no sooner has her in his arms than his attention turns to her white neck. Luckily he is foiled by the crowing of a cock . . .

So much for exposition: now for development. Suffering from shock, Marianne is found at the side of the road by the driver of a coach taking Dr Van Helsing to Badstein. Though both friendly and resourceful, he seems rather vague as to exactly what has brought him to the district: 'I am aware of an evil that exists in this province, and my reason for being here is to seek it out and destroy it.'

After he has cheered her, Marianne feels well enough to take up her appointment at the academy under pompous Mr Lang, who makes the somewhat hilarious initial mistake of reproving Marianne for bringing along a gentleman friend, until Van Helsing curtly introduces himself as a doctor . . . of philosophy, theology and metaphysics. (Which is most useful, one wonders, in combating vampires?) Having seen Marianne settled with a new friend called Gina, Van Helsing returns to the troubled village, where, as he tells the nervous curé, the most recently buried victim of the vampire must be staked:

> Those who have been infected by the kiss of the vampire must themselves infect others. The cult must spread: that is the rule of the undead. She will rise again from the grave . . . unless I stop her.

But when Van Helsing arrives in the churchyard to perform his unpleasant task, he finds he has been forestalled by mad old Greta, who in a quite unnerving scene is squatting on the grave, murmuring baby talk to the undead as she scrapes helpfully at the earth:

> Be patient, be patient, my little one. Greta is with you. Greta is here to take you to your master. To your master, little one. Come, my sweet one, come.

Suddenly the soil becomes disturbed, and a hand shoots through, clawing blindly at the air. Slowly the sad white-draped form of the murdered girl appears, and as she gains her full height a withered funeral wreath slithers to the ground. Van Helsing is about to take forcible action when the hysterical curé stumbles foolishly into the scene, and the vampiress gets away in the confusion. When Van Helsing tries to follow, he is attacked by a huge swooping black bat, which must have surprised him very much since in the previous film he was heard to declare that the ability of a vampire to transform himself into an animal was 'a common fallacy'. And by the way, if the baron *could* so transform himself, where was the purpose in his being shackled?

The trail leads back to the castle, where Van Helsing finds no baron and no coffin, but the undead form of the baroness. 'You will never destroy him,' she says. 'He is too clever for you.' Van Helsing gazes at her more in sorrow than in anger: 'By taking the blood of his own mother, he has broken the laws of darkness. If I do not destroy him, he will eventually be destroyed by his own kind.' The baroness nods in silent submission, and for herself placidly agrees to be staked, so that she may rest in peace. Meanwhile the baron is occupying himself usefully at the girls' academy, drawing the snobbish Mr Lang into acquiescence and turning the once spirited Marianne into a willing accomplice who will procure for him delectable morsels of female flesh. By the time Van Helsing pays another visit to the establishment, having had little enough luck elsewhere so far, it is too late for Gina, who has sprouted a fine set of fangs and has to be promptly staked. And when the local doctor, in the chubby form of Miles Malleson, is trotted on for a comic interlude, he is too absorbed by his own hypochondria to be concerned about his patients. ('Here, better take these, can't be too careful. There's been a lot of death about this year, lot of death. Still, that's life, isn't it?')

Van Helsing is delighted to find that Marianne can still be saved. ('He has taken just enough of you to hold on to him, then he left you till he needs you again, so that you may find others for his enjoyment.') She gratefully leads Van Helsing to an old mill, where the count and Greta are in hiding with a number of disciples. The old crone is soon disposed of by a fall downstairs, but the baron is a more dramatic adversary. Seizing an opportunity, he sinks his fangs into Van Helsing's shoulder: 'Now you are one of us,' he leers. But after a few moments of nausea Van Helsing steels himself to take the only possible course of action, branding his own wounds with an iron from a nearby brazier, and pouring on to the smoking result a phial of secret liquid from his little black bag. The slight setback overcome, he is again ready for a fight. When the baron returns with Marianne, Van Helsing whisks her into a pentacle which he has skilfully drawn on the floor. The baron dare not enter, especially since a magic mist rises at the perimeter; and from the centre Van Helsing declaims his judgment:

> I indict you, Baron Meinster, by the very code of your own loathsome sect. You have flouted even the evil laws of darkness. You have taken the blood of your mother. You have taken the blood of this girl, and yet permitted her to live to satisfy your desires. This is forbidden among the undead . . . I demand the penalty! Creatures of the night, I summon you from the grave, from the necropolis of the undead, from the depths of darkness itself. Come, give justice to your code. Destroy this evil being!

The wind rises to a shriek and is joined by a new sound, a murmur as though from a thousand insects. Terrified, the baron begins to back away, but even as he does so the mill is suffused with the sound of softly beating wings. Bats! Black, noisome bats fill the whole area except the space within the pentacle. The baron sinks to the floor under a cloud of them . . . and for good measure Van Helsing arranges the windmill's sails so that they fix the stricken baron in the shadow of the cross as the mill itself goes up in flames, and Marianne makes her escape with Van Helsing. Who could wish for a more thoroughgoing climax?

The secret key to *The Brides of Dracula* is sex, and that, in this thickly suggested form, is something new in vampire films. Lee had certainly wallowed in it, but here everybody does so. The title brings it first to our attention. The school is full

THE BRIDES OF DRACULA (1960). The American advertising seems to be for a rather different film, but on examination it is not quite untrue to the plot.

of foolish virgins. The baroness is a super madam. Marianne, despite herself, is a procuress. The baron is a lecher who violates his own mother, thus allowing the Hammer hierarchy to rub its hands at having got a little incest under the nose of the then very staid British censor. *The Brides of Dracula* is even very well acted, especially by the little-used newcomer David Peel, who has more to do than Lee in the previous film yet is billed fifth. However arrived at, the mix is most satisfactory, providing a true fairy tale for grown-ups; but it does accentuate the curious poverty of imagination in the next three Draculas starring Christopher Lee.

Before them, in fact, Hammer slipped in a rather good, well-paced yarn about another disciple of the old Count. The only trouble with *Kiss of the Vampire* is that it contains no surprises. Once again the setting, supposedly Bavaria, was all too clearly Black Park. It is 1910, and an English honeymoon couple (Gerald Harcourt and his wife, again Marianne) run out of petrol and have to spend the night in a local inn, though not before Marianne has been warned away by wide-eyed Dr Zimmer, who turns out to be a vampire hunter. The young people decide to stay, and receive a mysterious invitation to dine with Dr Ravna, who owns a nearby castle, and promises to get them some petrol. He has no such intention, for he and his children are vampires in search of prey. There is a sinister masked ball; Marianne is vampirized; Dr Zimmer turns up to offer help and conjures up thousands of bats which, together with garlands of garlic, destroy the evil band, bringing Marianne back to normality in the process.

Apart from the garlic this is a virtual reprise of *The Brides of Dracula*, though the script this time is credited to John Elder★. What makes it tolerable is good acting all round, especially from Noel Willman as the villain, and if it lacks frissons, there is a splendid finale with the white-robed disciples being attacked en masse by the black bats. Come to think of it there is also a pleasant little moment when a lady vampire looking for company scrabbles at the soil of a grave and murmurs: 'Why have you not been to see us, my sweet?'

The time had come to revive Dracula himself, and the best brains of Hammer had found a way, though they did it in a singularly unpersuasive film with little plot development apart from some rather crudely objectionable staking. *Dracula Prince of Darkness* was also shot in CinemaScope, totally robbing it of any opportunity for suspense. Paucity of imagination was demonstrated by the fact that its first five minutes are a re-run of the last five minutes of *Dracula*, with the count's dust being blown away. There was now postulated the existence in Dracula's retinue of a sinister servant named Klove; no doubt budget economies had prevented us from meeting him before. Klove it was, apparently, who carefully gathered up all the dust and hid it in a sarcophagus in the basement, biding his time until Christopher Lee could be lured back into the series.

Actor and agent having been satisfied, the right time dramatically for the reappearance turns out to be when four foolhardy travellers, despite the predictable local warnings and genuflections, insist on passing the night in the supposedly derelict Castle Dracula. After a few eerie happenings one of the men is kidnapped and killed by Klove, who hangs the body upside down over the

★ John Elder was the pseudonym of Hammer producer Anthony Hinds.

sarcophagus and slits its throat. Blood pours on to the ashes of Dracula, who promptly rises naked from the seething mess, with the predictable evil smile on his lips. Klove is ready with suitable clothing, and within seconds it is clear that enough dust was saved to rematerialize the Count exactly in his previous form. The two ladies in the party are naturally his first conquests, and for one of them, in a scene taken from Bram Stoker, he opens a vein in his chest so that she can suck *his* blood and become a vampire in every sense of the word. The Van Helsing figure in this thinly spun tale is one Father Sandor from the local monastery, where another disciple of Dracula lurks also, to ensure that right does not prevail too easily; but at length prevail it does, after the violent disposal of one screeching lady vampire played by the delectable Barbara Shelley, the saving in the nick of time of the other lady in the party, and a fine chase by landau. The climax is a battle on the ice, which Father Sandor shoots till it cracks, so that a terrified Dracula is trapped below in a bow to the half-forgotten tradition that vampires are allergic to running water.

Dracula Prince of Darkness was unpleasant and sadly cheap-looking. It had no style. Its sets were cardboard, its back-projected skylines quite unnecessarily inept. Lee's appearances were reduced to the absolute minimum and dialogue denied him altogether, so that instead of a saturnine villain one was presented with an unconvincing bogey man who sprang out whenever the audience least expected him. The lack of Van Helsing was another problem, for the necessary sense of antagonism between monster and avenger was almost totally lacking: a priest after all is *expected* to preach the gospel, and this particular priest was if anything less sympathetic than his quarry.

By 1968, when *Dracula Has Risen from the Grave* emerged, the producers had managed rather better to get the hang of the thing. In Britain the censor obliged with the highly commercial 'X' certificate, but the American distributors chose to regard the new offering as a jolly jape for the younger element. 'General audiences' were admitted, and advertisements included an image of sticking plaster across a girl's neck, with the slogan:

Dracula has risen from the grave . . . obviously.

There was also an ad depicting the fearsomely grimacing Count as he removed a huge stake from his own chest. This bore the caption:

You can't keep a good man down.

Humour, actually, was sadly lacking in the film itself, and Dracula never rose from the grave at all, rather from under the ice where we last left him: by means we won't go into, blood trickled through the cracks, and with one bound Drac was free. But no matter. The film starts with a swing when the huge bell of the local church won't ring, and is found to contain a most unusual clapper: the upside-down body of a naked girl. Just who was responsible for this picturesque outrage is never clarified, since Dracula is still under the ice; but then, James Bond prologues seldom connect with the rest of the film either. The terrified priest who

DRACULA HAS RISEN FROM THE GRAVE (1968). Christopher Lee is about to retire . . . if he can get into that coffin, that is. Unless it's a trick of perspective, he and the lid seem to belong elsewhere, and the inscription on the plate looks like: Gizela Syms 1885–1903.

witnesses the Count's resurrection promptly becomes his acolyte. Dracula can't get back into his own castle because a cross has been carelessly left against the door, so he vows revenge on priests in general and sets about upsetting the monastery. Sometimes he can't even be bothered to vampirize his victims, and kills them in more regular ways. At one point he is indeed staked, but the Hammer version of the legend now insists that additional prayers are necessary for his permanent demise, which is why he is able to unstake himself with comparative ease, as shown in the posters. Finally he hypnotizes a victim into removing the cross from the castle door, but it tumbles into a gully: during a subsequent struggle the Count falls upon it and is impaled. Before he can wriggle out of this predicament the necessary prayers are murmured, causing the Count to weep blood and break up into red powder. Another problem for the writers of the next episode.

Taste the Blood of Dracula (1969) removed the scene to Victorian England, and provided a comparatively complex plot with characters and relationships far more interesting than had been the case in the last two sagas of the noble bloodsucker. With less stolid direction it could even have been exciting, as it made some attempt to follow the sequence, by initially focusing on a vial of the red powder, scooped up by a frightened onlooker from the site of Dracula's last impalement.

DRACULA HAS RISEN FROM THE GRAVE (1968). The Rolls-Royce of hearses takes the Count to his favourite hunting ground, the woods near Black Pond, Iver, Bucks.

The existence of the vial becomes known to evil Lord Courtney, and he invites three wealthy degenerates (who frequent a brothel cunningly concealed in the rear of a workhouse) to join him in a kind of Dracula fan club. ('Would you be willing to sell your souls to the devil?') Part of the ritual is to drink some blood made from the powder, but the effect on the three is unexpected: revulsion at their own debauchery makes them kill their leader. This act of semi-sacrilege stimulates an enraged Count Dracula to regenerate himself (via some rather unpersuasive special effects), from the remains of his disciple, seeking revenge against the three men through their children. ('They have destroyed my servant. They will be destroyed!') The children of the unholy trio are then persuaded gleefully to kill their parents, in a kind of short story portmanteau. The development is efficient enough, but it adds up to too much plot and too little mood, and although Geoffrey Keen, John Carson and Peter Sallis are effective as the unhappy disciples, their progeny are an unattractive lot. Dracula is finally cornered in a church full of crosses, and falls to an apparent death, rather unconvincingly and unmagically, from the top of the high altar. Once again only red dust remains.

And once again someone kindly gathers it together. The Hammer/Dracula films by now were retracing a too-familiar pattern against far too familiar sets; they followed no logic save that of Grimm's fairy tales, which would not have been too bad a model had a little more imagination been applied to avoid repetition. The aim in *Scars of Dracula* seems to have been the allocation of more time to Christopher Lee (who may have decided at last to come cheaper). This time a vampire bat contrives to spill blood on the dusty remains of Dracula, enabling the Count to rise again and reinhabit his old castle, much to the distress of those rhubarbing villagers, who promptly set fire to it without pausing to render it entirely uninhabitable to a vampire. Three young people then become over-night guests in the ruins, and the mysterious servant Klove returns. (It all sounds like a re-run of *Dracula Prince of Darkness*, and we *thought* Klove had been killed off at the end of that.) The ensuing cross-currents are unengaging, especially since they result in the survival of a particularly boring pair of young lovers. The scars of the title are presumably those which the Count burns into Klove's back for unfaithfulness to the cause; Klove is then fried when lightning strikes a rod he is holding as a weapon, and Dracula falls in flames from a rooftop. It was all pretty yawnworthy, and in addition to the listless plot audiences were presented with muddy colour and clumsy trick work. Everything pointed to a lack of excitement on both sides of the camera.

At the box office Dracula was now distinctly subject to the law of diminishing returns; a little fresh blood had to be injected somehow. *Dracula A.D. 1972*, a rather confining title for a tiresome piece filled with what would later have been called punk rockers, was the result. (One might have liked it better under the once-touted alternative, *Dracula is Dead and Well and Living in London*.) The patently bad idea was to confront the suave snarling Count with fast cars, mini-skirts and hip dialogue, and a moment's thought would have told the producers that such a modern concept must inevitably rob the show of any period style or mystery it might have inherited from its occasionally distinguished forebears, especially since the London life depicted is fatuous in the extreme. Lee himself claims to have been totally against the idea, but in need of money. At least the script restored Peter Cushing as Van Helsing, but not the original Abraham. We see *him* killed off in an introductory period encounter with his arch-enemy, who is himself impaled on a broken wheel and suffers yet another disintegration. We are already in London, though the reason is unexplained, and Dracula's ashes are buried in a City churchyard, only to be brought back to vivid life a hundred years later by a hip-swinging no-good descendant of Dracula called Johnny Alucard. (You remember how to spell it.) Among the modish group of spectators is the alluring granddaughter of Van Helsing's grandson (coincidence runs thick and fast in this one), and once the Count is rematerialized it is she, naturally, whom he selects for his first act of vengeance. All rather confusing, but of course Granddad Van Helsing is still around to protect her, and all ends in a spectacular blaze of violence. Johnny, who must be a very dirty young man, because he has a vampiric phobia about running water, is dissolved simply by being pushed into a bath and having the water turned on. Dracula himself, increasingly accident-prone these days, has the misfortune to fall into a pit primed with wooden stakes, and it's back to the dust for him. A ho-hum reaction was the best that could be expected from all this, though Lee was curiously proud of having inserted into the script a rather clumsy line from Bram Stoker's original:

DRACULA A.D. 1972 (1972). The Count regenerates himself from generation to generation, but Van Helsing (Peter Cushing) is now the grandson of his original adversary.

You would play your brains against mine . . . against one who has commanded
nations!

There was some talk at this time of an episode tracing back Dracula's heritage to
the historical figure Vlad the Impaler (plenty of bloody possibilities there, but no
fantasy), with Dracula eventually being conquered in Victorian times by Sherlock
Holmes and Dr Watson. It never happened. Instead, Hammer came up with a
rather sober and complex film called *The Satanic Rites of Dracula*. Horror was
going out of fashion, and this turned out to be Hammer's last regular Dracula
adventure (one off-beat exception will be noted), so it seems worth careful
examination. In essence it is a sequel to *Dracula A.D. 1972*, and Van Helsing III is
again the Count's adversary, but its canvas is wider. We are still in London, and
the Count has forgotten none of his tricks. High-placed disciples have rescued and
revived him from his burial plot, over which, during the two years which have
passed, there has risen a vast modern concrete block housing a conglomerate
known as the D. D. Denham Group of Companies, which is busily buying up
London properties. The script, though not free from sluggishness, is packed with
surprising new political and cinematic references, suggesting fresh directions
which the myth might have taken had not Hammer's long-faithful audience
signalled its current indifference. The reclusive chief executive ('No one sees Mr
Denham – ever!' says the commissionaire) is obviously screenwriter Don
Houghton's pot-shy at Howard Hughes (first new reference), the American
mystery millionaire who in the early seventies took over the penthouse suite of
London's Inn on the Park and was seen by nobody for several months. It also
seems fitting that Dracula should have become a property speculator (second new
reference) after the national scandals of Rachman and Poulson, wielding their evil
power over innocent city dwellers. In his nefarious aims he is assisted by a modern
version of the eighteenth-century Hellfire Club (third new reference), consisting
of a general, a minister, a professor and a lord whose wit has gone astray. They
have convinced themselves that their dabbling in evil is for the ultimate good of
mankind, a kind of cleansing by immersion. Dracula calls them (fourth new
reference) 'the four horsemen of *my* apocalypse!'
    The story begins with a graphic human sacrifice by stabbing. The victim is a
nubile and fairly naked girl (for this is 1973) who has just had fresh cockerel's
blood poured over her stomach; and no harm is done, for a few moments later,
after the appropriate magic passes, her wounds heal quite magically. The occasion
is a secret black mass (fifth new reference) attended by the disciples at night in a
bogus research institute. An MI5 agent has been captured and awaits their
attention upstairs, but after throttling a guard he just makes it back to HQ before
expiring, despite the lethal attentions of two helmeted, machine-gunning motor
cycle guards (sixth new reference, *Orphée*). His report is received with a mixture
of determination and disbelief; but of the five photographs he has taken, purport-
ing to show the five members of the secret coven, four are easily recognized but
the fifth is suspiciously blank. (We know of course that vampires do not reflect in
mirrors nor cast shadows, but non-photographability is surely a seventh new
reference.) Meanwhile the audience sees the top MI5 man's girl secretary violently

kidnapped and vampirized. Baffled by the occult elements of the case, Colonel Matthews assigns to it two stalwart heroes – a plain clothes cop and a secret agent. They decide after 22 minutes of film have elapsed to call in that famous vampire specialist Professor Lorrimer Van Helsing, who takes what they say very seriously indeed and waves away their apologies for bothering him with something so seemingly childish. 'Those who adhere to the cult of vampirism,' he tells them, 'are usually mature sophisticated adults.' Of course, that could be a sop for Hammer audiences.

Van Helsing recalls that one of the disciples, Professor Keeley, is an old acquaintance, and calls to see him (Freddie Jones with a splendid case of the shakes). 'Evil exists, you know, it really does,' he babbles, casting admiring

THE SATANIC RITES OF DRACULA (1973). A modern Van Helsing confronts his grandfather's old adversary.

glances at his shelf of cultures containing enough bubonic plague to wipe out the world at D. D. Denham's bidding. (We are now in the sphere of an eighth new reference, Fu Manchu.) The professor (a Nobel Prize winner, no less) is obsessed by his new discoveries: 'the thrill of disgust, the beauty of obscenity'. Alas, he talks too much. A skulking motor cyclist knocks him down and strings him up, having previously shot Van Helsing (but carelessly enough only to nick him across the forehead).

Our heroes meanwhile are paying an absurd 'routine call' by night at the Institute, telling the scornful Chinese housekeeper that neighbours had complained of noises. (The nearest house appears to be about two miles away.) Quite unaccountably they take with them Van Helsing's tomboyish granddaughter, who certainly should have known better after her experiences in the last episode (though one has to admit that she is played here by a different actress). While the clumsy cops are showering themselves with suspicion upstairs, the daring young miss penetrates the cellar, and is attacked by late-rising lady vampires who hiss a great deal but seem only to maul her without doing any permanent damage to her metabolism. Her screams bring down the heroes, who stake at least one of the lethal ladies (allowing a quick display of gory breast) but entirely fail to make any of the arrests one might have expected in the circumstances. It is possible that the scene has got out of sequence and they didn't know what they were doing, since in this version only subsequently does Van Helsing give them his customary little lecture on the provenance, capabilities and weak spots of vampires. He lists all the methods of disposal to which faithful filmgoers have become accustomed, and adds a couple of fresh ones. Ninth new reference: they live in mortal fear of silver. Tenth new reference: they abhor the hawthorn bush, from which Christ's crown of thorns was made. (Was it?) Van Helsing's face grows grim as he realizes that the time has come for positive action. 'I destroyed Dracula two years ago, but this creature can live again – by reincarnation!' Eleventh new reference, but if it means that the soul of Dracula is inhabiting someone else's body, we hear no more about it.

While Van Helsing, with the aid of a little fireside kit for melting silver, fashions a deadly bullet, he works out to his own satisfaction D. D. Dracula-Denham's evil super-plan: the monster has tired of the life of the undead, and wishes to obtain a final peace but to bring down the whole world with him – 'the biblical prophecy of Armageddon!' (Twelfth new reference.) Meanwhile our two inept heroes, who should surely be drummed out of the service, have again taken the girl with them as they stake out the Institute from afar; but not so far that they can't be sniped at by the motor-cyclists. Colonel Matthews, who hasn't had much to do except look doubtful about the entire plot, is shot in the head, apparently through a car windscreen without breaking the glass. Agent hero is also shot dead; cop hero is captured, along with the girl of course. While she is being prepared for the inevitable sacrifice (but more decorously than her predecessor, for after all Joanna Lumley is a sort of star) he manages to escape and melt three of the lady vampires with water from the sprinkler system (a possibility tried out in the last episode, but the way it's done here is reminiscent of the witch's demise in *The Wizard of Oz*). And he finally stakes the Chinese housekeeper, who has become too toothily

amorous for a well-brought-up London cop to tolerate. Meanwhile Van Helsing
is arriving at the Denham building and, to the commissionaire's astonishment,
finding himself expected. While the lift shoots him up to the top floor, viewers
with long memories may be recollecting that although this was supposed to be a
Dracula film, 62 minutes have now passed with only a couple of brief unexplained
shots of Christopher Lee, striding down Institute corridors. But of course DDD is
none other than the wily old Count himself, complete with a mouthful of fangs
and a phoney Transylvanian accent (which seemes rather odd, for in his previous
incarnations he spoke perfect English). Alas, Van Helsing's aim with the silver
bullet (wasn't that for werewolves?) is deflected by the surviving disciples, who
appear from the shadows and overpower the investigator. 'Kill him!' they cry in
violent tones unsuited to men of their standing. But Dracula, only slightly injured
by Van Helsing's wiles, demurs, like all good villains. 'It cannot be made so
simple. Not for him. Nor for his granddaughter.' Besides, the film badly needs a
climax.

The showdown takes place at the Institute. Granddaughter lies naked (we
imagine) on the altar, and Dracula makes public his shock horror plan. 'I choose
the spawn of your blood, Van Helsing, to be my consort.' Dirty old Dracula.
Luckily for the forces of right, the minister accidentally breaks one of the vials of
plague germ, causing a natural diversion among those present. Oddly enough, in
view of Dracula's game plan, the resultant fast-growing fungus, far from
contaminating the world, seems to attack only the chap holding it. The others
manage to flee when our wandering cop hero, who has escaped from his bonds,
accidentally sets the building on fire. It remains only for Dracula to chase Van
Helsing into the woods and get himself rather unconvincingly caught up on a
convenient hawthorn bush, from which (it seemed from where I was sitting) he
could have plucked himself free in a moment. (If it was supposed to encircle him,
then a better effect was needed.) But who's quibbling? Dracula's consequent
helplessness makes it easy for Van Helsing, almost at leisure, to select a stave from
a nearby picket fence and plunge it into the monster's heart, thus turning the
Count into the usual pile of dust (a browny-grey this time) over which the credits
roll somewhat peremptorily as though to conceal the less convincing moments of
the special effects.

Dracula having recovered from far worse plights, this does seem an inappropri-
ate moment for Hammer to take their leave of him; but they made no more in the
series apart from an eccentric production of the following year. *The Legend of the
Seven Golden Vampires* was a cheap co-production with the Far-Eastern entrepreneur Run Run Shaw, shot entirely in Hong Kong and attempting to combine
the familiar vampire thrills with those of the martial arts. Though the *Satanic Rites*
team was transferred to it almost intact, the result was no more than a feeble
pantomime, its shoddy sets, atrocious make-up and spineless plot accentuated by
the decision to shoot in Panavision and a colour process which floods the indoor
events in the gaudy colours of the old-time British music hall. At least Peter
Cushing was again present as Van Helsing to provide a still centre for the violent
nonsense, and Dracula made a guest appearance in the person of John Forbes
Robertson, who seemed on the whole a rather better actor than Christopher Lee,

and even in his two scenes was allotted more lines than usually fell to the well-known star. The year is 1804 (well before Bram Stoker was even thought of) as a Chinese disciple makes his weary way to Dracula's castle to pay tribute. At his final approach a very plastic-looking stone coffin opens by apparent remote control and the figure of Dracula stiffly rises from horizontal to perpendicular. (The stone slab, incidentally, has disappeared entirely from the following shots.) 'Who dares to invade the sanctity of Dracula?' booms the Count in resonant tones; and yes, sanctity does seem a curious word for him to choose. His guest replies in sub-titles, presumably because the Chinese actor could not cope with English:

> My name is Kah . . . I am high priest of the Seven Golden Vampires in Ping Kwei in the province of Szechwan. My temple was the centre of all power in the area. The people bore allegiance to me. But now the vampires sleep and the people go their own ways . . .

What Kah needs, he says, is the help of the king of vampires, but Dracula draws himself up to his full height and replies that he does no favours, not even from his present predicament in the confines of a 'miserable place, this mausoleum'. But suddenly a rather splendid idea occurs to him, and he grips his visitor by the shoulders:

> I need your mortal coil . . . I need the form of your miserable carcass . . . I need your vile image. I will return to your temple in your image. I will recall the seven golden vampires as my own host . . . tools of my vengeance on mankind!

When the swirling mists clear, the Count has absorbed himself into the body of Kah, who stalks off with great western determination (which he will need for the long walk back to Szechwan). But the great plan does not seem to work very well, because after the main titles we find ourselves in Chungking a hundred years later, where Professor Van Helsing is lecturing to Chinese students about vampirism and recollecting elements of the local legends about them. So limited has been Dracula's influence that Van Helsing does not even know the name or location of the village, and can only recount a story which has been passed down to him about a farmer who (armed in the flashback with what looks like a gardening hoe) goes out one night to rescue seven virgins, shackled toe to toe round a cauldron of blood in the dreaded pagoda. He manages to destroy one of the vampires by snatching its bat-shaped golden medallion and releasing the steam from its innards. Kah/Dracula is present but seems rather limited in personal power, preferring to summon by gong an army of Chinese zombies, who rise from their graves and shuffle in slow motion after the terrified farmer. This unfortunate ends up having his throat cut by one of the remaining vampires, who all for some unexplained reason look as though they are wearing mud packs.

The sophisticated Chungking students are all highly disbelieving of this story, as their spokesman points out:

> Professor Van Helsing, these monsters may find sanctuary in the minds of the peasants of Transylvania, but China has a sophistication which has flowered and

bloomed over the course of 3000 years. You cannot diminish that sophistication with wicked tales of devil monsters and grotesque beings . . . Credit us with some intelligence, sir.

So much for Van Helsing's scholarly reputation through so many adventures. The professor perseveres with details:

In Europe, the vampire walks in dread of the crucifix. Here, it could be the image of the Lord Buddha . . .

No go: the students all walk out on him. All except one, who turns out (did you expect less?) to be the grandson of the murdered farmer, and when Van Helsing's son Leyland (who oddly calls his father 'primarily an anthropologist') meets a rich adventuress who can't wait to hunt vampires, an expedition is quickly set up, led by Van Helsing in a solar topi which never gets dirty despite the many trials and tribulations endured by the travellers. These consist chiefly of attacks every five minutes by either bandits or vampires, leading to mass displays of the martial arts. Meanwhile the Chinese girl leader falls for Van Helsing Jnr, and the farmer's grandson for the rich provider, though he later has to stake her when she is vampirized. Well, you can't have too happy an ending in a horror movie, and Van Helsing does once again reduce Dracula to dust.

The Legend of the Seven Golden Vampires came as a distinct confirmation that fangs weren't what they used to be. Every costume and prop had all too clearly been dusted off from some long-disused storeroom, the post-synching left a lot to be desired, and the credits even managed to misspell the name of composer James Bernard, to whom Hammer had good reason to be grateful. It was of course intended as no more than a romp, but it did not even succeed on those terms, and the Hong Kong connection was clearly unwise. The Hammer studios virtually folded soon after, though the name was kept going by long-time accountant Brian Lawrence and producer Roy Skeggs, who managed over the next ten years to produce two short-run television series of 'Hammer House' thrillers based on scripts which had clearly been a long time in the story editor's drawer.

During Hammer's heyday, various other low-budget attempts were naturally made to emulate their success with the Dracula legend, which had conveniently lapsed so far as literary copyright was concerned. Blood of Dracula, for instance, was a natural successor to American International's I Was a Teenage Werewolf, which had emerged in 1957 to predictable critical disdain but astonishing box-office success. The Dracula item, disappointingly, claimed no real link with the celebrated Transylvanian line, though it might still have been more enticingly titled I Was a Teenage Vampire. It centres on a neurotic girl named Nancy, whose teacher owns a medallion which might once have belonged to Dracula. Whenever Nancy gets frustrated and holds it in her hands, it turns her into a kind of living vampire with fangs and high-arched furry eyebrows, and the picture proceeds more on the level of Dr Jekyll and Mr Hyde than anything else, with Nancy's evil side showing through at the most inconvenient moments. Eventually the teacher is killed by the transmogrified student, who then impales herself accidentally on an upright piece of wood.

In the same year a routine item called *The Vampire* took pains to demonstrate that its unfortunate hero was not a real vampire at all, only the victim of a new type of drug which gives him a bat face and buck teeth, and sends him out on killing sprees. John Beal can't stop the production from seeming very silly, especially when, again like Dr Jekyll, he finds he can't stop transforming even when he leaves the drug in the medicine cabinet.

A few months later the same production team, encouraged by undeservedly good returns, had a go at a disguised version of the original Dracula story. *The Return of Dracula* begins in the Balkans, where a group of Van Helsing's more ardent followers aim to stake the count in his tomb. But the coffin when they reach it is empty: Dracula is aboard a railway train, where he commits a murder and then steals the identity of his victim, en route to visit unknown relatives in a small town in midwestern America. When the train steams into their quiet little depot Bellac does not step from it as expected, though a casket-shaped box in his name is off-loaded. The fact is that the sun is still up, so the vampire has to materialize later on in the forest. (All this is strongly reminiscent of *Son of Dracula*.) From then on he is more or less accepted as Bellac despite his curious nocturnal habits. Mysterious deaths are eventually laid at his door, though not until he has vampirized Jenny, a local girl who kills for him in the guise of a white wolf. The sceptical local authorities finally accept the truth when Bellac's image does not show up on a group photograph; the unfortunate Jenny is tracked down and staked; and Dracula falls down a pit conveniently equipped with sharp wooden props. It was all very predictable, though certainly watchable in an uninvolving way. Francis Lederer played the count with sufficient mittel-European style, though he surprisingly lacked any supernatural aura. The British distributor, incidentally, falsified this intense little black-and-white shocker by calling it *The Fantastic Disappearing Man*, no doubt an attempt to cash in on *The Incredible Shrinking Man* and *The Amazing Colossal Man*. (*The Incredible Melting Man* was still way in the future.)

A rather curious British chiller turned up in 1958 under the title *Blood of the Vampire*. Most people who saw it probably thought it came from Hammer Productions, and indeed its script was the work of Hammer regular Jimmy Sangster, who seems, though he begins with an account of the exact nature of the vampire problem, to have adapted his plot from an old Frankenstein script. *Blood of the Vampire* was never an attractive film, too crudely set and thickly coloured, with a nose for more unpleasant detail than Hammer ever dared to foist upon us; and in the mad doctor role, in place of Peter Cushing's fussiness, we have as Callistratus the Grand Guignol personality of Donald Wolfit, a fearsome monster in a leather apron constantly smeared with blood. He is technically the governor of a prison for the criminally insane; presumably the authorities don't know that he is also one of the undead who needs constant transfusions and organ transplants to keep him going. And where better than in his present occupation could he find an ample supply of material, especially when he has a mad one-eyed hunchback to help him? Despite a strong cast *Blood of the Vampire* is a somewhat unpleasant entertainment to watch, the impression it gives being that all the characters, good and bad, live in a pit on the brink of hell, somewhere never penetrated by the sun.

BLOOD OF THE VAMPIRE (1958). Following the tradition of distinguished thespians letting their hair down in horror romps, Donald Wolfit plays the sadistic asylum keeper with secret passions. He is flanked here by Barbara Shelley and Vincent Ball.

But it does have flashes of humour, as when Callistratus enquires unctuously of his housekeeper: 'The practical side of my work distresses you?'

In 1960 an Italian film usually called *Mask of the Demon* or *Black Sunday* gained some notoriety through its bravura style and the sensual, hissing performance of its leading lady, Barbara Steele. She is a vampire witch whose execution at the start involves having a mask with interior spikes pounded into her face. Two hundred years later the mask is removed, the blood of an attacking bat falls on to the skull, and Miss Steele is restored to her former activities. What happens next is inventive though predictably unattractive. Mario Bava, the director of this repulsive gem, also gave to the world three years later a horror omnibus called *Black Sabbath*. In the story entitled 'The Wurdelak', Boris Karloff appears as the hunter of a vampire which particularly savours the blood of his own family. While beheading the monster he is turned into a wurdelak himself, and on returning home infects his own kith and kin.

True horror fans were appalled in 1966 by the appearance of an extremely low-budget American potboiler called *Billy the Kid Versus Dracula*, which was available as part of a double bill with *Jesse James Meets Frankenstein's Daughter*. Production values were atrocious, but the story line proved more relevant than might have been expected, and John Carradine had been lured back to his old role as the Count, now seeking his victims in the American West, and confiding at one point that he 'might just sleep all day' (though he does not carry his earth-filled coffin with him and seems to have immunized himself to the rays of the sun). Billy has predictably been whitewashed into a hero; the almost-vampirized heroine wears the usual blank look and white satin; and although bullets have no effect on the Count he is eventually killed, against tradition, by a surgeon's scalpel.

By now familiarity had bred contempt, and Dracula was fair game for catchpenny producers in Italy, Mexico, the Philippines, and especially Spain. Christopher Lee was lured to Madrid by the promise of a Dracula closely based on the original book, but the result, usually known simply as *Count Dracula*, was handicapped by language problems and a lack of style. Under the same title a few years later Louis Jourdan had better luck with a BBC prestige production, except that he was very boring indeed in the role. Meanwhile there was a black Dracula (*Blacula*), a homosexual Dracula (*Does Dracula Really Suck?*), a porn Dracula (*Dracula the Dirty Old Man*), even a romantic one (*The Great Love of Count Dracula*). Two films called *Dracula vs Frankenstein* (see Chapter 2) figured among the multi-monster extravaganzas which proliferated. Legend and space fiction came together: *Goliath Versus the Vampires, Planet of the Vampires*. None of these titles seriously merits the attention of the film historian, and nor alas does Roman Polanski's highbrow would-be satire *The Fearless Vampire Killers, or: Pardon Me, Your Teeth Are in My Neck*. Despite expensive mounting and a valiant British cast this so-called comedy proved uninventive and dolefully dull, apart from a single moment with a Jewish bloodsucker played by Alfie Bass, who when confronted by the crucifix chuckles to himself, does an Oliver Hardy camera look, and responds: 'Hoi! Hev you got the wrong vampire!'

Andy Warhol made, or appended his name to, a truly disgusting frolic called *Blood for Dracula* (actually directed by his friend Paul Morrissey). David Niven was misguided enough to appear fanged in a sad spoof called *Vampira*, or *Old Dracula*. Bela Lugosi had come to Britain in the early fifties to make *Mother Riley Meets the Vampire*, but the film was appalling and he was only a crook masquerading as a monster. One mentions only in passing such titles as *The Mad Love Life of a Hot Vampire, Drakulita, The Dead Eyes of Dr Dracula, Dracula Meets the Outer Space Chicks, Guess What Happened to Count Dracula, Dracula's Vampire Lust, Dracula in the Year 2000* and *The Secret Sex Life of Dracula*. The Germans came up however with a mordant political satire called *Jonathan*, in which neo-Nazis are depicted as vampires; and I have a soft spot for a puppet movie made by Rankin-Bass under the title *Mad Monster Party*. Here Boris von Frankenstein (using Karloff's sibilant voice and gaunt features) invents a new explosive which will make him rich, but finds his own daughter plotting with Count Dracula to disinherit his named successor. It would have made a good storyline for Universal.

No account of the Dracula myth on film can ever be complete: new videos constantly spring up out of nowhere, and very often one can't even trace the country in which the film was made. References to Dracula abound in every kind of film and book; dozens of comic-strip paperbacks purport to tell the original Bram Stoker story. But even this brief account must not be terminated without a further glance at the distaff side, following Dreyer's *Vampyr* (which we will examine shortly) and Universal's 1935 venture with *Dracula's Daughter*. Both of these were very distantly based on a short novel of 1872 called 'Carmilla', which when published must have caused something of a sensation, being the first known account in English fiction of lesbian love. Its author, Sheridan Le Fanu (pronounced Leffanew, with the accent on the first syllable) was a semi-invalid who on the death of his wife became a writer and something of a Dublin recluse. He produced a number of semi-classical stories of mystery and the supernatural, including 'Green Tea' and 'Uncle Silas', but he is not an easy writer to appreciate, his emphasis often seeming to be on irrelevant detail while the sensational nub of the matter is glossed over, so that one misses the point on first reading and has to go back. 'Carmilla' is, like *Dracula*, written in the form of letters, quite unnecessarily in this case; but nothing can detract from the compulsive horror of its climax, which is most un-Victorian in its insistence on the goriest of detail. The principal narrator is a girl named Laura, daughter of an Englishman who served in the Austrian army. She tells of the time when he was widowed and they lived a lonely life in a Styrian *Schloss*, three miles from the nearest buildings, which comprise a ruined village and church once belonging to her mother's side of the family, the now-extinct Karnsteins. Laura tells first of a strange experience when she was six years old: a beautiful woman appeared at her bedside and inflicted puncture marks in her neck. She then moves on to the time when she was nineteen, and to an evening when she and her father have just heard of the death of a young girl, ward of a distant neighbour named General Spielsdorf, who declares obscurely that he must devote his remaining days to 'tracking and extinguishing a monster'. Details are vague in the extreme, and Laura makes no connection at first between this letter and a curious accident which gives them an unexpected house guest. A carriage containing two ladies overturns in a lane near the house. Luckily no one is seriously hurt, but the younger of the two travellers is stunned, and the proposal is soon made (by Laura) that she should stay in the *Schloss* for a few days and recover. The mother accepts this invitation with such alacrity that the reader may suspect her of having that precise intention all along; she goes about her business, and though weeks pass she does not reappear.

Meanwhile, when the stunned girl wakes up in bed, her first remark to Laura is that she saw her in a dream twelve years back; and Laura realizes with a shock that her guest, Carmilla, is the strange lady of her own twelve-year-old experience. Carmilla brushes away the oddity with a shake of the head:

> 'I don't know which should be most afraid of the other,' she said, again smiling. 'If you were less pretty I think I should be very much afraid of you, but being as you are, and you and I both so young, I feel only that I have made your acquaintance twelve years ago, and have already a right to your intimacy; at all events, it does seem as if we were destined, from our earliest childhood, to be friends. I wonder whether you feel as strangely drawn towards me as I do to you; I have never had a friend – shall I find one now?' She sighed, and her fine dark eyes gazed passionately on me.
>
> Now the truth is, I felt rather unaccountably towards the beautiful stranger. I did feel, as she said, 'drawn towards her,' but there was also something of repulsion. In this ambiguous feeling, however, the sense of attraction immensely prevailed. She interested and won me; she was so beautiful and so indescribably engaging.

I perceived now something of languor and exhaustion stealing over her, and hastened to bid her goodnight.

'The doctor thinks,' I added, 'that you ought to have a maid to sit up with you to-night; one of ours is waiting, and you will find her a very useful and quiet creature.'

'How kind of you, but I could not sleep, I never could with an attendant in the room. I shan't require any assistance – and, shall I confess my weakness, I am haunted with a terror of robbers. Our house was robbed once, and two servants murdered, so I always lock my door. It has become a habit – and you look so kind I know you will forgive me. I see there is a key in the lock.'

She held me close in her pretty arms for a moment and whispered in my ear, 'Goodnight, darling, it is very hard to part with you, but goodnight; tomorrow, but not early, I shall see you again.'

She sank back on the pillow with a sigh, and her fine eyes followed me with a fond and melancholy gaze, and she murmured again, 'Goodnight, dear friend.'

Young people like, and even love, on impulse. I was flattered by the evident, though as yet undeserved, fondness she showed me. I liked the confidence with which she at once received me. She was determined that we should be very dear friends.

They become intimate; but Laura has another shock when she finds that Carmilla is the living image of the countess Mircalla Karnstein (crossword addicts will spot the anagram) whose portrait hangs in the hall with a given death date of 1698.

'I am descended from the Karnsteins; that is, mamma was.'

'Ah!' said the lady, languidly, 'so am I, I think, a very long descent, very ancient. Are there any Karnsteins living now?'

'None who bear the name, I believe. The family were ruined, I believe, in some civil wars, long ago, but the ruins of the castle are only about three miles away.'

'How interesting!' she said, languidly. 'But see what beautiful moonlight!'

She rose, and each with her arm about the other's waist, we walked out upon the pavement.

In silence, slowly we walked down to the drawbridge, where the beautiful landscape opened before us.

She kissed me silently.

'I am sure, Carmilla, you have been in love; that there is, at this moment, an affair of the heart going on.'

'I have been in love with no one, and never shall,' she whispered, 'unless it should be with you.'

How beautiful she looked in the moonlight!

Shy and strange was the look with which she quickly hid her face in my neck and hair, with tumultuous sighs, that seemed almost to sob, and pressed in mine a hand that trembled.

Her soft cheek was glowing against mine. 'Darling, darling,' she murmured, 'I live in you; and you would die for me, I love you so.'

The two girls become almost like lovers, but Carmilla's remarks are sometimes inexplicable. 'Love will have its sacrifices,' she says: 'no sacrifice without blood.' And Laura begins to have terrifying dreams:

I had a dream that night that was the beginning of a very strange agony.

I cannot call it a nightmare, for I was quite conscious of being asleep. But I was equally conscious of being in my room, and lying in bed, precisely as I actually was. I saw, or fancied I saw, the room and its furniture just as I had seen it last, except that it was very dark, and I saw something moving round the foot of the bed, which at first I could not accurately distinguish. But I soon saw that it was a sooty-black animal that resembled a monstrous cat. It appeared to me about four or five feet long, for it measured fully the length of the hearthrug as it passed over it; and it continued to-ing and fro-ing with the lithe sinister restlessness of a beast in a cage. I could not cry out, although as you may suppose, I was terrified. Its pace was growing faster, and the room rapidly darker and darker, and at length so dark that I could no longer see anything of it but its eyes. I felt it spring lightly on the bed. The two broad eyes approached my face, and suddenly I felt a stinging pain as if two large needles darted, an inch or two apart, deep into my breast. I waked with a scream. The room was lighted by the candle that burnt there all through the night, and I saw a female figure standing at the foot of the bed, a little at the right side. It was in a dark loose dress, and its hair was down and covered its shoulders. A block of stone could not have been more still. There was not the slightest stir of respiration. As I stared at it, the figure appeared to have changed its place, and was now nearer the door; then, close to it, the door opened, and it passed out.

I was now relieved, and able to breathe and move. My first thought was that Carmilla had been playing me a trick, and that I had forgotten to secure my door. I hastened to it, and found it locked as usual on the inside. I was afraid to open it – I was horrified. I sprang into my bed and covered my head up in the bedclothes, and lay there more dead than alive till morning.

The next occasion is even more unpleasant:

Certain vague and strange sensations visited me in my sleep. The prevailing one was of that pleasant, peculiar cold thrill which we feel in bathing, when we move against the current of a river. This was soon accompanied by dreams that seemed interminable, and were so vague that I could never recollect their scenery and persons, or any one connected portion of their action. But they left an awful impression, and a sense of exhaustion, as if I had passed through a long period of great mental exertion and danger. After all these dreams there remained on waking a remembrance of having been in a place very nearly dark, and of having spoken to people whom I could not see; and especially of one clear voice, of a female's, very deep, that spoke as if at a distance, slowly, and producing always the same sensation of indescribable solemnity and fear. Sometimes there came a sensation as if a hand was drawn softly along my cheek and neck. Sometimes it was as if warm lips kissed me, and longer and more lovingly as they reached my throat, but there the caress fixed itself. My heart beat faster, my breathing rose and fell rapidly and full drawn; a sobbing, that rose into a sense of strangulation, supervened, and turned into a dreadful convulsion, in which my senses left me, and I became unconscious . . .

One night, instead of the voice I was accustomed to hear in the dark, I heard one, sweet and tender, and at the same time terrible, which said, 'Your mother warns you to beware of the assassin.' At the same time a light unexpectedly sprang up, and I saw Carmilla, standing, near the foot of my bed, in her white nightdress, bathed, from her chin to her feet, in one great stain of blood.

I wakened with a shriek, possessed with the one idea that Carmilla was being murdered. I remember springing from my bed, and my next recollection is that of standing on the lobby, crying for help.

Madame and Mademoiselle came scurrying out of their rooms in alarm; a lamp burned always on the lobby, and seeing me, they soon learned the cause of my terror.

I insisted on our knocking at Carmilla's door. Our knocking was unanswered. It soon became a pounding and an uproar. We shrieked her name but all was vain.

We all grew frightened, for the door was locked. We hurried back, in panic, to my room. There we rang the bell long and furiously. If my father's room had been at that side of the house, we would have called him up at once to our aid. But, alas! he was quite out of hearing, and to reach him involved an excursion for which we none of us had courage.

Servants, however, soon came running up the stairs; I had got on my dressing-gown and slippers meanwhile, and my companions were already similarly furnished. Recognising the voices of the servants on the lobby, we sallied out together; and having renewed, as fruitlessly, our summons at Carmilla's door, I ordered the men to force the lock. They did so, and we stood, holding our lights aloft, in the doorway, and so stared into the room.

We called her by name; but there was still no reply. We looked round the room. Everything was undisturbed. It was exactly in the state in which I left it on bidding her goodnight. But Carmilla was gone.

Carmilla reappears next day, having apparently been walking in her sleep, but concern about her increases from that morning on. Some time later, Laura and her father meet their old friend General Spielsdorf near Karnstein, and hear for the first time the full details of his tragic loss. At a ball he and his ward had met a noblewoman with a beautiful daughter. The mother had more or less inveigled them into inviting her Millarca to stay while the older woman was away on business. It seemed no problem at first:

'There soon, however, appeared some drawbacks. In the first place, Millarca complained of extreme languor – the weakness that remained after her late illness – and she never emerged from her room till the afternoon was pretty far advanced. In the next place, it was accidentally discovered, although she always locked her door on the inside, and never disturbed the key from its place, till she admitted the maid to assist at her toilet, that she was undoubtedly sometimes absent from her room in the very early morning, and at various times later in the day, before she wished it to be understood that she was stirring. She was repeatedly seen from the windows of the schloss, in the first faint grey of the morning, walking through the trees, in an easterly direction, and looking like a person in a trance. This convinced me that she walked in her sleep. But this hypothesis did not solve the puzzle. How did she pass out from her room, leaving the door locked on the inside. How did she escape from the house without unbarring door or window?

'In the midst of my perplexities, an anxiety of a far more urgent kind presented itself.

'My dear child began to lose her looks and health, and that in a manner so mysterious, and even horrible, that I became thoroughly frightened.

'She was at first visited by appalling demons; then, as she fancied, by a spectre, something resembling Millarca, sometimes in the shape of a beast, indistinctly seen, walking round the foot of the bed, from side to side. Lastly came sensations. One, not unpleasant, but very peculiar, she said, resembled the flow of an icy stream against her breast. At a later time, she felt something like a pair of large needles pierce her, a little below the throat, with a very sharp pain. A few nights after, followed a gradual and convulsive sense of strangulation; then came unconsciousness.'

I could hear distinctly every word the kind old General was saying, because by this time we were driving upon the short grass that spreads on either side of the road as you approach the roofless village which had not shown the smoke of a chimney for more than half a century.

You may guess how strangely I felt as I heard my own symptoms so exactly described in those which had been experienced by the poor girl who, but for the catastrophe which followed, would have been at that moment a visitor at my father's chateau. You may suppose, also, how I felt as I heard him detail habits and mysterious peculiarities which were, in fact, those of our beautiful guest, Carmilla!

As they approach the ruined village of Karnstein, the general explains that his mission is one of vengeance. A learned doctor from Vienna, having examined the general's daughter in her decline, had sent a written opinion that she was suffering from the attentions of a vampire:

'Nothing, you will say, could be more absurd than the learned man's letter. It was monstrous enough to have consigned him to a madhouse. He said that the patient was suffering from the visits of a vampire! The punctures which she described as having occurred near the throat, were, he insisted, the insertion of those two long, thin, and sharp teeth which, it is well known, are peculiar to vampires; and there could be no doubt, he added, as to the well-defined presence of the small livid mark which all concurred in describing as that induced by the demon's lips, and every symptom described by the sufferer was in exact conformity with those recorded in every case of a similar visitation.

'Being myself wholly sceptical as to the existence of any such portent as the vampire, the supernatural theory of the good doctor furnished, in my opinion, but another instance of learning and intelligence oddly associated with some hallucination. I was so miserable, however, that, rather than try nothing, I acted upon the instructions of the letter.

'I concealed myself in the dark dressing-room, that opened upon the poor patient's room, in which a candle was burning, and watched there till she was fast asleep. I stood at the door, peeping through the small crevice, my sword laid on the table beside me, as my directions prescribed, until, a little after one, I saw a large black object, very ill-defined, crawl, as it seemed to me, over the foot of the bed, and swiftly spread itself up to the poor girl's throat, where it swelled, in a moment, into a great, palpitating mass.

'For a few moments I had stood petrified. I now sprang forward, with my sword in my hand. The black creature suddenly contracted toward the foot of the bed, glided over it, and, standing on the floor about a yard below the foot of the bed, with a glare of skulking ferocity and horror fixed on me, I saw Millarca. Speculating I know not what, I struck at her instantly with my sword; but I saw her standing near the door, unscathed. Horrified, I pursued, and struck again. She was gone! and my sword flew to shivers against the door.

'I can't describe to you all that passed on that horrible night. The whole house was up and stirring. The spectre Millarca was gone. But her victim was sinking fast, and before the morning dawned, she died.'

The general now intends to decapitate the vampire:

The next day the formal proceedings took place in the Chapel of Karnstein. The grave of the Countess Mircalla was opened; and the General and my father recognised each his perfidious and beautiful guest, in the face now disclosed to view. The features, though a hundred and fifty years had passed since her funeral, were tinted with the warmth of life. Her eyes were open; no cadaverous smell exhaled from the coffin. The two medical men, one officially present, the other on the part of the promoter of the enquiry, attested the marvellous fact, that there was a faint but appreciable respiration, and a corresponding action of the heart. The limbs were perfectly flexible, the flesh elastic; and the leaden coffin floated with blood, in which to a depth of seven inches, the body lay immersed. Here then, were all the admitted signs and proofs of vampirism. The body, therefore, in accordance with the ancient practice, was raised, and a sharp stake driven through the heart of the vampire, who uttered a piercing shriek at the moment, in all respects such as might escape from a living person in the last agony. Then the head was struck off, and a torrent of blood flowed from the severed neck. The body and head were next placed on a pile of wood, and reduced to ashes, which were thrown upon the river and borne away, and that territory has never since been plagued by the visits of a vampire.

There remains only to be introduced a character who was clearly the original of Stoker's Van Helsing. He is an immensely tall, thin, black-garbed man named Baron Vordenberg, and his account of the vampire's habits may usefully be compared with that given later by Bram Stoker:

> How they escape from their graves and return to them for certain hours every day, without displacing the clay or leaving any trace of disturbance in the state of the coffin or the cerements, has always been admitted to be utterly inexplicable. The amphibious existence of the vampire is sustained by daily renewed slumber in the grave. Its horrible lust for living blood supplies the vigour of its waking existence. The vampire is prone to be fascinated with an engrossing vehemence, resembling the passion of love, by particular persons. In pursuit of these it will exercise inexhaustible patience and stratagem, for access to a particular object may be obstructed in a hundred ways. It will never desist until it has satiated its passion, and drained the very life of its coveted victim. But it will, in these cases, husband and protract its murderous enjoyment with the refinement of an epicure, and heighten it by the gradual approaches of an artful courtship. In these cases it seems to yearn for something like sympathy and consent. In ordinary ones it goes direct to its object, overpowers with violence, and strangles and exhausts often at a single feast.

'Carmilla' then proceeds to its happy ending:

> The following Spring my father took me a tour through Italy. We remained away for more than a year. It was long before the terror of recent events subsided; and to this hour the image of Carmilla returns to memory with ambiguous alternations – sometimes the playful, languid, beautiful girl; sometimes the writhing fiend I saw in the ruined church; and often from a reverie I have started, fancying I heard the light step of Carmilla at the drawing-room door.

We have noted the slight influence of this haunting story on *Dracula's Daughter*, but three years earlier, and indeed just a few months after *Dracula* itself, another film was released which actually credited itself as an adaptation of 'Carmilla'. This was *Vampyr*, which turned out to have almost nothing in common with its original but has become, by critical consensus, probably the best vampire film of them all, though likely to remain caviare to the general. On its first appearance it had a hard time even obtaining a public showing, and seems to have survived only by courtesy of film societies and private collectors. It also set back by ten years the career of its Danish director Carl Dryer, because its remote, cold treatment branded him as totally uncommercial, despite the sensational nature of his subject. It is difficult now to guess why Dreyer wanted to make it, except that he seems to have had a preoccupation with death and witchcraft. His previous film was *The Passion of Joan of Arc*, which contrived to be superbly pictorial and cinematic

VAMPYR (1931). Carl Dreyer's film has little enough plot, but a number of memorable images. Here the sinister man with a scythe is only tolling the bell for the ferry; but the 'cemetery hag' makes a disturbing first appearance in a barn full of wheels, and finally in the hero's dream of his own death she peers at him through a glass plate in his coffin lid.

without ever leaving the courtroom in which Joan was condemned to be burnt at the stake; his next would be *Day of Wrath*, still one of the most solemnly horrific pictures I have ever seen, with its vivid depiction of the execution of an old woman in seventeenth-century Denmark. (Supposed to be a witch, she is hounded and burned alive by religious fanatics, only to pass on her curse to the wife of one of them.) Within his own more sombre predilections, *Vampyr* may have seemed to Dreyer like a concession to popular taste, but it did not turn out that way: the treatment was so distant and the narrative so desultory that the public was left cold.

Vampyr is available now only in faded prints from a battered negative, and although a version was made with English dialogue it seems to have disappeared, so that the viewer must put up with misspelt sub-titles which offer a character called 'the cemetery bag'. (Presumably 'the cemetery hag' was intended.) Nevertheless it is a fair bet that any genuine fan who begins to watch *Vampyr* will find his gaze riveted until it ends, for the 70-minute film unfolds as a series of hypnotic, almost surrealist images which don't have to make narrative sense in order to weave their cinematic spell. There is in fact a story of sorts, but it is constantly interrupted by mysterious digressions, and all that is left of 'Carmilla' is the central fact of a girl being turned into a vampire by another woman. The production was mounted with great difficulty. Scenes were shot over a period of twelve months, and the leading role was played by the principal investor, Baron Nicolas de Gunzberg, who is billed as Julian West and portrays a character called David Gray, introduced as follows:

> There are human beings whose lives are bound by invisible chains to the supernatural. They crave solitude. To be alone and dream . . . Their imagination is so developed that their vision reaches beyond that of most men. David Gray was thus mysterious. One evening, lured by a fascination of the unknown, he came, after sunset, to the inn which is by the river in the village of Courtempierre . . .

David Gray is a tall, dark-eyed young man of somewhat immobile expression. He wears a dark city suit throughout the picture's strange goings-on, no doubt symbolic of his inhabiting a different world, and initially he carries a fishing net, perhaps to suggest his search for experience. The fact is that if you look for sinister undertones you can find them even in the most outwardly innocent circumstances, and David is looking. The doors of the inn are locked. 'Go in the other way,' calls a girl from the skylight; but the other way is locked too. Finally about to enter, David is distracted by the sight of a man carrying a scythe who rings a bell for the ferry boat, and somehow that irrelevant image is among the most memorable in the film. A glimpse of an old man with a crippled face makes David lock his bedroom door, and the sub-titles continue to insist on the air of dislocation:

> David Gray has retired for the night, but an atmosphere laden with mystery has kept him awake . . .

And of course someone comes in through the apparently locked door. It's a gaunt old man who stands in the middle of the room and cries 'Silence!' though nobody has spoken. He adds: 'She must not die, do you hear?' And he leaves a packet marked: 'To Be Opened After My Death'.

> Is it a ghost? Is it a dream? Or some poor creature seeking his help?

These self-dramatizing sub-titles would have become a bore in any other film, but with Dreyer they simply enhance the weird atmosphere – in which nothing very weird, so far, has happened. Next morning David's vision seems to be impaired, or perhaps he is just getting used to the supernatural atmosphere he was looking for. At any rate he sees in the river a reflection which has no original. Then there is a shot in reverse. And the shadow of a one-legged policeman which only in its own time comes to rest in accord with the policeman's body. Finally in a barn David sees more shadows, of a witch's sabbat conducted by a white-haired old crone, the 'cemetery hag' of the opening titles. Back in the inn he meets a little man who starts a very peculiar conversation:

> – Did you hear it?
> – Yes, a child.
> – Child?
> – Yes, a child.
> – There is no child here.

– And the dog?

– There is neither child nor dog. Good night.

When David has gone, the little man leads into his room the cemetery hag, and a chinless skull on his desk swivels round to face her.

This is all preliminary. Up at the castle a girl, Leone, lies in bed with marks on her throat. 'The wound is nearly healed,' says the nurse. 'Do not go to bed before the doctor comes,' says an old man, her father . . . yes, the old man who came into David's room. But just as David arrives at the house the old man is shot – by shadows – and while they all wait for the police David opens the package, which contains a book entitled *Strange Tales of the Vampyres*. 'Some say these creatures are betrayed souls,' David reads. 'Some say they are criminals. Either way,

The passage of these monsters is strewn with actions reeking of death and blood.'

The dead man's other daughter sees Leone wandering off through the trees, and when she and David follow her it is to find her lying on a bench with the cemetery hag bending over her throat. Brought back to her room, the invalid begins by wishing she could die, but then in a superb shot an evil smile slowly lights her face as she contemplates her sister's neck . . .

No wonder the regular audiences of 1932 grew bored with this half-hour of shadowy suggestion, but it is marvellous stuff all the same, and it has lasted. It seems likely that *Vampyr* was conceived in the spirit of an undergraduate caper, heavily influenced by surrealist films such as *Un Chien Andalou*, and essentially it aims to do no more than evoke an unsettling atmosphere. All but two of the performers were amateurs approached in the street because they looked right, and indeed no real acting is required of them, only the ability to pose in whatever attitude is required for each shot. Such dialogue as exists is muffled or muttered, like the fragments Jacques Tati allowed in his comedies; the eyes, not the ears of the audience are what matter.

Yet the last portions of *Vampyr* are chilling by any standards. The doctor comes to treat the vampirized girl, and he is of course the little Einstein with whom David had so unsatisfactory a conversation. As he enters the sick room, the untroubled sister asks a question which lingers: 'Why does he always come at night?' At the doctor's request, David gives blood for a transfusion, and during the operation he dreams of his own funeral. He is locked in a coffin with a glass window, through which the hag peers down at him in eager anticipation as he is being carried to a grave in the local cemetery – which is where he awakes unharmed. With the help of a servant he locates the hag's grave, and stands back while an iron pole is rammed into her heart. The evil doctor, clearly the centre of the outbreak of vampirism, is driven by his own guilty conscience into a plaster mill where the machinery starts and he is suffocated, his black-garbed figure finally obliterated by falling white dust. (His eyeglasses are the last items to disappear.) Leone and the world return to normal, and David walks with the other sister through forest glades in hazy sunshine.

No synopsis can possibly do justice to *Vampyr*. But nor is there any doubt of its classic status.

COUNTESS DRACULA (1970). The delightful Ingrid Pitt grows monstrously old before our very
eyes.

Hammer first jumped into the muddy pool of female vampirism in 1970 with a
film which wasn't what it seemed. *Countess Dracula* was the title, but it told the
story not of a fictional vampiress but of a historical character called Elisabeth
Bathori, who was born in Hungary in 1560 and seems to have known more about
orgies than the Marquis de Sade. When she grew older, having explored every
known perversion, she discovered, or imagined, that the application of female
blood to her skin made it young again. This was an obvious cue for murder, and it
was not long before she was bathing in the blood of virgins. Rumour had it that
600 girls were killed for her cosmetic requirements. She was finally tried for the
crimes and died in prison. The Hammer film version elaborated this amazing
story with transformation scenes which followed the Hollywood tradition of
lap-dissolves, with a reversed process at the end when the countess's real age
catches up with her. Ingrid Pitt had a field day in the leading role, but it was an
unpleasant story and the superimposed plot added confusions of its own. Oddly
enough, it provoked several continental imitations: Delphine Seyrig played a
modernized version of the role in *Daughters of Darkness*, a Belgian film of 1973,
and the same year saw a German version called *The Bloody Countess*, while Ewa
Aulin appeared in something called *Blood Ceremony* which had a remarkably
similar storyline.

Meanwhile Hammer had finally taken the plunge with a long-considered
version of *Carmilla* which they thought they could get past the censor. They did
have the example of Roger Vadim's 1960 version called *Et Mourir de Plaisir* (*Blood
and Roses*), but that was almost as rarefied as *Vampyr*, and certainly not an

audience-grabber. The *Monthly Film Bulletin* reported that 'this expensive attempt at an art/horror film is nothing short of a travesty, both of the genre and of Le Fanu's marvellous short story. Though Vadim's direction leans heavily on Cocteau, it remains for the most part awkward and pedantic: there is none of that essential intensity and conviction you find in a film like *L'Eternel Retour*. The psychological explanation, lesbianism, comes over as unsubtle and sensational . . . the film suffers badly from comparison with Dreyer's much freer adaptation of the story, *Vampyr*, a work of genuine imagination and atmosphere.' Vadim had modernized the settings but aimed for a dreamlike atmosphere in which perversion might be romanticized. The Karnstein history has become a family curse, and the vampire is a modern girl who simply takes on the identity of her ancestor, to find her personality changing for the worse and her amorous inclinations settling on her cousin's fiancée. She is finally killed when an explosion blasts a paling through her heart. In 1963 an Italian company had hired Christopher Lee to appear in a slightly distended version of the same story, released internationally as *Terror in the Crypt*. But in 1970 these fumbling attempts had been forgotten, and Hammer had the field to itself. An eager co-producer was found in American International, thus guaranteeing world markets. The result was *The Vampire Lovers*, a film which succeeded within its own limits but was found by most audiences to be too distasteful. Besides, where was the fun in women loving

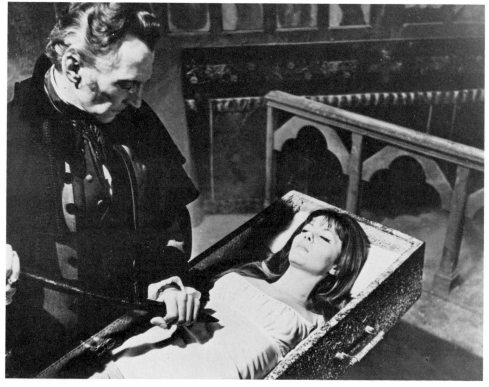

THE VAMPIRE LOVERS (1970). Once more Peter Cushing sharpens his stake. Ingrid Pitt is the victim this time.

LUST FOR A VAMPIRE (1970). Nudity and lesbianism are now added to the mixture. Yutte Stensgaard, Suzanna Leigh.

women? Only a very small percentage of the audience could get any vicarious enjoyment out of that.

Certainly the script remained as true to its source as anyone had a right to expect. In the prologue a vengeful nobleman destroys all but one of the undead of Karnstein Castle. The survivor is of course the beautiful Carmilla, sensuously played by Ingrid Pitt in the busiest year of her career. Years later she turns up in high society, escorted by an equally mysterious countess, and now going by the name of Marcilla. She inveigles her way into the home of General Spielsdorf, whose daughter Laura subsequently dies. As Carmilla, she then menaces Laura's friend Emma, but the General is now on to her and, with the help of the experienced vampirist Baron Hertzog, Carmilla is tracked down and staked. *The Vampire Lovers* was well enough made, but did not seem to command a sequel. One turned up, however, within a year, and *Lust for a Vampire* received more critical praise than its predecessor although it ventured only a few obvious variations on the same foundation, and its excitements were nothing more than red-rimmed eyes, sharp fangs and heaving bosoms, plus the final blood-letting. This time Mircalla was somewhat miraculously revived (considering that her head had been cut off) by the evil Count Karnstein, played by Mike Raven to look as much like Christopher Lee as possible. He enrols her in the girls' academy which now occupies Karnstein Castle, and a research student comes under her spell and is killed by her. His friend discovers her secret but nearly goes the same way; luckily when the villagers set the castle on fire she is killed by a burning rafter. These warmed-over titbits were directed with some style by Jimmy Sangster, but audiences were not particularly impressed, perhaps because the story lacked a Van Helsing figure with whom the watchers could identify. Surprisingly, Hammer pressed on in the following year with yet another sequel, *Twins of Evil*, in which the Count reincarnates Mircalla and invites her to corrupt the twin daughters of his puritan arch-enemy Gustav Weil, a witch hunter. At least the puritan sect added a new dimension to the heavy breathing, and visually the movie had quite a lot to offer. Nevertheless Tudor Gates, who had written all three 'Carmilla' scripts, seemed now to be at the end of his tether, and the last two European vampire Hammers were from other imaginers. *Vampire Circus* very nearly scored a bullseye of some kind, establishing an atmosphere more gently evocative of Hollywood magic than the usual Bray mixture of jolting shocks and heaving bosoms. It also seemed to draw from several rather superior Hollywood sources. There was a little girl victim of the monster, carried away in her father's arms. There were villagers with flaming torches. There was a village cut off (by plague in this case) from the rest of the world; it was infiltrated by sinister alien beings, very much in the manner of *Invasion of the Body Snatchers*. There was a gypsy ringmistress of the type who has seen everything, not at all like Maria Ouspenskaya but full of spirit. 'Why have you come?' she is asked, and answers: 'To steal the money from dead men's eyes.' The menace reached the remote community in the guise of a travelling show, as in *House of Frankenstein*, and also as in that movie there was a revenge plot on the burgomaster, conceived by the master showman to settle the previous killing of one of his ilk. These pleasant nuances from the past were however lost whenever sex reared its not necessarily ugly but certainly irrelevant head. 'One lust feeds another,' murmurs the vampire-in-chief as with much heavy breathing he shifts his attention from his nubile victim's neck to elsewhere; and the finale, a fight between the upright hero and the revived, bloodthirsting Count Mitterhouse, was a routine physical set-to. The revenge theme was reinstated in *Captain Kronos, Vampire Hunter*, but the film did not seem to know whether or not it was meant seriously. Since technically it was fairly slapdash, interest withered and died long before Wanda Ventham, as a vampiress preying on young boys, shrivelled away in the light of the sun. *Kronos* had a very limited release, and it was clearly time for Hammer to call it a day.

The Hammer moguls had become millionaire victims of their own success: the need they had filled with such spectacular success no longer existed. Every new film was in some measure a recyling of an older one, and the older ones were coming round with increasing frequency on television. The company had tried to diversify with Stone Age spectaculars and feature versions of TV comedies, but despite occasional box-office bullseyes, Hammer was linked in the public mind with horror. When that commodity came back into fashion, it would be of a kind to shock even the pseudonymous John Elder and Henry Younger: emetic 'modern' nastiness, with teenagers being unpleasantly murdered by madmen wielding chainsaws. High Gothick was already well out of fashion.

Still the Dracula image exerted its hold on the public consciousness, and the Count has probably made more film appearances than any other character, if one

Count Yorga. Two advertisements cover his entire sensational career.

BEWARE OF THE STARE!

These are the eyes that paralyze!

Yorga, the DEATHMASTER is back from beyond the grave.

THE RETURN OF COUNT YORGA

a michael macready-bob kelljan production "the return of count yorga" **GP** ALL AGES ADMITTED ‡ Parental Guidance Suggested

starring
robert quarry · mariette hartley · roger perry · yvonne wilder · edward walsh · guest stars george macready · and walter brooke

as bill nelson

written by bob kelljan and yvonne wilder · based on characters created by bob kelljan · produced by michael macready · directed by bob kelljan · music by bill marx · color by movielab · released by american international pictures

© 1971 American International Pictures, Inc.

includes the brief impersonations. Robert Quarry appeared in two films as the bloodlusting Count Yorga, and in the second there was a Dracula lookalike contest. There were two films also about Dr Phibes, with whom the Count had much in common. *The Deathmaster* was a Californian beach party imitation. Werner Herzog produced a crude, almost scene for scene, revamping of *Nosferatu*, and in the 1979 *Dracula* Laurence Olivier was persuaded to play Van Helsing to Frank Langella's Count; it was all quite unsuitably widescreened, there was far too much heavy breathing, and Olivier stumbled through his routine Albert Bassermann impersonation. Some of this activity was encouraged by the Broadway success, later repeated to some extent in London, of two versions of the original stage play, which ran simultaneously and became highly fashionable. At least they drew the emphasis away from the gore of such corruptions as Paul Morrissey's *Blood for Dracula*, in which the Count can subsist only on the blood of virgins, who have to be deflowered as protection; Dracula in this case is chopped to pieces with an axe, which may sound very final but in his case probably isn't. Other variations included *Not of This Earth*, a neat little thriller about aliens from outer space in search of human blood (a theme more recently repeated in the science fiction TV serial '*V*'). 1959 had brought a western vampire in *Curse of the Undead*, but that experiment was not repeated. Richard Matheson's story *I Am Legend*, about the last man left in a world populated by vampires, was twice filmed unsatisfactorily, first with Vincent Price as *The Last Man on Earth*, and then with Charlton Heston as *The Omega Man*. Portmanteau horror films had a fashion, four or five stories to the film, with a linking story à la *Dead of Night*, and usually one of the stories was a Dracula rip-off. In *Dr Terror's House of Horrors*, Max Adrian was a doctor who persuades a man that his wife is a vampire and must be staked; when this is accomplished, the doctor looks into the camera and sniggers: 'There's only room for one vampire in a small town . . .' In *The House That Dripped Blood* Jon Pertwee, in a role intended for Christopher Lee, is a film actor who makes such a good job of Dracula that the undead invite him to join their club. In *Vault of Horror* a man murders his sister for her inheritance, then retires to celebrate at a restaurant where he finds her and her friends waiting: they are vampires who intend to partake of his blood, having proved that he isn't one of them by his rejection of the tomato juice cocktail. The French variation I like best (it also has Frankenstein connotations) is *Traitement de Choc* (*Shock Treatment*, unaccountably released in Britain as *Doctor in the Nude*). This is a subtle thriller about a health spa where the staff of Portuguese never seem well. A determined lady patient discovers that this is because their vital fluids are being drained off for injection into the rich, who want to stay young. (Somerset Maugham and Winston Churchill are among those who in real life were said to have retreated to Dr Niehans' Swiss clinic which had similar objectives, but there at least the rejuvenating source was restricted to unborn ewes.) Most commercially successful of the spoofs and semi-spoofs was *Love at First Bite*, in which George Hamilton as the vampire Count in New York cut such a dashing figure that one would have liked to see him play the part in a 'serious' version. And 1985's *Fright Night* had a suave disciple (Chris Sarandon) settling cosily into a Californian suburb, suspected only by a teenage neighbour adept at vampire-spotting.

Nor was television slow to cash in on the vampire myth. The two horror comedy series of 1964 both had a vampire figure, the wife played by Carolyn Jones in *The Addams Family*, and in *The Munsters*, Al Lewis's Grandpa, who although retired from active service was always talking about 'putting the bite' on someone. A soap opera called *Dark Shadows* was an immense success in America in the late sixties: it centred on a Gothic house, and its leading character was a vampire called Barnabas. There were also Renfield and Van Helsing figures, and the 'posse' consisted of policemen with crucifixes instead of villagers with torches. Two TV movie versions followed, but they never quite reached the popularity of *The Night Stalker*, about a modern vampire terrorizing Las Vegas. (The investigator, Kolchak, was later given his own series and met every monster the producers could think of.) *The Norliss Tapes* aimed to run as a similar series of creepshows, but never got beyond a genuinely frightening pilot about a gentle-man who, though officially dead, absolutely refused to lie down. The various thriller anthologies (*The Outer Limits, One Step Beyond, Twilight Zone, Night Gallery*) all put the vampire theme to good use. *Thriller* included a particularly effective episode called *Masquerade*, in which the young couple seeking shelter for the night in a cobwebbed spooky house (actually the Bates house from *Psycho*) turn out themselves to be the vampires who are striking fear into the inhabitants. Having scared everyone else away, the travellers settle down for the night in their coffins in the cellar. Universal in 1978 tried to establish a weekly package of serials called *Cliffhangers*, one of which was *The Curse of Dracula* with Michael Nouri; but the idea was a bit camp for prime time, and the show folded after thirteen weeks. Television however did give us in 1979 a mini-series which turned out to be the medium's most potent restatement of the original, by now conventional, vampire theme. Two hundred minutes is of course a great deal of screen time over which to spread what amounts to no more than a reprise of the middle and end sections of Bram Stoker's novel, i.e. the infection of members of a community by the plague of vampirism, brought in by a stranger from across the sea, and the eventual stamping out of the plague by bold individuals. But in *Salem's Lot*, from the novel by the prolific Stephen King, the dialogue is reasonably intelligent, the characters moderately interesting, the production highly efficient and the colour sharp yet subdued. The whole thing is roughly on the level of Siodmak's *Son of Dracula*, which is not a bad level for this kind of endeavour. Directorially, Tobe Hooper achieves his frequent climaxes with genuine cinematic suspense rather than the lashings of gore which had become too conventional in his theatrical films, though he is a shade too fond of fixing our attention on a dramatically empty frame into which something exceedingly nasty erupts after a beat of three.

Salem's Lot is the name of the community, and of course for Americans it has overtones of witchcraft; but the menace here comes in the form of an elderly, sober-suited, rather smarmy antique dealer who sets up shop in town under the shingle Straker and Barlow (though Barlow seems always to be 'away travel-ling'). Straker has taken over the sinister old house above the town, long a source of local rumour and legend. He is curiously secretive about his activities in it, and at first one suspects him to be the monster, the Dracula figure who by night is fanging and corrupting young boys (an inevitable modern twist) who thereafter rise from their graves with yellow pinprick eyes, to hover eerily in clouds of mist outside the bedroom windows of their next intended victims. There is a particu-

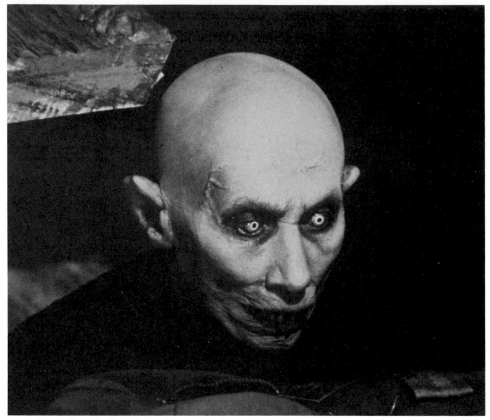

SALEM'S LOT (1979). Even in 20th-century America the vampire master looks pretty much like his 19th-century predecessors.

larly effective shock moment when the gravedigger, left alone in growing darkness to fill in the grave after a service, is silently willed to leap down and open the yet unburied coffin. After what seems an age of silence and uncertainty we are allowed to see the horrid eyes of the undead corpse staring up at him. Then with a sigh he squats down on the lower end of the coffin so that we see his left profile at screen right. Promptly there springs into view at screen left the right profile of the young vampire, out for blood. Deliciously shuddersome.

It shortly transpires that Straker is not the real menace at all; but then, since he faces daylight with equanimity, how could he be? Straker, played with saturnine suavity by James Mason, is merely the minder, the watchdog, the Renfield, for the demonic Barlow, who hisses as he unfurls himself from the chaos of a kitchen floor, having just hurled himself at full force through the window. Black cloaked and malevolent, he has yellow eyes and teeth which seem to glow three-dimensionally from a bald, matt, purple face: surely this is no mere vampiric disciple, but Satan himself. His reign in Salem's Lot, however, is short, his undoing brought about less by the investigating young author-on-a-visit than by the young boy who has lost his parents to the evil but can resist because he has made a thorough study of the Hollywood monsters, and keeps their posters above his bed. ('Unhealthy!' cry both parents in unison shortly before Barlow erupts to bash their skulls together.)

Alas, all virtues disappear in the last forty minutes, when author and boy, now seeming awfully like Batman and Robin, converge in the *Psycho*-styled house, which though all windows seem intact is ludicrously carpeted with feathers and bird-droppings, not to mention a few rats left over from the 1931 version. There is a Tom-and-Jerry sequence in which everybody just misses each other; then the heroine, who has foolishly, and traditionally, ventured inside on her own, is abducted by the smiling Straker and fed to the vampires in the cellar. For an ordinary man Straker next, surprisingly, assumes enough superhuman strength to pick up a stray intruder and impale him on a wall of stags' horns; he is then rather disappointingly shot at the top of a flight of stairs, and proves to possess no invulnerability to bullets. Down below, as the light fades, Barlow rises amid his company of undead, but he is rather too easily staked, after which the house very predictably goes up in flames. There is an epilogue in Ximico, Guatemala (of all places) where, clearly at the end of a long search, Batman and Robin track down the vampirized girl friend and put her to rest; after which the deadly duo set out wearily in search of fresh fiends to conquer. Ah well, the first three hours were good. As to why the monsters came to Salem's Lot in the first place – 'How the hell should I know?' asks Batman. It's as good an answer as any.

Meanwhile the absurdities continued to proliferate: a rock musical stage version; a porno item called *Vampire Hookers*; another called *Dracula Sucks*, which more or less followed Stoker's novel but postulated some bizarre sexual romping in Dr Seward's sanatorium; and something entitled *The Velvet Vampire*, starring one Diane LeFanu. And so did the radio versions and comic strips and television impersonations in comedy shows and commercials.

An ingenious if not very likeable 1977 variation was *Dracula's Dog*, otherwise known as *Zoltan, Hound of Dracula*. Here it is a long-undead servant of Count Dracula (called Veidt Smit and played by the cadaverous Reggie Nalder) who, accidentally resurrected when his master's tomb is investigated, decides to wreak a little mayhem in America and takes along for persuasive purposes the Count's vampire hound. Smit determines to find himself a new master in the person of Dracula's last living descendant, who has almost forgotten his family taint and resents the intrusion. During the friction which follows, our hero's dogs are all torn to bits by Zoltan, who finally falls on to a picket fence; and at the fade-out a dead pup, which was not properly staked, is scrabbling up out of the earth. Unpleasantness to dogs is generally sensed as less tolerable than unpleasantness to humans, and Zoltan did not become a cult figure, though a more diabolically-inspired canine starred a year later in a TV movie called *Devil Dog: the Hound of Hell*.

Dracula's P.R. man is doing a great job. Even in the field of literary scholarship Dracula has made inroads: Professor Leonard Wolf, himself a native of Transylvania, produced a version of Bram Stoker's novel with learned annotations and appended essays (from which one can learn, if one wishes, that in the original edition the Count is present, in human, animal, or suggested form, on only 62 pages out of 390). There is also a calendar for 1887, which Professor Wolf considers the most probable year for the adventure, with every incident assigned to a date, each (naturally) with its times of sunrise and sunset.

The total number of films, books, comics, plays, variety acts and jokes about Dracula is way beyond counting. No doubt the chief reason for the popularity of the theme is its slick packaging of horror and sex; yet many have found humour in it too. In 1982 a slim volume called *Dracula's Diary*, 'edited' by Michael Geare and Michael Corby, gave an 'authentic' account of the nineteen-year-old Dracula's visit to London before entering Eton in the 1870s. He meets socially, *inter alia*, Dr Henry Jekyll (with Mr Hyde alternating), Algernon Swinburne, Dr John H. Watson, and Sherlock Holmes, to whom he is introduced by his English cousin:

> 'Mr Roy Dracula I think I know: but his companion?'
> We all looked at the detective; I think I heard the doctor give a resigned sigh.
> Holmes contemplated me. 'From your voice and appearance, sir, you are a Scot: that dark, Celtic look, that over-perfect English speech. Evidently strong and healthy, probably of a careful medical family. So you'll be a Scots medical student, much concerned with your college games, unless I'm mistaken, since your limp from some sporting injury. Am I not right, sir?'
> 'Close,' said I. 'Quite close. In fact, I'm Count Dracula from Transylvania, and I'm limping because I've got a stone in my shoe.'

In Eton the Count's nocturnal transformations can have unfortunate results, as when in canine form he prowls the by-ways and is approached by an enormous Alsatian:

> The last thing I wanted was a fight with a dog . . . however, it appeared that the animal's intentions were not violent but amorous.
> 'Go away,' I said. 'I'm not a normal dog.'
> 'Nor am I, duckie,' he replied in rather a piping voice, and leaped at me.

Ah well: the eighties have even brought a series of children's books about a character called Vlad the Drac. Perhaps one day stuffed dolls of the cadaverous Count will replace teddy bears by our babies' pillows.

THE FEAR OF FRANKENSTEIN

It was the freak commercial success of *Dracula* which brought *Frankenstein* to the serious attention of Universal Studios. The play version, the latest of many, which toured the States in the late twenties had, like all current theatrical offerings, been processed by the studio's story department, which very likely considered it unsuitable material for the sophisticated talkie screen. Should any conscientious department head have troubled to check back on the original novel, he must have been doubly convinced, for despite being written by an intelligent and apparently vivacious girl of 19 it is a heavy-going piece of work expressed in a cumbersome style which probably seemed old-fashioned even when first published in 1818. In 1930, a monster story more stimulating to the commercially minded must have been that of *The Golem*, silent versions of which had been successfully produced in Germany. Studio photographer Karl Freund had even worked on the most recent of them, which had been widely released in the US, and Germany had been systematically drained by the Hollywood studios of all the creative talent connected with it. Here, in a medieval setting, was a rather amiable clay monster which, when its talisman is stolen, comes to life in a manner fearful but not too threatening, and wreaks assorted havoc before being pacified. The trouble may have been that it was a specifically Jewish monster, and that would not do for a Hollywood in which, despite a vague national mood of anti-Semitism, Jews predominated. Almost no film of the thirties clearly labelled Jews as such. (Even in *The Life of Emile Zola* no mention of Dreyfus' heritage was permitted, and as late as 1942, in *To Be or Not to Be*, the nearest a character named Greenberg can get is to tell a ham actor: 'What you are I wouldn't eat.')

Still, a second supernatural or monstrous role had to be found for Bela Lugosi, the language-mangling star of *Dracula*, and although elements of *The Golem* were finally combined with it, *Frankenstein* came to seem the most desirable property, especially since it was well out of copyright and therefore free. There had been film Frankensteins before, one as early as 1908, but now the era of sound had dawned, and something like genius would be required to prevent the story from seeming absurd. Trial posters were hurriedly designed and distributed, toning down the grave-robbing aspect and generating instead a comic-strip ambience featuring a macho young giant with searchlight eyes. This image scarcely suited

SCENE FROM
FRANKENSTEIN
FILM No. 6604

EDISON FILMS TO BE RELEASED
FROM MAY 11 TO 18 INCLUSIVE

FRANKENSTEIN (1908). It reached London two years late, and by all accounts can't be said to have set the Thames on fire; but it survives historically as the first in an honourable line, despite the fact that you *can* see the join.

the rather desiccated Lugosi, and the project might have foundered entirely had not Universal's latest directorial acquisition from England, James Whale, been looking around for a subject with which to make his American name. His reputation having derived entirely from his direction of *Journey's End* on the London stage (and the moderate success of the Anglo-American film version), Whale turned out to be a fastidious homosexual eccentric who even on the hottest Hollywood day dressed in tweeds and accompanying haberdashery. His penchant for macabre humour was as yet untapped and even unknown; he would in fact refrain from displaying much of it in *Frankenstein*; but he did see in the project something strange and compelling which appealed not only to his sense of style but to his rather lost, wandering soul. For inspiration, being a careful man, he undoubtedly went back to the Mary Shelley novel; and here, after he had discounted the rather clumsy framework, are some of the passages which may have inspired him.

The novel opens strikingly enough as Victor Frankenstein (whose friend and confidant is Henry – the names were curiously reversed in the play and film) pursues across the frozen ice, north of Archangel, a strange misshapen giant of a man. The figure disappears among the icebergs. To the British explorer who saves him, our exhausted hero tells a strange story:

At the University of Ingolstadt, Frankenstein, the scion of a noble family, had studied alchemy as well as modern science, and gradually became obsessed with the hope that he might discover the elixir of life. After nights of near-madness spent in the examination of bodily decay in charnel houses, he became convinced that the great secret resided in the ultraviolet ray, electrically transmitted. His more advanced studies involved vivisection, grave robbing, and the stealing of remains from slaughter houses; and from the parts thus assembled he created an eight-foot giant in human form.

> One of the phenomena which had peculiarly attracted my attention was the structure of the human frame, and, indeed, any animal endued with life. Whence, I often asked myself, did the principle of life proceed? It was a bold question, and one which has ever been considered as a mystery; yet with how many things are we upon the brink of becoming acquainted, if cowardice or carelessness did not restrain our inquiries. I revolved these circumstances in my mind, and determined thenceforth to apply myself more particularly to those branches of natural philosophy which relate to physiology. Unless I had been animated by an almost supernatural enthusiasm, my application to this study would have been irksome, and almost intolerable. To examine the causes of life, we must first have recourse to death. I became acquainted with the science of anatomy: but this was not sufficient; I must also observe the natural decay and corruption of the human body. In my education my father had taken the greatest precautions that my mind should be impressed with no supernatural horrors. I do not ever remember to have trembled at a tale of superstition, or to have feared the apparition of a spirit. Darkness had no effect upon my fancy; and a churchyard was to me merely the receptacle of bodies deprived of life, which, from being the seat of beauty and strength, had become food for the worm. Now I was led to examine the cause and progress of this decay, and forced to spend days and nights in vaults and charnel houses. My attention was fixed upon every object the most insupportable to the delicacy of the human feelings. I saw how the fine form of man was degraded and wasted; I beheld the corruption of death succeed to the blooming

James Whale (1886–1957) in mischievous mood. The lad from Dudley, Worcs., has just arrived in Hollywood and is preparing to make the world's flesh creep with *Frankenstein*.

cheek of life; I saw how the worm inherited the wonders of the eye and brain. I paused, examining and analysing all the minutiae of causation, as exemplified in the change from life to death, and death to life, until from the midst of this darkness a sudden light broke in upon me – a light so brilliant and wondrous, yet so simple, that while I became dizzy with the immensity of the prospect which it illustrated, I was surprised, that among so many men of genius who had directed their inquiries towards the same science, that I alone should be reserved to discover so astonishing a secret.

Remember, I am not recording the vision of a madman. The sun does not more certainly shine in the heavens, than that which I now affirm is true. Some miracle might have produced it, yet the stages of the discovery were distinct and probable. After days and nights of incredible labour and fatigue, I succeeded in discovering the cause of generation and life; nay, more, I became myself capable of bestowing animation upon lifeless matter . . .

No one can conceive the variety of feelings which bore me onwards, like a hurricane, in the first enthusiasm of success. Life and death appeared to me ideal bounds, which I should first break through, and pour a torrent of light into our dark world. A new species would bless me as its creator and source; many happy and excellent natures would owe their being to me. No father could claim the gratitude of his child so completely as I should deserve theirs. Pursuing these reflections, I thought that if I could bestow animation upon lifeless matter, I might in process of time (although I now found it impossible) renew life where death had apparently devoted the body to corruption.

These thoughts supported my spirits, while I pursued my undertaking with unremitting ardour. My cheek had grown pale with study, and my person had become emaciated with confinement. Sometimes, on the very brink of certainty, I failed; yet still I clung to the hope which the next day or the next hour might realise. One secret which I alone possessed was the hope to which I had dedicated myself; and the moon gazed on my midnight labours, while, with unrelaxed and breathless eagerness, I pursued nature to her hiding-places. Who shall conceive the horrors of my secret toil, as I dabbled among the unhallowed damps of the grave, or tortured the living animal to animate the lifeless clay? My limbs now tremble and my eyes swim with the remembrance; but then a resistless, and almost frantic, impulse urged me forward; I seemed to have lost all soul or sensation but for this one pursuit. It was indeed but a passing trance that only made me feel with renewed acuteness so soon as, the unnatural stimulus ceasing to operate, I had returned to my old habits. I collected bones from charnel houses; and disturbed, with profane fingers, the tremendous secrets of the human frame. In a solitary chamber, or rather cell, at the top of the house, and separated from all the other apartments by a gallery and staircase, I kept my workshop of filthy creation: my eye-balls were starting from their sockets in attending to the details of my employment. The dissecting room and the slaughter house furnished many of my materials; and often did my human nature turn with loathing from my occupation, whilst, still urged on by an eagerness which perpetually increased, I brought my work near to a conclusion.

It was on a dreary night of November that I beheld the accomplishment of my toils. With an anxiety that almost amounted to agony, I collected the instruments of life around me, that I might infuse a spark of being into the lifeless thing that lay at my feet. It was already one in the morning; the rain pattered dismally against the panes, and my candle was nearly burnt out, when, by the glimmer of the half-extinguished light, I saw the dull yellow eye of the creature open; it breathed hard, and a convulsive motion agitated its limbs.

How can I describe my emotions at this catastrophe, or how delineate the wretch whom with such infinite pains and care I had endeavoured to form? His limbs were in proportion, and I had selected his features as beautiful. Beautiful! – Great God! His yellow skin scarcely covered the work of muscles and arteries beneath; his hair was of a lustrous black, and flowing; his teeth of a pearly whiteness; but these luxuriances only formed a more horrid contrast with his watery eyes, that seemed almost of the same colour as the dun white sockets in which they were set, his shrivelled complexion and straight black lips.

The different accidents of life are not so changeable as the feelings of human nature. I had worked hard for nearly two years, for the sole purpose of infusing life into an inanimate body. For this I had deprived myself of rest and health. I had desired it with an ardour that far exceeded moderation; but now that I had finished, the beauty of the dream vanished, and breathless horror and disgust filled my heart . . .

That night, Victor's sleep is filled with horrid dreams, including one of his mother's corpse in her shroud, with 'grave worms crawling in the folds of the flannel':

I started from my sleep with horror; a cold dew covered my forehead, my teeth chattered, and every limb became convulsed: when, by the dim and yellow light of the moon, as it forced its way through the window shutters, I beheld the wretch – the miserable monster whom I had created. He held up the curtain of the bed; and his eyes, if eyes they may be called, were fixed on me. His jaws opened, and he muttered some inarticulate sounds, while a grin wrinkled his cheeks. He might have spoken, but I did not hear it; one hand was stretched out, seemingly to detain me, but I escaped, and rushed down stairs. I took refuge in the courtyard belonging to the house which I inhabited; where I remained during the rest of the night, walking up and down in the greatest agitation, listening attentively, catching and fearing each sound as if it were to announce the approach of the demoniacal corpse to which I had so miserably given life.

Oh! no mortal could support the horror of that countenance. A mummy again endued with animation could not be so hideous as that wretch. I had gazed on him while unfinished; he was ugly then; but when those muscles and joints were rendered capable of motion, it became a thing such as even Dante could not have conceived.

I passed the night wretchedly. Sometimes my pulse beat so quickly and hardly that I felt the palpitation of every artery; at others, I nearly sank to the ground through languor and extreme weakness. Mingled with this horror, I felt the bitterness of disappointment; dreams that had been my food and pleasant rest for so long a space were now become a hell to me; and the change was so rapid, the overthrow so complete!

Morning, dismal and wet, at length dawned, and discovered to my sleepless and aching eyes the church of Ingolstadt, its white steeple and clock, which indicated the sixth hour. The porter opened the gates of the court, which had that night been my asylum, and I issued into the streets, pacing them with quick steps, as if I sought to avoid the wretch whom I feared every turning of the street would present to my view. I did not dare return to the apartment which I inhabited, but felt impelled to hurry on, although drenched by the rain which poured from a black and comfortless sky.

I continued walking in this manner for some time, endeavouring, by bodily exercise, to ease the load that weighed upon my mind. I traversed the streets, without any clear conception of where I was, or what I was doing. My heart palpitated in the sickness of fear; and I hurried on with irregular steps, not daring to look about me:

> Like one who, on a lonely road,
>   Doth walk in fear and dread,
> And, having once turned round, walks on,
>   And turns no more his head;
> Because he knows a frightful fiend
>   Doth close behind him tread.

Victor thus deserts his creation, and suffers for months from remorse and from physical revulsion at having created it. The creature disappears entirely. Then

Victor has word from home that his younger brother has been foully murdered, and near the end of his hasty journey to comfort his family he sees on the hillside something which makes him cringe with guilt . . .

I perceived in the gloom a figure which stole from behind a clump of trees near me; I stood fixed, gazing intently: I could not be mistaken. A flash of lightning illuminated the object, and discovered its shape plainly to me; its gigantic stature, and the deformity of its aspect, more hideous than belongs to humanity, instantly informed me that it was the wretch, the filthy demon, to whom I had given life. What did he there? Could he be (I shuddered at the conception) the murderer of my brother? No sooner did that idea cross my imagination, than I became convinced of its truth; my teeth chattered, and I was forced to lean against a tree for support. The figure passed me quickly, and I lost it in the gloom. Nothing in human shape could have destroyed that fair child. *He* was the murderer! I could not doubt it. The mere presence of the idea was an irresistible proof of the fact. I thought of pursuing the devil; but it would have been in vain, for another flash discovered him to me hanging among the rocks of the nearby perpendicular ascent of Mont Salêve, a hill that bounds Plainpalais on the south. He soon reached the summit, and disappeared.

I remained motionless. The thunder ceased; but the rain still continued, and the scene was enveloped in an impenetrable darkness. I revolved in my mind the events which I had until now sought to forget: the whole train of my progress towards the creation; the appearance of the work of my own hands alive at my bedside; its departure. Two years had now nearly elapsed since the night on which he first received life; and was this his first crime? Alas! I had turned loose into the world a depraved wretch, whose delight was in carnage and misery; had he not murdered my brother?

No one can conceive the anguish I suffered during the remainder of the night, which I spent, cold and wet, in the open air. But I did not feel the inconvenience of the weather; my imagination was busy in scenes of evil and despair. I considered the being whom I had cast among mankind, and endowed with the will and power to effect purposes of horror, such as the deed which he had now done, nearly in the light of my own vampire, my own spirit let loose from the grave, and forced to destroy all that was dear to me.

When he arrives home, Victor discovers that a servant girl, Justine, is suspected of the murder. He knows her to be innocent: Justine, however, is caught and hanged, which naturally aggravates Victor's guilt complex. Later, on a glacier below Mont Blanc . . .

. . . I suddenly beheld the figure of a man, at some distance, advancing towards me with superhuman speed. He bounded over the crevices in the ice, among which I had walked with caution; his stature, also, as he approached, seemed to exceed that of man. I was troubled: a mist came over my eyes, and I felt a faintness seize me; but I was quickly restored by the cold gale of the mountains. I perceived, as the shape came nearer (sight tremendous and abhorred!) that it was the wretch whom I had created . . .

'Devil,' I exclaimed, 'do you dare approach me? and do not you fear the fierce vengeance of my arm wreaked on your miserable head? Begone, vile insect! or rather, stay, that I may trample you to dust! and, oh! that I could, with the extinction of your miserable existence, restore those victims whom you have so diabolically murdered!'

'I expected this reception,' said the demon. 'All men hate the wretched; how, then, must I be hated, who am miserable beyond all living things! Yet you, my creator, detest and spurn me, thy creature, to whom thou art bound by ties only dissoluble by the annihilation of one of us. You purpose to kill me. How dare you sport thus with life? Do your duty towards me, and I will do mine towards you and the rest of mankind. If you will comply with my conditions, I will leave them and you at peace; but if you refuse, I will glut the maw of death, until it be satiated with the blood of your remaining friends.'

'Abhorred monster! fiend that thou art! the tortures of hell are too mild a vengeance for thy crimes. Wretched devil! you reproach me with your creation; come on, then, that I may extinguish the spark which I so negligently bestowed.'

My rage was without bounds; I sprang on him, impelled by all the feelings which can arm one being against the existence of another.

He easily eluded me, and said –

'Be calm! I entreat you to hear me, before you give vent to your hatred on my devoted head. Have I not suffered enough that you seek to increase my misery? Life, although it may only be an accumulation of anguish, is dear to me, and I will defend it. Remember, thou hast made me more powerful than thyself; my height is superior to thine; my joints more supple. But I will not be tempted to set myself in opposition to thee. I am thy creature, and I will be even mild and docile to my natural lord and king, if thou wilt also perform thy part, the which thou owest me. Oh, Frankenstein, be not equitable to every other, and trample upon me alone, to whom thy justice, and even thy clemency and affection, is most due. Remember, that I am thy creature; I ought to be thy Adam; but I am rather the fallen angel, whom thou drivest from joy for no misdeed. Everywhere I see bliss, from which I alone am irrevocably excluded. I was benevolent and good; misery made me a fiend. Make me happy, and I shall again be virtuous.'

'Begone! I will not hear you. There can be no community between you and me; we are enemies. Begone, or let us try our strength in a fight, in which one must fall.'

'How can I move thee? Will no entreaties cause thee to turn a favourable eye upon thy creature, who implores thy goodness and compassion? Believe me, Frankenstein: I was benevolent; my soul glowed with love and humanity: but am I not alone, miserably alone? You, my creator, abhor me; what hope can I gather from your fellow-creatures, who owe me nothing? they spurn and hate me. The desert mountains and dreary glaciers are my refuge. I have wandered here many days; the caves of ice, which I only do not fear, are a dwelling to me, and the only one which man does not grudge. These bleak skies I hail, for they are kinder to me than your fellow-beings. If the multitude of mankind knew of my existence, they would do as you do, and arm themselves for my destruction. Shall I not then hate them who abhor me? I will keep no terms with my enemies. I am miserable, and they shall share my wretchedness. Yet it is in your power to recompense me, and deliver them from an evil which it only remains for you to make so great that not only you and your family, but thousands of others, shall be swallowed up in the whirlwinds of its rage. Let your compassion be moved, and do not disdain me. Listen to my tale: when you have heard that, abandon or commiserate me, as you shall judge that I deserve. But hear me. The guilty are allowed, by human laws, bloody as they are, to speak in their own defence before they are condemned. Listen to me, Frankenstein. You accuse me of murder; and yet you would, with a satisfied conscience, destroy your own creature. Oh, praise the eternal justice of man! Yet I ask you not to spare me: listen to me; and then, if you can, and if you will, destroy the work of your hands . . .

'It is with considerable difficulty that I remember the original era of my being: all the events of that period appear confused and indistinct. A strange multiplicity of sensations seized me, and I saw, felt, heard, and smelt, at the same time; and it was, indeed, a long time before I learned to distinguish between the operations of my various senses. By degrees, I remember, a stronger light pressed upon my nerves, so that I was obliged to shut my eyes. Darkness then came over me, and troubled me;

Mary Wollstonecraft Shelley was in her nineteenth year when she wrote *Frankenstein*.
This, her only known portrait, was painted in her forties, but there is still a glimmer of
the rebellious teenage authoress. When the story was devised, she and her husband-to-be
were spending a weekend at Diodati by Lake Geneva with their friends Lord Byron and
his physician John Polidori. *Frankenstein* was the most direct result of the ghost stories
they told to each other. (See over, and page 26.)

George Gordon, Lord Byron, the poet and man of action whose rebellious spirit stirred many a heart to adventure.

but hardly had I felt this, when, by opening my eyes, as I now suppose, the light poured in upon me again. I walked, and, I believe, descended; but I presently found a great alteration in my sensations. Before, dark and opaque bodies had surrounded me, impervious to my touch or sight; but I now found that I could wander on at liberty, with no obstacles which I could not either surmount or avoid. The light became more and more oppressive to me; and, the heat wearying me as I walked, I sought a place where I could receive shade. This was the forest near Ingolstadt; and here I lay by the side of a brook resting from my fatigue, until I felt tormented by hunger and thirst. This roused me from my nearly dormant state, and I ate some

John Polidori, Byron's doctor and somewhat jealous friend. The Lake Geneva weekend inspired him to write *The Vampyre*, one of the precursors of *Dracula*. (See page 26.)

berries which I found hanging on the trees, or lying on the ground. I slaked my thirst at the brook; and then lying down, was overcome by sleep.'

A garrulous monster indeed. He goes on to describe at great length how he stayed with a blind man who could not see his ugliness (an incident which Whale would reserve for his sequel four years later). Finally he tells how he came upon the small boy and murdered him because he was of the Frankenstein family:

'He struggled violently. "Let me go," he cried; "monster! ugly wretch! you wish to eat me, and tear me to pieces – You are an ogre – Let me go, or I will tell my papa."

'"Boy, you will never see your father again; you must come with me."

'"Hideous monster! let me go. My papa is a Syndic – he is M. Frankenstein – he will punish you. You dare not keep me."

'"Frankenstein! you belong then to my enemy – to him towards whom I have sworn eternal revenge; you shall be my first victim."

'The child still struggled, and loaded me with epithets which carried despair to my heart; I grasped his throat to silence him, and in a moment he lay dead at my feet.

'I gazed on my victim, and my heart swelled with exultation and hellish triumph: clapping my hands, I exclaimed, "I, too, can create desolation; my enemy is not invulnerable; this death will carry despair to him, and a thousand other miseries shall torment and destroy him." . . .'

The being finished speaking, and fixed his looks upon me in expectation of a reply. But I was bewildered, perplexed, and unable to arrange my ideas sufficiently to understand the full extent of his proposition. He continued –

'You must create a female for me, with whom I can live in the interchange of those sympathies necessary for my being. This you alone can do; and I demand it of you as a right which you must not refuse to concede.'

The latter part of his tale had kindled anew in me the anger that had died away while he narrated his peaceful life among the cottagers, and, as he said this, I could no longer suppress the rage that burned within me.

'I do refuse it,' I replied; 'and no torture shall ever extort a consent from me. You may render me the most miserable of men, but you shall never make me base in my own eyes. Shall I create another like yourself, whose joint wickedness might desolate the world! Begone! I have answered you; you may torture me, but I will never consent.'

Frankenstein has plenty of thinking to do. Eventually he retreats from the society he knows and sets up a new laboratory in a remote part of the Orkneys. Here under the crudest conditions, and despite his initial horror at the idea, he prepares to build a bride for the monster. The original creature, however, is so impatient that the pair of them fall out, and Frankenstein sets out once more on his desperate travels.

But there is no escape for poor Victor. The monster next murders his friend Henry, and Victor is imprisoned for three months before his innocence is established. Then at last he marries his Elizabeth and sets off to honeymoon in Evian. But he should have heeded the monster's warning of further revenge to come. The honeymoon night is a tragic one.

She left me, and I continued some time walking up and down the passages of the house, and inspecting every corner that might afford a retreat to my adversary. But I discovered no trace of him, and was beginning to conjecture that some fortunate chance had intervened to prevent the execution of his menaces, when suddenly I heard a shrill and dreadful scream. It came from the room into which Elizabeth had retired. As I heard it, the whole truth rushed into my mind, my arms dropped, the motion of every muscle and fibre was suspended; I could feel the blood trickling in my veins and tingling in the extremities of my limbs. This state lasted but for an instant; the scream was repeated, and I rushed into the room.

Great God! why did I not then expire! Why am I here to relate the destruction of the best hope and the purest creature of earth? She was there, lifeless and inanimate, thrown across the bed, her head hanging down, and her pale and distorted features half covered by her hair. Everywhere I turn I see the same figure – her bloodless arms and relaxed form flung by the murderer on its bridal bier. Could I behold this and live? Alas! life is obstinate and clings closest where it is most hated. For a moment only did I lose recollection; I fell senseless on the ground.

When I recovered, I found myself surrounded by the people of the inn; their countenances expressed a breathless terror; but the horror of others appeared only as a mockery, a shadow of the feelings that oppressed me. I escaped from them to the room where lay the body of Elizabeth, my love, my wife, so lately living, so dear, so worthy . . .

While I still hung over her in the agony of despair, I happened to look up. The windows of the room had before been darkened, and I felt a kind of panic on seeing the pale yellow light of the moon illuminate the chamber. The shutters had been thrown back; and, with a sensation of horror not to be described, I saw at the open window a figure the most hideous and abhorred. A grin was on the face of the monster; he seemed to jeer as with his fiendish finger he pointed towards the corpse of my wife. I rushed towards the window and, drawing a pistol from my bosom, fired; but he eluded me, leaped from his station, and running with the swiftness of lightning, plunged into the lake.

The report of the pistol brought a crowd into the room. I pointed to the spot where he had disappeared, and we followed the track with boats; nets were cast, but in vain. After passing several hours, we returned hopeless, most of my companions believing it to have been a form conjured up by my fancy. After having landed, they proceeded to search the country, parties going in different directions among the woods and vines.

I attempted to accompany them, and proceeded a short distance from the house; but my head whirled round, my steps were like those of a drunken man, I fell at last in a state of utter exhaustion; a film covered my eyes, and my skin was parched with the heat of fever. In this state I was carried back and placed on a bed, hardly conscious of what had happened; my eyes wandered round the room as if to seek something that I had lost.

When Victor sets out on more rather aimless wanderings in pursuit of his demon, the novel threatens to turn into a world tour. The Rhône, the Mediterranean, the Black Sea, Tartary, Russia are all explored in vain. But sometimes the monster taunts Victor with clues and messages, and one of these sets him on a new tack: 'My reign is not yet over. You live, and my power is complete. Follow me: I seek the everlasting ices of the north, where you will feel the misery of cold and frost to which I am impassive. You will find near this place, if you follow not too tardily, a dead hare: eat, and be refreshed. Come on, my enemy: we have yet to wrestle for our lives: but many hard and miserable hours must you endure until that period shall arrive.' Victor follows the trail across the Arctic ocean until his dogs die one by one and, as we have seen, he is rescued half dead to tell his story. The monster eludes him still.

Oh! when will my guiding spirit, in conducting me to the demon, allow me the rest I so much desire; or must I die and yet he live? If I do, swear to me, Walton, that he shall not escape; that you will seek him and satisfy my vengeance in his death. And do I dare to ask of you to undertake my pilgrimage, to endure the hardships that I have undergone? No; I am not so selfish. Yet, when I am dead, if he should appear; if the ministers of vengeance should conduct him to you, swear that he shall not live – swear that he shall not triumph over my accumulated woes, and survive to add to the list of his dark crimes. He is eloquent and persuasive; and once his words had even power over my heart: but trust him not. His soul is as hellish as his form, full of treachery and fiendlike malice. Hear him not; call on the names of William, Justine, Clerval, Elizabeth, my father, and of the wretched Victor, and thrust your sword into his heart. I will hover near and direct the steel aright.

After several days Victor dies, and in a letter home his rescuer adds a footnote:

Great God! what a scene has just taken place! I am yet dizzy with the remembrance of it. I hardly know whether I shall have the power to detail it; yet the tale which I have recorded would be incomplete without this final and wonderful catastrophe.

I entered the cabin where lay the remains of my ill-fated and admirable friend. Over him hung a form which I cannot find words to describe; gigantic in stature, yet uncouth and distorted in its proportions. As he hung over the coffin his face was concealed by long locks of ragged hair; but one vast hand was extended, in colour and apparent texture like that of a mummy. When he heard the sound of my approach he ceased to utter exclamations of grief and horror and sprung towards the window. Never did I behold a vision so horrible as his face, of such loathsome yet appalling hideousness. I shut my eyes involuntarily and endeavoured to recollect what were my duties with regard to this destroyer. I called on him to stay.

He paused, looking on me with wonder; and, again turning towards the lifeless form of his creator, he seemed to forget my presence, and every feature and gesture seemed instigated by the wildest rage of some uncontrollable passion.

'That is also my victim!' he exclaimed: 'in his murder my crimes are consummated; the miserable series of my being is wound to its close! Oh, Frankenstein! generous and self-devoted being! what does it avail that I now ask thee to pardon me? I, who irretrievably destroyed thee by destroying all thou lovedst. Alas! he is cold, he cannot answer me.'

His voice seemed suffocated; and my first impulses, which had suggested to me the duty of obeying the dying request of my friend, in destroying his enemy, were now suspended by a mixture of curiosity and compassion. I approached this tremendous being; I dared not again raise my eyes to his face, there was something so scaring and unearthly in his ugliness. I attempted to speak, but the words died away on my lips. The monster continued to utter wild and incoherent self-reproaches. At length I gathered resolution to address him in a pause of the tempest of his passion: 'Your repentance,' I said, 'is now superfluous. If you had listened to the voice of conscience, and heeded the stings of remorse, before you had urged your diabolical vengeance to this extremity, Frankenstein would yet have lived.'

'And do you dream?' said the demon; 'do you think that I was then dead to agony and remorse? – He,' he continued, pointing to the corpse, 'he suffered not in the consummation of the deed – oh! not the ten-thousandth portion of the anguish that was mine during the lingering detail of its execution. A frightful selfishness hurried me on, while my heart was poisoned with remorse. Think you that the groans of Clerval were music to my ears? My heart was fashioned to be susceptible of love and sympathy; and when wrenched by misery to vice and hatred it did not endure the violence of the change without torture such as you cannot even imagine.

'After the murder of Clerval I returned to Switzerland heartbroken and overcome. I pitied Frankenstein; my pity amounted to horror: I abhorred myself. But when I discovered that he, the author at once of my existence and of its unspeakable torments, dared to hope for happiness; that while he accumulated wretchedness and despair upon me he sought his own enjoyment in feelings and passions from the indulgence of which I was for ever barred, then impotent envy and bitter indignation filled me with an insatiable thirst for vengeance. I recollected my threat and resolved that it should be accomplished. I knew that I was preparing for myself a deadly torture; but I was the slave, not the master, of an impulse which I detested, yet could not disobey. Yet when she died! – nay, then I was not miserable. I had cast off all feeling, subdued all anguish, to riot in the excess of my despair. Evil thenceforth became my good. Urged thus far, I had no choice but to adapt my nature to an element which I had willingly chosen. The completion of my demoniacal design became an insatiable passion. And now it is ended; there is my last victim!'

I was at first touched by the expressions of his misery; yet, when I called to mind what Frankenstein had said of his powers of eloquence and persuasion, and when I again cast my eyes on the lifeless form of my friend, indignation was rekindled within me. 'Wretch!' I said, 'it is well that you come here to whine over the desolation that you have made. You throw a torch into a pile of buildings; and when they are consumed you sit among the ruins and lament the fall. Hypocritical fiend! if he whom you mourn still lived, still would he be the object, again would he become the prey, of your accursed vengeance. It is not pity that you feel; you lament only because the victim of your malignity is withdrawn from your power.'

'Oh, it is not thus – not thus,' interrupted the being; 'yet such must be the impression conveyed to you by what appears to be the purport of my actions. Yet I seek not a fellow-feeling in my misery. No sympathy may I ever find. When I first sought it, it was the love of virtue, the feelings of happiness and affection with which my whole being overflowed, that I wished to be participated. But now that virtue has become to me a shadow and that happiness and affection are turned into bitter and loathing despair, in what should I seek for sympathy? I am content to suffer alone while my sufferings shall endure: when I die, I am well satisfied that abhorrence and opprobrium should load my memory. Once my fancy was soothed with dreams of virtue, of fame, and of enjoyment. Once I falsely hoped to meet with beings who, pardoning my outward form, would love me for the excellent qualities which I was capable of unfolding. I was nourished with high thoughts of honour and devotion. But now crime has degraded me beneath the meanest animal. No guilt, no mischief, no malignity, no misery, can be found comparable to mine. When I run over the frightful catalogue of my sins, I cannot believe that I am the same creature whose thoughts were once filled with sublime and transcendent visions of the beauty and the majesty of goodness. But it is even so; the fallen angel becomes a malignant devil. Yet even that enemy of God and man had friends and associates in his desolation; I am alone . . .

'Fear not that I shall be the instrument of future mischief. My work is nearly complete. Neither yours nor any man's death is needed to consummate the series of my being, and accomplish that which must be done; but it requires my own. Do not think that I shall be slow to perform this sacrifice. I shall quit your vessel on the ice-raft which brought me thither, and shall seek the most northern extremity of the globe; I shall collect my funeral pile and consume to ashes this miserable frame, that its remains may afford no light to any curious and unhallowed wretch who would create such another as I have been. I shall die. I shall no longer feel the agonies which now consume me, or be the prey of feelings unsatisfied, yet unquenched. He is dead who called me into being; and when I shall be no more the very remembrance of us both will speedily vanish. I shall no longer see the sun or stars, or feel the winds play on my cheeks. Light, feeling, and sense will pass away; and in this condition must I find my happiness. Some years ago, when the images which this world affords first opened upon me, when I felt the cheering warmth of summer, and heard the rustling of the leaves and the warbling of the birds, and these were all to me, I should have wept to die; now it is my only consolation. Polluted by crimes, and torn by the bitterest remorse, where can I find rest but in death?

'Farewell! I leave you, and in you the last of human kind whom these eyes will ever behold. Farewell, Frankenstein! If thou wert yet alive, and yet cherished a desire of revenge against me, it would be better satiated in my life than in my destruction. But it was not so; thou didst seek my extinction that I might not cause greater wretchedness; and if yet, in some mode unknown to me, thou hast not ceased to think and feel, thou wouldst not desire against me a vengeance greater than that which I feel. Blasted as thou wert, my agony was still superior to thine; for the bitter sting of remorse will not cease to rankle in my wounds until death shall close them for ever.

'But soon,' he cried, with sad and solemn enthusiasm, 'I shall die, and what I now feel be no longer felt. Soon these burning miseries will be extinct. I shall ascend my funeral pile triumphantly, and exult in the agony of the torturing flames. The light of that conflagration will fade away; my ashes will be swept into the sea by the winds. My spirit will sleep in peace; or if it thinks, it will not surely think thus. Farewell.'

He sprung from the cabin window, as he said this, upon the ice-raft which lay close to the vessel. He was soon borne away by the waves and lost in darkness and distance.

While James Whale was still pondering various possible treatments of *Frankenstein* – and one should bear in mind that at the beginning of the thirties sound techniques were still very restrictive – he had a great stroke of luck, allegedly one lunchtime in the studio commissary. Across the crowded tables he glimpsed a solitary actor whom he knew by sight but not by name. Another Englishman, Whale surmised: that gaunt upper-class face and the bony back of the head could emanate from nowhere else. When the man stood up to leave, Whale was reminded too of his curious loping gait, like a thing about to run out of control. Now, if only the man could act, he might make a highly photogenic monster, one with real star quality.

The man of course was Boris Karloff, and the rest is history. Or, at least, it would become history when Whale had forced Robert Florey, the original studio choice for director and co-writer, off the *Frankenstein* project Florey was given *Murders in the Rue Morgue* to direct, starring Lugosi who had finally turned down the monster role because it now contained no dialogue. All Whale had to do then was settle on the right mood, the right script, and the right actor for the half-crazed baron. In the end he put the spotlight on his old colleague from *Journey's End*, Colin Clive, a nervous fellow-homosexual who as the officer under pressure had done such a fine job of chewing up the scenery. As for script, Whale finally approved something which had been produced by the usual studio technique of having a series of contractees each improving on the work of the other. The screen credits run as follows:

> from the novel by Mrs Percy B. Shelley
> adapted from the play by Peggy Webling
> based upon the composition by John L. Balderston
> screen play: Garrett Fort, Francis Edwards Faragoh
> scenario editor: Richard Schayer

No mention was made of the discarded Florey, who many years later claimed himself to have blocked out the treatment finally used. His descent from glory was final: *Murders in the Rue Morgue* proved an awkward flop.

The principal elements being assembled, Whale evolved a stark, rather jagged narrative technique, with a no-holds-barred opening sequence in which earth falls on to a coffin being lowered into its grave, while from behind a row of spiky

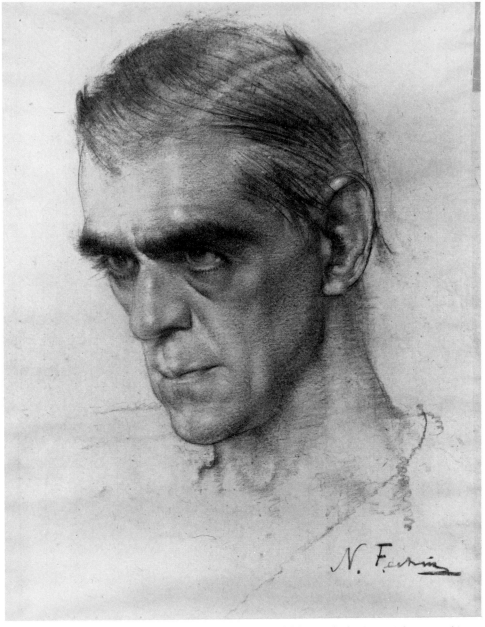

Boris Karloff was rather a quiet person, but with a useful lisp and a loping gait he created in the Frankenstein monster a figure of impenetrable moods and frightening power.

railings Frankenstein and his grave-robbing assistant wait with ill-concealed eagerness. (Dwight Frye, the Renfield of *Dracula*, played the hunchbacked Fritz, and someone at Universal must have thought he brought good luck to both productions, for he appeared in many more of the studio's horror films before his death in 1942.) As soon as the ceremony is over, and the mourners have moved tearfully away, the ghouls make haste to undo the sexton's work, for Frankenstein needs a fresh corpse to provide parts for the new creature which he hopes to endow with artificial life. Just to make sure he has enough spares in stock, he waits on the way home while Fritz appropriates another rotting specimen from a wayside gibbet. All this was strong stuff for 1931, and the sequence still reduces most audiences to cold shivers, especially when bathed in the green light used at its première.

This first time round in the saga he had unwittingly begun, Whale permits no infusion of humour save in the occasional interjections of Frankenstein's elderly father, who despite the German setting, the beret and the meerschaum pipe is clearly a silly ass of the old Piccadilly school. 'What's the matter with my son?' he asks Henry's friend Victor. (Remember the reversal of names.) 'Why does he go messing about in an old ruined windmill when he has a decent house, a bath, good food and drink and a damned pretty girl to come back to? Hm? Will you tell me that?' Victor won't, or can't; he hasn't much of a role at all, and in the final version doesn't even get the girl. But the audience knows the reason well enough.

After that first sequence Henry is well stacked with bodies, and needs only a really good brain. Carelessly he sends the not-too-bright Fritz to get one from the anatomy school – without asking, of course. To begin with, Fritz quite properly chooses the jar labelled 'normal brain', but a fright makes him drop it, and the contents splatter all over the polished floor. So he brings back instead the one labelled 'abnormal brain', the one we heard the professor describe as coming from a man of 'degenerate characteristics', a man 'whose life was one of brutality, of violence and murder'. (How odd that Frankenstein should not have noticed the label – perhaps Fritz tore it off.)

This anatomy professor, Dr Waldman, we have met before in *Dracula*, and will meet again. He is played by a grey-haired, walnut-faced actor called Edward Van Sloan, who was to be spotted in several horror films of the period, and who indeed appeared before the titles of this one, in an immaculate but somewhat more effete persona, to offer a few urgent words of welcome:

> How do you do. Mr Carl Laemmle feels that it would be a little unkind to present this picture without just a word of friendly warning. We are about to unfold the story of Frankenstein, a man of science, who sought to create a man after his own image, without reckoning upon God. It is one of the strangest tales ever told. It deals with the two great mysteries of creation, life and death. I think it will thrill you. It may shock you. It might even . . . horrify you. So then, if you feel that you do not care to subject your nerves to such a strain, now is your chance to . . . well, we've warned you!

Even today there is a Castle Frankenstein, a real one, not far from Frankfurt-am-Main, but it was mysteriously ruined in the Middle Ages and only a few walls are left. The film version of it is a warm and even cosy place, put in, one feels, partly for contrast with the starker horrors and partly to give full rein to designer Charles Hall's penchant for baronial sets full of striking if unlikely detail (such as a massive detached beam which slopes at an absurd angle across the main corridor). If anyone still thinks that ceilings on sets began with *Citizen Kane*, let him witness the splendid one which surmounts the baron's living room, complete with ornamental plasterwork whose cost can scarcely have been justified by the three or four seconds of its appearance on the screen. All this, as we say, is contrast, for the burden of the story locates itself in an abandoned old hilltop watch tower which, despite its obvious lack of modern conveniences, Henry is happy to use as an isolated workplace in which he is unlikely to be bothered by callers. Somehow he manages to generate his own electricity, plenty of it, enough to operate that famous hoist which, to the accompaniment of much crackling and flashing from assorted instruments, carries his inert creature up through a sliding roof to be brought to life by a lightning storm. In this, as in all the thrill sequences, Whale proves himself a master of fast cutting. In this film it is the rapid succession of hard unpleasant images which stirs the blood, rather than any whirling camera movement or background music. We come so close to Henry that we feel as mad as he is when he cries to Fritz: 'Think of it! No blood, no decay. Just a few stitches. And look, here's the final touch. The brain you stole – the brain of a dead man – waiting to live again in a body I made with my own hands!' (He's exaggerating, of course: he only assembled the parts.)

When at the height of the storm Henry's grossly neglected fiancée comes to call, bringing escorts in the shape of Dr Waldman and the faithful Victor, she is privileged to view the first faint stirrings of life in the artificially regenerated creature. When questioned, Henry is just a little vague about the means: 'I have discovered,' he says, 'the great ray that first brought life into the world.' This is a great suspense sequence for its day, right up to the close-up of the great hand with its sewn-up wrist, beginning to flex itself just as the scene fades out. The brilliant timing of this fade may have been made necessary by the need to cut Henry's final cry of triumph: 'In the name of God! Now I know what it feels like to *be* God!' The censor wasn't having that sort of sacrilege, not in a film already loaded with excess. He was probably disturbed too by the fact that Dr Waldman, up to now the film's voice of reason, is fired by Henry's enthusiasm. By the time we visit the tower again he has taken up permanent residence and is eagerly keeping the log, though concerned that the revived creature is allowed to wander around unfettered, and sceptical about the eventual outcome:

> Only evil will come of it. Your health will be ruined if you persist in this madness.

Well, Henry won't be the first horror hero to close his ears to the gypsy's warning; and of course, if he did there would be no film.

By now the entertainment is nearly half over, and it is time for us to meet our monster. Karloff, being unknown at the time, does not even appear among the main credits, which seem to indicate that the monster is played by a question mark. By the time the film was released, however, audiences must have been aware that they were to witness the birth of a new star, and Karloff does not disappoint them. Nor does Whale, who provides for the monster's first appearance a startling piece of cinematic legerdemain. The monster is heard stomping up the corridor. Henry and Waldman turn off the strong light. The door swings open, and there in the stone arch stands in silhouette a massive dark figure with its back to the audience. As he slowly turns, the camera cuts from long shot to head

FRANKENSTEIN (1931). The monster's first appearance: not quite as in the film, but a memorable enough image on its own account. Colin Clive and Edward Van Sloan wait apprehensively.

and shoulders and gives us our first view of that evil visage which has since become implanted in three generations of public consciousness. The chalk-white face with heavy-lidded eyes, the flat head, the untidy fringe, the neck electrodes, the one sunken cheek, all take our breath away. Then Whale surpasses his first effect. In swift succession he cuts from head and shoulders into full face, then from full face into eyes-nose-and-mouth, each shot taken from a disorientingly differ- ent angle. This triple darting from shot to shot is a trick he will use again in other films – it became a kind of signature – but never more effectively than he uses it here.

In the tense scene which follows we note the creature's lack of balance and its fear of light and fire; and we see what wonders of expression Karloff can bring into that totally false face, especially when compared with the stolid comic-strip vacuum offered by his several successors. It is almost true to say that every frame in which he appears makes a still picture worth hanging on the wall, and the shot in which he silently pleads for help and comfort, using eyes, mouth, hands and shoulders, is a moment to cherish. But a naked torch brings out the violence of his unhappy character, especially when Fritz misguidedly sees in it an easy means of controlling him. It works once, but even then three men are needed to overcome and subdue the raving beast, who is next seen chained and howling in the nearest the old tower can approach to a cell. Then Fritz gets a shade too daring, and is found hanged for his pains. After a savage struggle the monster is felled by a hypodermic, but by now Dr Waldman has had enough. Frankenstein's creation must be painlessly destroyed by injection.

It is a measure of Whale's bravura treatment that he now interrupts the cold horror of the last five minutes for a bumbling visit from Frankenstein senior, who insists on taking the obviously shattered Henry home for assiduous nursing. Waldman is left at the tower to do the necessary, but finds the creature's powers of resistance quite amazing, and unwisely stops to make a note about this before embarking on the dissection process. That means he fails to see the monster's eyes open. Goodbye, Dr Waldman: as you next crouch over the giant form, a hand will steal up behind you and grip you by the neck . . .

The creature is free now to go on the rampage, and we begin to see the cleverness of the make-up designed by Jack Pierce. Any light which catches the face gives it new shadows and highpoints, all of them alarming; the roadmender's boots, with their specially thickened soles and heels, give the already misshapen figure strange dimensions which add a further note of terror. Another ingenious touch is the shortening of the sleeves of the old black jacket; we are not told *why* they are cut almost to the elbow, but they add an impression of immense power to

FRANKENSTEIN (1931). The monster meets little Maria. A famous but unsatisfactory scene, developed from the similar one in *The Golem* (see page 10). The disappearance from reissue prints of the scene's climax created a forty-year *cause célèbre*.

the already large hands. Meanwhile Frankenstein, hearing nothing from the
doctor, recovers something of his old self and prepares to get married; but on the
very morning of the festive day, with the villagers in lederhosen dancing round
maypoles in the low-arched village set originally built for *All Quiet on the Western
Front*, a small girl up by the mountain lake picks wild flowers and tosses some of
the blooms into the water, curious to see whether they will float. They do, and
form a pretty pattern. Then, in a scene directly borrowed from *The Golem*, the
monster stalks ominously out of the bushes towards her . . . only to find that she
has no fear. 'I'm Maria,' she says coyly. 'Will you play with me?' The monster is
touched and temporarily humanized; willingly he gets on his knees to join in her
game. First he imitates her by tossing flowers into the water. Then he reaches out
for Maria . . .

For fifty years, from around 1936, the rest of this scene was mysteriously
eliminated from all circulating prints, and also from the negative at Universal
City. Some call it an absurd act of censorship; others attribute the cut to the
distaste shown for the scene by Boris Karloff himself. Both motives backfired, for
when we next see Maria's father carrying the dead child through the streets we
assume the monster must have raped her. In fact all he did – as is shown by the
missing footage now found in an ancient print at the National Film Archive – was
throw her into the lake in the expectation that she would float like the flowers. The

FRANKENSTEIN (1931). The scene in which the monster abducts Mae Clarke on her wedding
morn is clearly borrowed from Cesare's abduction of the white-robed heroine in *The Cabinet
of Dr Caligari* (right).

fact that she didn't adds to his bewildered distraction; but now the hunt for him is on. The rhubarbing villagers are dipping their torches in long-burning tar, and up at the castle the bride-to-be must wait in her white gown for the excitement to blow over. Needless to say, the monster, in a scene of horrid suspense, finds her with no difficulty; and as he makes a grab for her, and her white train spills across the screen, we are reminded of a very similar scene in *The Cabinet of Dr Caligari*, when the heroine was abducted by the white-faced, black-garbed somnambulist played by Conrad Veidt. In this case the bride is rescued in the nick of time, but the

wedding is firmly postponed until the monster has been caught, and Victor fulfils
his thin role of general comforter:

VICTOR: Easy, old man, she'll be all right.
HENRY: Our wedding day!
VICTOR: Steady. The wedding will only be postponed a day at most.
HENRY: There can be no wedding while this horrible creation of mine is still alive. I
    made him with these hands and with these hands I will destroy him . . . You stay
    here and look after Elizabeth. I leave her in your care. Whatever happens, do you
    understand? In your care.

That last line was written for the original version, when Henry was supposed to
be killed off for his sins, leaving Victor to succeed him in matrimony; but that was
before the Universal moguls suspected a hit of such colossal proportions as to
demand a sequel.

It is almost dark by the time the posse sets off, with Henry, whom nobody
seems to blame, leading one of its three platoons. ('The woods . . . the mountains
. . . the ravines.') The camera naturally follows Henry, whose route leads him
between some of Universal's least convincing papier-mâché rocks and past at least
one distinctly crinkled backdrop; but the sudden, silent appearance of the monster
put a chill even on that, especially since he is no longer frightened by the torch's
fire, and easily overcomes his creator. Clumsily he drags off the inert Henry to a
nearby windmill, but the sniffer dogs are soon on to him. (It is held in some

FRANKENSTEIN (1931). A wonderful mixture of anguish and evil plays on the face of Boris
Karloff during the climax in the windmill.

quarters that Whale's interest in the Frankenstein project was first clinched by the windmill signs which advertised a local Los Angeles bakery, and still do, though now in blue neon; he thought a mill would make an original locale for the story's climax.) The finale is all quick shots of menace and fear and flames, the villagers having helpfully set fire to the wooden building in which man and superman are trapped. The monster stalks Henry round some rumbling machinery, then vengefully throws him from a high balcony; but the young nobleman's fall is luckily broken by a sail. Our last view of the snarling monster has him trapped by a beam as flames approach ever nearer, and since the whole mill is reduced to ashes he is presumed destroyed; but the old serial heroes got out of tougher spots than that, and even in 1931 hardened filmgoers must have had their doubts. Meanwhile a couple of hastily added lines establish that Henry still lives and breathes. The original sombre coda was jettisoned before release; and the replacement scene shows the old baron leaving the invalid's chamber, intercepting a glass of great-grandmother's wine, and drinking to the prospect of a son for the house of Frankenstein.

How did the world receive this startlingly innovative entertainment? Here is the somewhat astonished review from the trade paper *Variety*, published in December 1931:

> A click from the start of the Mayfair engagement, holding a crowd out on a rainy opening night, 'Frankenstein' establishes itself as a notable box-office subject.
>
> Looks like a 'Dracula' plot touching a new peak in horror plays and handled in production with supreme craftsmanship. Exploitation, which dwells upon the shock angle, is also a punchful asset with hair-raising lobby and newspaper trumpeting.
>
> Appeal is candidly to the morbid side and the screen effect is up to promised specifications. Feminine fans seem to get some sort of emotional kick out of this sublimation of the bedtime ghost story done with all the literalness of the camera.
>
> Maximum of stimulating shock is there, but the thing is handled with subtle change of pace and shift of tempo that keeps attention absorbed to a high voltage climax, tricked out with spectacle and dramatic crescendo, after holding the smash shiver on a hair trigger for more than an hour.
>
> Picture starts out with a wallop. Midnight funeral services are in progress on a blasted moor, with the figure of the scientist and his grotesque dwarf assistant hiding at the edge of the cemetery to steal the newly-buried body. Sequence climaxes with the gravedigger sending down the clumping earth upon the newly-laid coffin. Shudder No. 1.
>
> Shudder No. 2, hard on its heels, is when Frankenstein cuts down his second dead subject from the gallows, these details being presented with plenty of realism. These corpses are to be assembled into a semblance of a human body which Frankenstein seeks to galvanize into life, and to this end the story goes into his laboratory, extemporized in a gruesome mountain setting out of an abandoned mill. But first our scientist must have a brain, which leads to another sock touch of the creeps, when the dwarf crawls into a medical college's dissecting room to steal that necessity. If you think these episodes have exhausted the repertoire of gruesome props they are but preliminaries.
>
> Laboratory sequence detailing the creation of the monster patched up of human odds and ends is a smashing bit of theatrical effect, taking place in this eerie setting during a violent mountain storm in the presence of the scientist's sweetheart and others, all frozen with mortal fright.
>
> Series of successive jolts continue through the moment when the monster creeps

upon the scientist's waiting bride, probably the prize blood-curdler of the picture, and its final destruction when the infuriated villagers burn down the deserted windmill in which it is a prisoner. Finish is a change from the one first tried, when the scientist also was destroyed. The climax with the surviving Frankenstein (Frankenstein is the creator of the monster, not the monster itself) relieves the tension somewhat at the finale, but that may not be the effect most to be desired.

Subtle handling of the subject comes in the balance that has been maintained between the real and the supernatural, contrast that heightens the horror punches. The figure of the monster is a triumph of effect. It has a face and head of exactly the right distortions to convey a sense of the diabolical, but not enough to destroy the essential touch of monstrous human evil.

In like manner the feeling of horror is not once let go past the point at which it inspires disbelief, where out of excess it would create a feeling of make-believe. This is the trick that actually makes the picture deliver its high voltage kick. The technique is shrewd manipulation. After each episode dealing with the weird elements of the story there is a swift twist to the normal people of the drama engaged in their commonplace activities, a contrast emphasizing the most eerie detail.

Playing is perfectly paced. Colin Clive, the cadaverous hero of 'Journey's End,' is a happy choice for the scientist driven by a frenzy for knowledge. He plays it with force, but innocent of ranting. Boris Karloff enacts the monster and makes a memorable figure of the bizarre figure with its indescribably terrifying face of demoniacal calm, a fascinating acting bit of mesmerism.

Mae Clarke makes a perfunctory ingenue role charming, and John Boles is satisfying as a family friend, playing with neat elegance a part that loses much with the alternative finale.

Photography is splendid and the lighting the last word in ingenuity, since much of the footage calls for dim or night effect and the manipulation of shadows to intensify the ghostly atmosphere. It took nerve for U to do this one and 'Dracula', all of which may track back to the gruesomeness in 'The Hunchback of Notre Dame', which was also produced by this company. The audience for this type of film is probably the detective story readers and the mystery yarn radio listeners. Sufficient to insure financial success if these pictures are well made.

The picture, which had cost nearly half-a-million dollars, a tidy sum at that time even though there were four dollars to the pound, took five million dollars on its first domestic release, and nobody in the film business needs telling how frequently it was reissued in the cinemas, or that it is still a popular favourite on television 55 years later. Many more recent films date badly, but *Frankenstein* seems to have lost none of its stark style, though the romantic scenes, in which Whale clearly took no interest, might have been treated more realistically. It remains more truly frightening than any of our modern horror sagas filled with bloody corpses and severed eyeballs. And it retains this effect because Whale intuitively used his camera to get through to fears and hopes which lurk within all of us; also because in Colin Clive and Boris Karloff he chose two actors who in these particular roles could not possibly have been bettered.

A sequel was naturally called for, and that without delay. Alas, of the rather thin directorial roster at Universal only Whale could be expected to bring off such a thing, and he wasn't interested in repeating himself. In the hope of tempting him, various treatments were drummed up under the title *The Return of Frankenstein*; but he merely smiled and sent them back to the story department. He willingly created other films more macabre than frightening – *The Old Dark House, The*

Invisible Man – but more than four years passed before he agreed to the Franken-stein sequel as part of a deal which would also send the studio's elaborate production of *Showboat* his way, and incidentally included a contract increase which would make him independent for life. He found that the Frankenstein treatments all focused on the manufacturing of a bride for the monster, a possibility mentioned in Mary Shelley's novel but not touched in the first film. That was all right by Whale, but this had to be his own kind of horror film, something with more black comedy than outright terror, a tale peopled by eccentrics of his own choosing and decorated with the little twists of black fancy in which he had come to delight. He was given a massive budget to work with, and a newly-imported composer named Franz Waxman who thought it would be amusing to herald the birth of the monster bride with music which sounded like a Polynesian love song. The somewhat impractical laboratory equipment shown in the old film was replaced by items of far greater sophistication: there was enough electricity flashing in the creation scene to light a small town. Whale's favourite photographer, John Mescall, was a brilliant composer of weird images, more so when drunk than when sober; and so, though seldom sober, he was retained. Whale kept the period German setting, but playfully brought in an all-English cast to support Karloff, who now was billed, by surname only, in letters twice as big as the title (or the director), and was apparently getting untypical delusions of grandeur, talking airily about the monster's motivation. Colin Clive was still a fine hysteric, but there could be no sustained interest four years later in a continuing battle of wills between creator and created, especially since the monster was to turn half-sympathetic. What was required was a new villain to bring out the worst in both of them, a man of indisputable black evil to show up against their off-white and grey. Whale found his man in an emaciated, indeed skeletal-looking English stage actor called Ernest Thesiger, who, as well as writing a book on embroidery, had brilliantly played the vacillating Horace Femm in *The Old Dark House*. You wouldn't think so from the billing, but Thesiger was the real star of *The Bride of Frankenstein*, as the new film came to be called. Even Claude Rains, who was once mooted for the role of Dr Septimus Pretorius, could scarcely have done a finer job; and Bela Lugosi, the studio's first favourite, would have given the production a horror comic ambience.

It is Pretorius who persuades the reluctant Henry to continue with his monster-making, and Pretorius who surreptitiously brings the monster under his own control and sends him out on more missions of murder. All this he accomplishes by fluttery, limp-wristed gestures and prissy remarks which only the monster seems to appreciate; and when all else fails he has the monster kidnap Henry's wife, a juicy piece of blackmail which forces the scientist to finish his task. Thesiger was not a popular figure in Hollywood and worked there no more, but for his two performances under Whale's direction he richly deserved an Academy Award.

For writers Whale had more or less preserved his original team, but it was at his suggestion rather than theirs that the sequel somewhat disconcertingly begins in an eighteenth-century Gothic residence, obviously Diodati in 1816, high on a romantic mountainside during a thunderstorm. Here sit none other than both

Shelleys and Lord Byron, all discussing the enormous commercial potential of
Mary's book; she, in the person of Elsa Lanchester, proffers an occasional demure
comment but keeps her eyes on her needlework. Every means of studio pressure
was brought upon Whale to omit this scene, with its obvious excess of verbiage
and consequent lack of direct appeal to audiences in Pittsburgh or Pocatello,
Idaho. Even his friends thought it a merely frivolous impediment to the horror he
was supposed to be creating. But he was adamant, and although throughout the

The villains of *The Bride of Frankenstein* (1935), arguably the best horror film ever made. The skeletal, effeminate Ernest Thesiger (left) makes a useful assistant of the wandering monster (Boris Karloff), now sadder but wiser despite the singeing of his hair and the apparent treachery of all the friends he has tried to make.

world many cinemas did cut it, preferring an abrupt start to the main story, it survives in the abbreviated form to which Whale finally agreed. Since that short version omits several points of explanation, including the matter of the telephone and of the gentlemen's curiously modern dress, the scene as originally written is here reproduced in full,★ with the subsequent omissions in square brackets:

★ The original script by John L. Balderston and William Hurlbut is reproduced by permission of Universal Pictures.

THE BRIDE OF FRANKENSTEIN (1935). Colin Clive as Frankenstein and Ernest Thesiger as Pretorius watch their creation (Elsa Lanchester) take her first tottering steps. But she and Frankenstein realize with horror, a few minutes later, that the monster is about to go on the rampage after her rejection of him.

BEHIND THE TITLES, the sounds of a storm – weird howling, thunder rolling and the sound of violins – eerie, unearthly music. It seems to be shrieking – and horrid – laughter, such as might come up from fiends in the pits of hell. This continues as we:

DISSOLVE TO

EXT. LANDSCAPE . . . (NIGHT) . . . (MINIATURE) . . . LONG SHOT

of a wild, storm-riven landscape – Lake Geneva with the mountains beyond. The CAMERA MOVES SWIFTLY over the landscape – menacing rock formations, a frightening precipice, trees bent and torn under the storm – TOWARD a distant light coming from a house set high and solitary in the hills.

As the CAMERA COMES TO REST here, MOVING UP before the lighted window, we see:

LORD BYRON . . . MED. CLOSE SHOT

Standing in the window is the figure of Lord Byron, the poet, gazing out at the storm. At his feet lie two great bloodhounds. He turns to look into the room, and we:

DISSOLVE TO

INT. SALON OF THE VILLA DIODATI . . . LONG SHOT

A richly furnished house of the period – 1816. The atmosphere is sentimentally luxurious – there is magnificent and ornate furniture of the French Empire (now barely yesterday's style) with the voluminous drapings at windows of the English Regency. The lights are delicately shaded, a cheerful fire burns in the grate – and the three occupants of the room set the tone of exquisite, soft elegance and luxury.

Seated before the fire is Mary Wollstonecraft Shelley, embroidering on a frame, her fingers almost as fine as the needle she uses – her fragile blonde beauty like a perfume in the room.

Near her sits Shelley, the poet, correcting some of his verses in manuscript.

CAMERA MOVES UP TO GROUP SHOT.

His beauty almost equals hers in perfection; the finely-cut features, the clear blue eyes, the delicate throat, the high-strung nerves, all mark him the poet that he was.

CUT TO

LORD BYRON . . . MED. CLOSE SHOT

at the window. He lets the curtain, which he has been holding back, fall across the window again as he turns to the others.

A liveried servant enters and leads away the two bloodhounds. Byron is smoking a cheroot as elegant as its length implies. He, too, has great beauty, but a flashing, virile beauty accentuated rather than marred by a misshapen foot. He pauses to take in the group to which he has turned from the storm outside. There is a flash of lightning and a clap of thunder.
    BYRON: How beautifully dramatic . . .

CUT TO

MARY AND SHELLEY . . . MED. TWO-SHOT

They both look up.

CUT TO

MARY, SHELLEY AND BYRON . . . MED. THREE-SHOT
    BYRON: The crudest savage exhibition of Nature at her worst without – and we
        three, we elegant three within . . .

THE BRIDE OF FRANKENSTEIN (1935). The 1816 party has apparently reassembled by Lake Geneva after the successful completion of Mary's novel. Gavin Gordon (Byron) exults in the thrills it gave him; Douglas Walton (Shelley) looks on admiringly. Elsa Lanchester, who later plays her own monster, is about to narrate the sequel.

A gesture to indicate the contrast, a pause to make his point.

CUT TO

MARY . . . CLOSE UP

She looks up with an appreciative smile.

CUT TO

BYRON . . . MED. CLOSE SHOT
    BYRON: I should like to think that an irate Jehovah was pointing those arrows of lightning directly at my head – the unbowed head of George Gordon Lord Byron – England's greatest sinner –
    (*It is evident that he relishes saying it*)
      – but I cannot flatter myself to that extent. Possibly the thunders are for our dear Shelley – heaven's applause for England's greatest poet.

CUT TO

SHELLEY . . . MED. CLOSE UP
    SHELLEY: *(handing written sheet to Mary)*
      What of my Mary?

CUT TO

BYRON . . . MED. CLOSE UP
BYRON: She is an angel.

CUT TO

MARY . . . MED. CLOSE UP
MARY: You think so.
(She reads in a low voice, strangely sweet)
['Lift not the painted veil which those who live
Call Life; though unreal shapes be pictured there,
And it would mimic all we would believe –'

At this moment there is a rolling peal of thunder as though it were in the nature of applause.

CUT TO

BYRON . . . MED. CLOSE UP
BYRON: You hear –]

CUT TO

MARY, SHELLEY AND BYRON . . . MED. THREE-SHOT

Even Shelley is brought out of his concentration to smile at his friend's fancy.
BYRON: Come, Mary – come and watch the storm.

He holds out his hand to her.

CUT TO

MARY . . . CLOSE UP
MARY: *(always demure, gently poised and mild)*
You know how lightning alarms me.

She chooses another skein of silks ready to thread her needle. There is a flash of lightning and crash of thunder.

I am trying not to hear the horrid thunder – or to see the lightnings. Shelley, darling, will you please turn up the lamps a little more?

BYRON . . . CLOSE UP

He has been regarding her during this.
BYRON: Astonishing creature . . .

CUT TO

MARY . . . CLOSE UP
MARY: I, Lord Byron?

CUT TO

MARY, SHELLEY AND BYRON . . . MED. SHOT
BYRON: Frightened of thunder – fearful of the dark – and yet you have written a tale that sent my blood into icy creeps.

CUT TO

MARY . . . CLOSE UP

She chuckles a little smile, but is centred upon threading her needle.

CUT TO

MARY, SHELLEY AND BYRON . . . MED. SHOT
BYRON: Look at her, Shelley, can you believe that bland and lovely brow conceived

a Frankenstein – a monster created from cadavers out of rifled graves. – Isn't it astonishing?

CUT TO

MARY AND BYRON . . . MED. TWO-SHOT
   [MARY: I don't know why you should think so – what could you expect? We are all three infidels, scoffers at all marriage ties, believing only in living fully and freely in whatever direction the heart dictates. Such an audience needs something stronger than a pretty little love story. You say look at me; I say look at Shelley – who would suspect that pink and white innocence, gentle as a dove, was thrown out of Oxford University as a menace to morality, had run away from his lawful spouse with innocent me but seventeen, that he was deprived of his rights as a father by the Lord Chancellor of England, and reviled by society as a monster himself. I am already ostracized as a free-thinker, so why shouldn't I write of monsters?]
   BYRON: No wonder Murray has refused to publish the book – says their reading public would be *too* shocked.

CUT TO

MARY . . . CLOSE UP
   MARY: *(in her mild, calm voice)*
   It will be published, I think.

CUT TO

SHELLEY . . . CLOSE UP
   [SHELLEY: Then, darling, you will have much to answer for. People, yet unborn, will lie awake of nights, unable to close their eyes because of the dreadful visions your story conjures up.

CUT TO

BYRON . . . CLOSE UP
   BYRON: It shall be published, if only to give the world a good shock! We're all for shocking 'em – eh, Shelley? 'The world is a bundle of hay; Mankind are the asses that pull.']

MARY . . . CLOSE UP
   MARY: The publishers did not see that my purpose was to write a moral lesson – the punishment that befell a mortal man who dared to emulate God.

CUT TO

MARY, SHELLEY AND BYRON . . . MED. CLOSE SHOT
   BYRON: Whatever your purpose may have been, my dear, I take great relish in savouring each separate horror – I roll them over on my tongue –
   MARY: Don't, Lord Byron; don't remind me of it tonight!
   BYRON: *(in no way interrupted)*
   What a setting in that churchyard to begin with . . .

As Byron speaks, we DISSOLVE INTO the shots from the old film – the voice coming over.
   (continuing)
   . . . the sobbing of women . . . the first clod of earth on the coffin . . . that was a pretty chill! . . . Frankenstein and the dwarf stealing the body out of its new-made grave . . . cutting the hanged man down from the gallows where he swung . . . creaking in the wind . . . the cunning of Frankenstein in his laboratory . . . taking dead men apart and building up another creature out of the charnel house, piece by piece until he had contrived a human monster . . . so

fearful, so horrible, that only a half-crazed brain could have devised – to be galvanized into life by the electrical storm . . . And then the devil's work . . . the murders . . . the old professor strangled . . . the little child drowned . . .

DISSOLVE BACK TO

BYRON: *(continuing)*
. . . and it was these fragile white fingers that penned the nightmare . . !

He takes her hand. – In doing this Mary has pricked herself with the needle.

CUT TO

MARY . . . CLOSE UP

MARY: *(cries out and winces)*
Oh, there! You've made me prick myself, Byron. Ugh – it's bleeding.

She turns her head squeamishly away from the sight of the drop of blood.

CUT TO

MARY AND SHELLEY . . . MED. TWO-SHOT

Shelley springs across to her – letting his papers fly – and staunches the tiny wound gallantly with his handkerchief.
SHELLEY: I do think it a shame, Mary, to end your story quite so suddenly – to kill off poor Frankenstein and burn up the Monster in that terrible fire at the mill.

Her wound staunched now, Mary picks up her needle again and goes on with her meticulously dainty handiwork.
MARY: *(dreamily)*
Fire is the most beautiful thing in the world! But, who said the monster was burned to death in it?

CUT TO

BYRON . . . CLOSE UP

BYRON: *(with intense interest)*
Wasn't it?

CUT TO

MARY . . . CLOSE UP

MARY: *(continuing in her bland manner)*
Oh, no, that wasn't the end at all. [I've taken the rest of the story far into the future – and made use of developments which science will some day know – a hundred years to come. I think you will find the new horrors are far more entertaining, Lord Byron.] Would you like to hear what happened after that?

CUT TO

MARY, SHELLEY AND BYRON . . . MED. CLOSE THREE-SHOT

As the thunder rolls, the lightning flashes, Byron draws closer – Shelley drops at her feet.
MARY: I feel like telling it – it's a perfect night for mystery and horror – the very air itself is filled with monsters –
BYRON: I am all ears! While Heaven blasts the night without – open up your pits of hell –
MARY: Well, then –

She launches into her recital without that offensively smug satisfaction of the born story-teller who has a waiting audience.

CUT TO

MARY . . . BIG CLOSE–UP

She lays down her work gently, and spreads out her beautiful hands before her descriptively.
>   MARY: Imagine yourselves standing near the wreckage of the mill . . . The fire has died down, and only the bare skeleton of the building is visible – the gaunt rafters against the sky . . .

The tale Mary tells is as follows:

After Henry has been carried off half dead to the castle, the villagers prematurely rejoice at the burning mill. One oldish man celebrates the apparent death of the monster by stamping too firmly in the ashes, and falls through the charred floorboards into a series of water cellars which rather surprisingly exist under the hilltop structure. It is with rather less surprise, but some shock, that the audience now learns of the monster's survival. Only slightly singed around the hairline, he too has fallen through to the stagnant waters, and, emerging suddenly from a side channel, makes short work of the victim who has practically dropped into his lap. Climbing a convenient ladder towards the night air, the monster is hauled the last few feet by the dead man's short-sighted wife (now widow), whom he tosses

THE BRIDE OF FRANKENSTEIN (1935). After its elegant introduction, the story proper begins with a shock, as a peasant falls through the smoking ruins of the windmill into an underground cavern, where he is promptly set upon by the undead monster.

rather casually, with a dismissive growl, into the pit after her husband. Minnie the castle maid (Una O'Connor, whom Whale retained from *The Invisible Man* because he so enjoyed her screaming act) is the sole witness to these proceedings, and after her own near-fatal brush with the monster runs hysterically home to announce to the half-conscious Henry that his work is unfinished. (The happy ending tacked on to the release print of the first film is here quite invalidated; the elder Frankenstein has already died offscreen from shock at the news of Henry's injuries. The audience is supposed to have a short memory.)

A marriage, of course, is still in view, after a decent period of mourning. Whale in fact delighted in the ambiguity of his title: was *The Bride of Frankenstein* Henry's own bride, or the one he was to create for the monster? (The latter is far more interesting than the former, given Valerie Hobson's incredibly stilted perform-ance.)* But while Henry is still convalescing, the night air is disturbed by a Macbeth-like clanging at the castle door. 'Let me in,' a strange figure tells Minnie, 'I must see the young baron tonight on a secret matter of grave importance.' The ensuing scene is given here:

Pretorius comes in. It is simple to write the words, 'he comes in' – but this man's entrance into the room is something to make a witch's skin creep.

CUT TO

MED. CLOSE THREE-SHOT . . . DR PRETORIUS, FRANKENSTEIN AND ELIZABETH
PRETORIUS: *Baron* Frankenstein, now, I believe?
HENRY: Won't you come in, sir?
PRETORIUS: Good evening, Herr Baron. I trust you will pardon my intrusion at so late an hour. I should not have ventured to come had I not a communication to make, which, I suspect, may be of the utmost importance to yourself.
HENRY: I remember you, of course, Herr Professor, and your lectures – vividly –

Elizabeth likes none of this – she is watching with a most inimical eye.
HENRY: *(introducing him)*
This is Professor Septimus Pretorius, who used to be doctor of philosophy at the University – but –
PRETORIUS: *(helping Henry out)*
but – who was booted – no less – out of the University, booted, my dear Baron, is the word, for knowing too much.

He gives a dry, mirthless laugh. He is approaching Henry as he speaks. Elizabeth instinctively draws away with a repugnance she is unconscious of.
ELIZABETH: He has been very ill – he should not be disturbed –
PRETORIUS: I am also a doctor, Baroness, – or – is it Baroness yet . . ?

Elizabeth ignores this, turns from him.
HENRY: *(his eyes fixed with an apprehensive and inimical look on Dr Pretorius)*
Why have you come here tonight?
PRETORIUS: *(glancing toward Elizabeth)*
My business with you, Baron, is private . . .

---

* To be charitable, her acting style may have been dictated by Whale in an obscure attempt at humour.

A look, an indication from Henry for Elizabeth to leave them. She obeys reluctantly, but does go. CAMERA MOVES UP TO TWO SHOT.

HENRY: *(waiting until the door is closed – then he leans eagerly forward)*
You know something about the . . .
(he stops without saying 'the Monster')

PRETORIUS: About your creature, – yes, Henry. I know everything. And I know more even than you, I think . . .

HENRY: What? What are you driving at?

PRETORIUS: The interesting result of your experiments, Herr Baron, is, so I understand, believed to have been destroyed in a fire which consumed the old mill.

HENRY: *(quickly, suspiciously)*
Yes . . .
(then with alarm)
So I believe, and so I trust.

PRETORIUS: Yes – that is the popular belief.

HENRY: *(sharply)*
Have you any reason to think otherwise? What do you know?

PRETORIUS: I hesitate to say I know anything in this specific instance, only as I am an investigator myself in these esoteric matters, I might merely offer a general suggestion, Herr Baron. It is possible that you have ventured farther than you think. Those who experiment in the creation of living organisms have been accused of impiety, even of blasphemy. . . Of course, as you and I, and as all men of learning know, such accusations are only made by the narrow, the bigoted and superstitious – but the creation of these forms of life involves something more than a temporary disturbance of the regular courses of nature. In fact, I have reason to believe that under some circumstances – one may create something which is, shall I say, immortal? Something which is practically indestructible.

HENRY: *(almost a smothered cry; his face aghast)*
What do you really know? Do you mean that the creature I made may still be living?

PRETORIUS: Oh, I have no positive legal evidence, but my own experiments have led me to believe that it would be best to be careful – always to be careful. That is really all I can say at the moment – here.

HENRY: It can't be! He was burned!

PRETORIUS: *(suddenly more forceful)*
The clumsiness of your effort is your worst crime . . . You were my pupil – you shared all my experiments – my *secret* experiments – then you, like a fool, went to work by yourself, crudely, unskilled, and fumbled my great discovery –

HENRY: The experiments were mine as well as yours!

PRETORIUS: Then you let the thing escape – you let the stupid world know. Your crime is against science.

HENRY: *(half to himself)*
My crime is against God.

PRETORIUS: Fiddlesticks. It was I who have had to suffer for this bungling. It was because of you that I have been kicked out of the University.
(Henry looks at him queerly.)
All *your* crime has been traced back to me . . . and as a result I am here knocking at your door – an outcast, my ambition ruined.

HENRY: What do you want?

PRETORIUS: We must work together.

HENRY: Never – I am through! I want no more of this hell's spawn. As soon as I am able I am to be married – and get away, –

PRETORIUS: I beg you to reconsider. You know, do you not, that it is you, really, who are responsible for all those murders . . ?

Henry turns a look of alarm on him.

PRETORIUS: *(continuing)*
There are penalties to pay for killing people . . . and with your creature still loose in the countryside . . .

HENRY: Are you threatening me?

PRETORIUS: Don't put it so crudely. I had ventured to hope that you and I together – no longer as master and student, but as fellow scientists . . . or if you prefer . . . you as master and I as your faithful assistant – I regret that my necessity forces me to say your *paid* assistant – I had hoped that we might together probe into the mysteries of life and death . . .

Henry recognizes the veiled threat back of all this.

HENRY: No more – no farther!

PRETORIUS: *(going inexorably on – paying no attention to this now)*
. . . and reach, between us, a goal not yet dreamed by science.

HENRY: I cannot take part in any further experiments – I have had a terrible lesson.

PRETORIUS: That is sad – very sad, but you and I have already gone too far to stop, and it cannot *be* stopped so easily. I also have continued with my experiments – and this is why I came tonight. You must see *my* creation.

HENRY: *(breathlessly)*
Have you succeeded in bringing the dead to life?

PRETORIUS: If you, Herr Baron, will be so good as to visit my humble abode, I think you will be interested in what I can show you. After twenty years of secret scientific research, and countless failures, I also have created LIFE, as they say, in God's own image.

HENRY: I must know – when can I see it?

PRETORIUS: I thought you might change your mind – Why not tonight? It is not very late.

HENRY: Is it far?

PRETORIUS: Not very, but you will need a coat.

What Pretorius has to show, when he ushers Frankenstein into his bachelor quarters, is essentially an irrelevant joke, but an amusing one. The baron has fashioned his creature from selected corpses, but Pretorius has grown his, 'from seed':

While you were digging into your graves, piecing together dead tissues, I, my dear pupil, went for my beginnings to the source of life. I grew my creatures, as Nature does . . . like cultures. I followed the process of Life, not the processes of Death.

Pretorius does not explain – perhaps cannot – how his so-logical experiments came to be tainted with an element of bonzai miniaturism, but the fact is that while full of life, and perfect in every detail, the results are no more than six inches high. He keeps them, impeccably costumed, in chemical jars: a queen, a very amorous king, a disapproving bishop, a devil (suspiciously resembling Pretorius himself), a ballerina, and a baby who according to the script was supposed to look like Boris Karloff, but in the film has been replaced by a mermaid. Pretorius has dreams of an astounding collaboration: a man–made race upon the face of the earth.

– Our mad dream is only half realised. You, alone, have created a man. Now, together, we will create his mate.
– You mean . . . ?
– Yes. A woman. That should be lots of fun.

The necessary time lapse for the new experiments to get under way is covered by the famous sequence in which the monster meets up in the forest with a blind and saintly hermit who gladly takes him in as a non-paying guest and teaches him to talk.★ Their idyll is broken when huntsmen pass by and recognize the monster for what he is. After various excitements, which leave the poor hermit's hut ablaze, the monster is trussed up (with a deliberate resemblance to Christ on the cross) and carried off to jail, where he is not only locked in a subterranean cell but stapled to the wall in an apparatus apparently kept handy for giant prisoners. After this the pompous Burgomaster washes his hands of the whole affair:

> Well, now *that's* done, I can get back to more important duties. Monster indeed – tush, tush! Just an escaped lunatic. Merely wanted somebody to handle it, that's all. Quite harmless.

Needless to say, he turns at this point to see the monster emerging from the jail, having broken all his imposing bonds . . . and the Burgomaster is among the people who scuttle in all directions. We see the monster, unaffected by rifle fire, shake and trample one man; then there is a short scene in which the body of a young girl is discovered outside a church; and at this point comes the giant cut which reduced the film from a reputed 85–90 minutes on its first public showings to the 75 we have now. The original script continues as follows:

[MED. SHOT . . . A SPOT IN THE WOODS

A hunting dog is howling with uncanny barks, over the body of a man . . . CAMERA MOVES UP and we see that it is the brother of the girl who fired at the monster, his fishing rod lying beside him.

DISSOLVE TO

LONG SHOT . . . HOUSE IN VILLAGE STREET

A group of the neighbours discussing the terror. A scream is heard coming from a house . . . all dash in . . . CAMERA FOLLOWS THROUGH DOOR. Inside they gather around a couch on which lies the slaughtered body. An axe lies near.
    A NEIGHBOUR: Poor old Neuman.

They are wringing their hands – looking from the axe to the body.
    ANOTHER NEIGHBOUR: Where is his wife, Frau Neuman?

One woman leaves the group.

CUT TO

LONG SHOT . . . HALL & STAIRWAY

The woman goes running up the stairs.
    WOMAN: *(calling)*
        Frau Neuman! Frau Neuman!

★ Boris Karloff thought the latter idea quite ludicrous: to him even the few words allowed ('Friend. Fire. Good . . .') diminished the monster's sinister presence. But in retrospect the sequence works perfectly, coming across as surprising, delightful and even moving.

THE BRIDE OF FRANKENSTEIN (1935). Examples of superior set design. The monster is trussed up, Christ-like, on a convenient tree trunk, and is about to fall forward into the hay cart. Later he escapes and runs amok through a Gothick graveyard.

LONG SHOT . . . GROUP BELOW

Who come out into hall, faces looking up . . .

CUT TO:

MED. CLOSE . . . WOMAN UPSTAIRS

Turns back from having looked into upstairs room . . . her face ashen.
 WOMAN: There's another one . . . in there . . . Frau Neuman.
 (she sobs)

DISSOLVE TO

MED. LONG SHOT . . . A MORTUARY

In an old stone building. A room is filled with frightened villagers . . . hats off.
Standing alongside a slab on which lies a corpse, and beside which stands the coroner.
The corpse is hidden by a sheet, but the hair, hanging to the floor, is that of a woman.
 CORONER: *(repeating in solemn official tones the legal form)*
  . . . wilful murder.

FADE OUT

FADE IN

LONG SHOT . . . BURGOMASTER'S OFFICE (MORNING)

The pompous officious Burgomaster sits at his chair of office. Beside are two village
police, standing very straight and self-important. The room . . . at a respectful
distance . . . is partly filled with villagers, all white and panicky-eyed with terror.

The Burgomaster has a written list before him and to which he refers . . . a list of the
slaughterings.

CUT TO

MED. SHOT . . . BURGOMASTER
 BURGOMASTER: Now then – I mean to get to the bottom of this monster business. I
  only want eye-witnesses and what they saw – No nonsense about what they
  think.
 (reading)
  Henry Kronstadt.

CUT TO

MED. SHOT

Henry, a big peasant youth steps forward.
 BURGOMASTER: Did you see your sister murdered?
 KRONSTADT: No sir, but I saw her afterward, and no human man could have done
  it.
 BURGOMASTER: There you are – you know nothing. – Next, please.
 (reading)
  A young huntsman found strangled.

Second huntsman steps forward.

CUT TO

CLOSE UP . . . BURGOMASTER
 BURGOMASTER: Any relation to the body?

CUT TO

MED. SHOT . . . HUNTSMAN
 HUNTSMAN: Brother.

CUT TO

MED. SHOT . . . BURGOMASTER
BURGOMASTER: Did you see him killed?

CUT TO

MED. TWO SHOT . . . BURGOMASTER AND HUNTSMAN
    HUNTSMAN: I hadn't left him more than a minute and when I came back the dog
        was barking and –
    BURGOMASTER: You did NOT see the deed done?
    HUNTSMAN: No, sir.

No one is crowding forward. They are all shrinking back.
    BURGOMASTER: That will do . . . that will do. Don't crowd forward. Now then –
    (reading)
    – the Neuman case – a double murder, wasn't it?

Minnie, Henry's housekeeper, steps forward. She has nosed in here, too.
    MINNIE: Yes, your Honour, the most horrible murders I ever did see – there was
        Mr Neuman all hacked to pieces with a big axe and his poor wife upstairs lying
        across the bed – a sight to scare the devil himself.
    BURGOMASTER: Tell me in detail exactly how the murders were committed.

CUT TO

CLOSE UP . . . MINNIE
    MINNIE: Oh! I didn't *SEE* it but it must have been horrible!

CUT TO

MED. SHOT . . . BURGOMASTER
    BURGOMASTER: *(jumping up, furious)*
        There you are! Nobody's seen anything. It's all nonsense and poppycock –
        probably some wild beast from the mountains and here you all are talking about
        Monsters and Devils like a pack of superstitious infidels! Clear the court – I
        won't hear another word!
    (shouting)
        Clear the court, I say! Go home and get to work, all of you! And let me hear no
        more of this Monster business!

CUT TO

MED. SHOT . . . BURGOMASTER'S OFFICE

There is a stampede for the door as they all start to tumble out, leaving the
Burgomaster muttering impotently, as he straightens up his official papers, cleans
pens, etc.
    BURGOMASTER: *(muttering)*
        Fools – stupid, ignorant fools – Monster, indeed. They can't make a fool of me!

CUT TO

LONG SHOT . . . BURGOMASTER'S OFFICE

The Monster's great shoulders appear in the window directly behind the Burgomaster.

CUT TO

CLOSE UP . . . BURGOMASTER

The Monster's hand reaches slowly in and throttles the words as the Burgomaster is
muttering them.

CUT BACK TO

MED. SHOT . . . BURGOMASTER

The Monster drags the Burgomaster out through the window. This all happens swiftly.

CUT TO

MED. SHOT . . . AT DOOR

At first, those at the door – as they look back – are too startled to exclaim – then there is a wild screaming of horror – a stampede.

CUT TO

MED. SHOT . . . BURGOMASTER

The screams come over while the CAMERA is on the Monster's actions.
   SOUND: Screams

CUT TO

MED. SHOT . . . OUTSIDE WINDOW

The Monster holds the struggling Burgomaster by his fist and cuffs him soundly, first from one side, then the other – and drops him, then turns away.

CUT TO

LONG SHOT . . . EXT. STREET

Of stampeding men and women. Amongst them are Glutz family.

CUT TO

MED. SHOT . . . GLUTZ FAMILY

Uncle and Auntie Glutz, fleeing with their nephew. The nephew is a bit of a village idiot. He follows, but is half-way interested to watch what has happened to the Burgomaster – he is looking back to see.
   UNCLE GLUTZ: Come, Karl – come, you fool!

Nephew keeps turning to look back – the incident has great attraction for him.

CUT TO

LONG SHOT OF THE VILLAGE STREET

Again – everyone running about like a chicken with its head cut off. The fire bells are clanging – whistles are tooting – there are shouts on all sides.
   SOUND: Fire bells, whistles, screams.

CUT TO

MED. SHOT . . . GLUTZ HOMESTEAD

Uncle and Aunt enter, both still panting from the run and fear.
   AUNT: Where is that good-for-nothing, Karl?
   UNCLE: Let him get murdered – a good riddance.

He stamps into bedroom.

CUT TO

MED. SHOT BEDROOM

Uncle Glutz goes over to bed, pulls back the mattress.

CUT TO

INSERT OF

Money bag in mattress.

CUT BACK TO

MED. SHOT . . . BEDROOM

Uncle takes out money bag from mattress and adds a packet of money to the secret hoard from his pocket. The money bag is seen bulging with money.

CUT TO

MED. SHOT . . . WINDOW

The nephew is watching.

CUT TO

CLOSE UP . . . NEPHEW

A sly look is darkening his face.

CUT TO

MED. SHOT . . . BEDROOM

The nephew steps – without making any noise – over the window sill and in one step he is behind his uncle. With a quick movement he throttles the old miser, lowers him to the floor, helps himself to what he wants of the money – listens to see that he is not detected – slips the bag back into the hiding place and is out of the window again. He has been an adept pupil of the Monster's.

CUT TO

MED. SHOT . . . OUTSIDE GLUTZ COTTAGE

CAMERA PANS with the nephew as he comes around and goes to the front door. He turns the knob, finds it locked and knocks.
>   AUNT: *(from inside)*
>   Who's there?
>   NEPHEW: It's only me, Auntie.

CUT TO

MED. SHOT . . . AUNT AT DOOR

She opens the door a little.

CUT TO

CLOSE UP . . . NEPHEW
>   NEPHEW: Where's Uncle?

CUT TO

MED. SHOT . . . INT. COTTAGE

The nephew pushes his way in. Keeping her eyes on him Auntie backs toward the bedroom
>   AUNTIE: Not one penny do you get.
>   *(to husband)*
>   Joseph, that good-for-nothing nephew is here again. Don't you give him any more money.

She turns to warn her husband. There is a pause – a shriek – her cries come over.
>   The Monster! The Monster has been here!

CUT TO

CLOSE UP . . . NEPHEW
   NEPHEW: *(before he starts to follow her)*
     Very convenient to have a Monster around.
   (he looks around the room)
     This is quite a nice cottage – I shouldn't be surprised if he visited *Auntie* TOO.
               FADE OUT]

Several reasons probably contributed towards the excision of this curious sequence from the release prints:

   (a) it shows the monster as destructive and malevolent, whereas Whale's general intention is to make him sympathetic;

   (b) it polishes off the Burgomaster, who is an amiably comic figure;

   (c) it keeps us for too long from any sight of the major characters of the story, and indeed introduces an entirely new, if brief, sub-plot.

One might also add that it does not seem particularly entertaining in its own right. For whatever reason, it disappeared from view, and was replaced by a short sequence of a group of gypsies having supper by the night fire. The oldest crone has barely time to say 'Pass the pepper and salt' (a splendid moment, comparable with Ernest Thesiger's 'Have a potato' in *The Old Dark House*) before the monster emerges from the bushes and destroys the whole encampment.

On the run again, the monster lopes through the churchyard and comes up against a huge El Greco-like figure of Christ. Seeing it as yet another pursuing figure, he overturns it, revealing a cavity which strikes him as a good hiding place. The dark hole leads him into a recess of the extremely cobwebby vault in which Pretorius is paying off the grave robbers who have helped him find a firm, fresh female corpse for his and Frankenstein's joint purposes. The ghouls leave, but not before one has inserted an outright comic tone by glancing back and muttering: 'If there's much more like this, pal, what do you say, we let them hang us?' Prissy Dr Pretorius has decided to stay for supper ('I rather like this place'), and sets out the elements of his meal on a handy slab below a pile of bones surmounted by a candle on a grinning skull. After a dissolve we find his meal completed; the doctor is even singing softly to himself as he enjoys a good cigar. So far he has not been aware of the monster's lurking presence, but now the music wells up as the giant figure emerges from the shadows and silently lopes towards him. A shot of Pretorius over the monster's shoulder seems to signal the end for him: the audience prepares itself to bid a reluctant farewell to its rather endearing mad doctor. Then the latter suddenly turns, sees the monster for the first time, and is not one whit discomposed. 'Oh,' he says casually. 'I thought I was alone.' (In the film he adds: 'Would you like a cigar? They're my only weakness.' This is almost certainly an interpolation by the actor himself, paralleling a similar remark about gin in *The Old Dark House*.)

A little later, man and monster are the best of friends, drinking and smoking like club cronies: the monster's growls of menace have become sighs of content- ment. As the script tells us, 'the glow from a pleased palate spreads over the monster's face': it must be the chicken carcass he has crunched. Thoughtfully looking at the display of human debris amid which they sit, he asks:

MONSTER: You make man, like me?
PRETORIUS: No. A woman. Friend for you.
MONSTER: Woman, for me. Yes, I want friend like me.
PRETORIUS: I think you can be very useful. And you will add a little force to the argument if necessary. Do you know who Henry Frankenstein is – and who you are?
MONSTER: Yes. I know. He made me from dead. I love dead. Hate living.
PRETORIUS: You are wise in your generation. We must have a long talk, and then I have an important call to make.
MONSTER: Woman. Friend. Wife . . .

And so Henry is blackmailed, by Pretorius's command of the monster, into continuing his experiments, and when Henry demurs further, his bride is kidnapped and threatened with death. It all comes to a climax in the renovated mill, as sparks again fly by night during a thunderstorm and a shrouded, inert figure is hoisted through the roof to receive the kiss of life from an electric sky, while the monster stalks around below like an expectant father, a nuisance to the extent that he has to be drugged into a temporary sleep. This creation sequence is a perfect masterpiece of direction, photography and editing, and could be used even now as a show piece for students who want to learn something about the film as a narrative art:

THE SKY

The figure on the table ablaze with electric sparks, seen against the background of the storm – a brilliant final flash of lightning and roar of thunder – enough to wake the dead, which it does.

CUT TO

INT. LABORATORY – CLOSE SHOT – HENRY

He works reverse levers.

CUT TO

INT. LABORATORY – LONG SHOT

The table is seen descending.

CUT TO

INT. LABORATORY – MED. CLOSE – HENRY

He is bending over the table, intently watching it for signs of life. The figure on the table is well lit, but the rest of the laboratory is either dark or filled with strange shadows.

CUT TO

THE HAND – CLOSE UP

It moves.

CUT TO

THE HEAD — CLOSE UP

A low moan comes from the bandages.

CUT TO

INT. LABORATORY — MED. CLOSE UP — HENRY

He feverishly begins to unwind the bandages from the eyes.

CUT TO

THE EYES — CLOSE UP

They flutter and gradually open. Vacant at first, they gradually focus in an intense stare. They seem to contain depths of unfathomable mystery.

CUT TO

HENRY — CLOSE UP

Henry gazing back into their strange unholy depths. He gives a cry of triumph.
    HENRY: She lives –! She is alive!

CAMERA PULLS BACK
Now both men, with flying fingers, unloose the straps, peel back the face coverings. They bend over the figure, between it and the CAMERA, as we

DISSOLVE TO

A RATHER LONG SHOT

Henry and Pretorius are still screening, by their positions, what they are actually doing. They step to each side of the now almost upright table, which has been tilted. The figure on it is stiffly lying back, but practically standing, against the table – giving something of the effect of an Egyptian mummy.

The CAMERA MOVES CLOSER and we see the figure dressed in a long garment, the wrappings removed except from her fingers, which are still wrapped and pointed. Her hair – though curled close to the head – hangs straight and dark at either side. With their hands ready at her elbows the two men see her make a first tentative, stiff-jointed movement toward walking. They step a little away, backing toward CAMERA. She advances – her movements strange and jerky, walking like a doll . . . but walking. Her eyes are fixed on Henry's face – she smiles – totters on towards Henry.

CUT TO

MONSTER . . . MED. LONG SHOT

He has risen from his doped sleep and is standing now – tense and still, his eyes fixed on what is taking place across the room.

CUT BACK TO

THE GROUP OF THREE . . . MED. SHOT

The two scientists, in their excitement, forgetting even – for the moment – that the Monster is there waiting.

She is moving onwards toward Henry – with Pretorius also breathlessly watching. She all but falls forward, but reaches Henry and clings to him – smiling and pleased as a child learning to walk. Henry balances her.

NOTE: The whole of the creation sequence has had the accompanying music of a weird symphonic storm which mounts in triumph at the final Fade Out.

CUT TO

MONSTER . . . MED. SHOT

He starts to move forward, his eyes fixed on their objective.

CUT TO

THE GROUP OF THREE . . . MED. SHOT

Henry releases her hands from clinging to him – and starts her off again. She makes small sounds of pleasure – and starts again to walk. But now she senses the alien, menacing presence of something else in the room. She is death still for a moment, then turns her head to look. Her eyes focus on . . .

CUT TO

MONSTER . . . MED. CLOSE SHOT

Steadily approaching.

CUT TO

THE FIGURE . . . CLOSE UP

She holds her look fixed upon the Monster – only a steady stare thus far.

CUT TO

MONSTER . . . MED. CLOSE

He takes it that she is accepting him – he advances more quickly with a stupefied sound of pleasure and excitement. Here at last is his friend . . . his mate.

CUT TO

THE FIGURE, HENRY & PRETORIUS . . . MED.

She is still not moving. Henry and Pretorius look at the Monster as he comes more swiftly forward. They – in their awe and excitement of this great moment – unconsciously step a little away – a little backward . . . as though to give the two principals a free hand to act out this drama. Now she is alarmed – a look of repulsion comes over her features – she utters a horrible cry of fright – a sound as strange as was the utterance of pleasure, but its extreme opposite. Her eyes still fixed on the Monster, she moves toward Henry.

CUT TO

MONSTER . . . MED. CLOSE

Coming on faster.

CUT TO

THE FIGURE . . . MED. CLOSE

Now she flies to Henry – as fast, that is, as her unruly joints can carry her. Monster enters the shot now and reaches out to grab her.
    PRETORIUS: Get back – get back!

The Monster now realizes that his mate is revolting from him. He stands still – his eyes dull with pain.

Pretorius and Henry step toward her and almost drag her – the feet trailing – away from the Monster around to the side of the table.

CUT TO

EXT. DOOR TO THE LABORATORY . . . LONG SHOT

Rudy, with Elizabeth in tow, comes up to the door. He releases her from a cloak which has been wrapped about her head – inserts a big key into lock and swings the door open for her. She rushes in frantically with eager steps.

CUT TO

ELIZABETH . . . CLOSE SHOT . . . INT. HALLWAY

Hurrying up the steps.

CUT TO

INT. LABORATORY . . . LONG SHOT

A shot taking in the whole situation, with Monster starting to lunge forward.

CUT TO

MONSTER . . . CLOSE SHOT

In his movement to rush around end of table he is almost in contact with the lever which controls the whole works. Pretorius rushes toward him, his hand gesturing.
    PRETORIUS: The lever – look out! The lever! There's enough voltage in that machine to blow us all and the mountain itself to atoms.

This halts the Monster. Pretorius's warning registers – the Monster's eyes go to the lever against which Pretorius is warning him.

THE CAMERA SWINGS AROUND for a moment to Henry and the figure. She is clinging to Henry, looking up to him, looking fearfully over her shoulder toward the Monster.

CUT TO

OUTSIDE THE LABORATORY DOOR . . . MED. CLOSE

Elizabeth, weak and panting, pounds on the door.

CUT TO

INT. LABORATORY . . . MED. SHOT

Henry looks with amazed start around towards the door.

CUT TO

MONSTER . . . MED. CLOSE
    MONSTER: She is like the rest . . .

With cold deliberation he moves the one step that brings him to the lever.

CUT TO

CLOSE UP . . . ELIZABETH
    ELIZABETH: *(knocking at door)*
      Henry! . . .

CUT TO

HENRY . . . CLOSE SHOT

He releases the figure's hold upon him – about to rush to the door when – a shout from Pretorius comes over.
    PRETORIUS: *(off)*
      Look out!

Henry turns to see what the warning shout means – a look of blind terror on his face – gives a desperate shout to Elizabeth whose pounding on the door comes over.
    HENRY: Go back . . . Go back!

CUT TO

MONSTER . . . MED. CLOSE UP

His hand is on the lever – in his eyes the gleam of a wild vengeance. He utters an ugly cry – and with one great gesture swings the deadly lever –

Then there are cries and shouts – a blinding flash – a blast like thunder – smoke, sparks – hell let loose.

DISSOLVE TO

EXT. RIDGE OF THE HILL AGAINST THE STORMY SKY

With the lightning and thunder of the heavens for accompaniment – the structure that was the laboratory collapses into a burning heap – the cloud of smoke and dust disperses a little and settles down over the scene – the thunders of a jealous and triumphant Jehovah roll – for positively the FINAL

FADE OUT

THE END*

By the end of the thirties Frankenstein was a household word throughout the world, though many adults confused the creator with the monster and had to be corrected by show-off children who had not been allowed to see the films but were diligently ploughing their way through the book, on loan from the local branch library, or from the more tantalizing abridgements in the fan magazines. The monster, for no good scientific reason, was by now assumed to be virtually indestructible, and could therefore be revived whenever Universal thought it commercially expedient to do so. After the enormous, and totally unexpected, success of the *Frankenstein/Dracula* reissue double bill in 1937, there was no doubt that the time was again drawing near, and Universal was sufficiently heartened to commission a major Frankenstein production in colour. Why the colour process was eventually abandoned is not clear: some sources say that scenes were shot and that the monster looked ridiculous with whatever colour and complexion they gave him. But *Son of Frankenstein* remains, at 97 minutes, the *longest* Frankenstein film ever, and is still a very striking show despite the absence as director of James Whale, who by then had blotted his copybook with Universal and was treading the slippery slope. Rowland V. Lee was the substitute, a maker of stolid films with good pictorial values but no dramatic pace and no particular talent with performers. In this case he certainly allowed Basil Rathbone and Boris Karloff to get out of hand, as he did with their follow-up film *Tower of London*, a kind of horror

---

* This can never have been a satisfactory scene in the form given here, which is a revision of the original intention. Henry was supposed to discover – too late – that the fresh female heart he had demanded for his new monster was supplied by Pretorius by the simple expedient of having his henchmen murder Elizabeth and bring hers, thus making the creation on the bench truly 'the bride of Frankenstein'. This was thought to be altogether too ghoulish, and so it probably was, but there seems little dramatic point in this version's alternative, which is to bring her to the laboratory floor only to die in the explosion. The final rewrite had her briefly inside, but this version had already been shot, and quick eyes will still spot her with Henry against a back wall in the shot of the explosion, even though in the version released the happy pair are allowed to survive, escaping at the monster's whim to a nearby hill as he keeps Pretorius and his hissing mate at bay while his hand rests on the mysterious lever which Pretorius has conveniently told him will blow the mill to atoms. 'You go,' he says. 'You live. We belong dead.' The last sequence of close-ups, which follows, is cinematically quite breathtaking.

An informal note: this really is Boris Karloff taking tea on the set of *Son of Frankenstein* (1939).
His hair, it will be noted, has grown back, but by his own request he can no longer speak. He
will look much more frightening in the picture.

version of the crimes of Richard III, with emphasis on a club-footed executioner;
on the other hand he drew from Bela Lugosi the most relaxed performance that
actor ever gave, and one of which few suspected he was capable.

John Balderston also, apparently, being out of favour with Universal, the small
matter of a script was handed to one Willis Cooper, whose original submission
was directly linked to the end of *Bride of Frankenstein*, or rather to the original
script of same with its unhappy ending. Frankenstein's son Wolf (and one might
enquire when he found time to be born, since Baroness Frankenstein showed no
signs of being even mildly pregnant when the monster exploded the tower) was
on reaching man's estate to return to the tower and uncover the skeletons of his
father and mother as well as Dr Pretorius, but to discover the monster, amazingly,
to be full-fleshed and merely dormant. A flash of lightning would then not merely
reactivate the creature but improve its intellect; when Wolf proved reluctant to
make friends, the monster would threaten to remove the brain of Wolf's young
son and transplant it into the skull of a corpse which the monster was keeping by
him. Eventually the villagers would be aroused and the monster would tumble
into a conveniently bottomless pit.

It is possible that such a downbeat tale could have been enlivened by wit, but one doubts whether that commodity was available, since there is none in the Cooper script eventually used. *Son of Frankenstein* is never less than watchable, but it does proceed at a rather leaden pace, its plotline is meagre, and most of its humour is unconscious. Again the time scale merits attention. In *Bride*, purportedly set in the future by Mary Shelley when she wrote it in 1816, one of the coffins has the date 1899 and the telephone is a new invention, so we might assume 1900. Allowing the happy ending, which as we have seen was tacked on, we might assume Wolf to have been born around 1901, and as played by Basil Rathbone he is clearly not much less than 40 years old, so one can take the story to be contemporary with the 1939 film. Yet it is set in a Germany with no sign of unrest or war, and not a Nazi on the streets; indeed, the Burgomaster and his town council operate in a way, and against backgrounds, more suggestive of Grimm's fairy tales. Details of place are equally puzzling. The little town where the deceased Frankensteins lived is no longer called Ingolstadt; in spite of their notoriety, it bears their family name. It also has a railway station with a German version of that inevitable American altitude sign: 938m Hohenlade. The castle no longer has a drawbridge or a courtyard: it is cramped around a hilly bend not far above the town, and directly across the road from it is the ruined stone tower where Frankenstein's researches took place. That tower was once a remote place in the distant hills, but no matter; some fans, however, must have vividly recalled how it was exploded into smithereens at the end of *Bride*, yet here it is seen to have suffered no more damage than having its roof blown off. And when Wolf explores it he will find to his great surprise (and ours) that it contains not only the family crypt but (quite remarkable on the side of a mountain) an open sulphur pit which has been bubbling at 800° Fahrenheit since the time of the Romans.

When we first see the castle it appears derelict, and an old mad shepherd called Ygor, who was hanged once for sheep stealing but released when it didn't take, is hiding behind an upper window from a mocking crowd. (He's OK now except that his head is set to one side and his neck reverberates when he taps it.) EINGANG VERBOTEN, it says on the door. But a snip of the editor's scissors shows us a train bringing Wolf and his family (dull wife and infuriating American-accented small son) coming to take up residence. Through the window, the weather and scenery are predictably bleak, every tree gnarled and bare. In fact, after Wolf makes the mistake of drawing our attention to this fact, quick eyes will spot the same tree coming round three times. At the station, the mayor waits reluctantly to greet his visitors, and bemoans the lot of his town: 'forsaken, desolate, shunned by every traveller – and why? – because of these damned Frankensteins'. The little reception ceremony takes place in a blinding rainstorm, which seems to have been a favourite device of the director: in *Tower of London* he would stage the Battle of Bosworth in one (with the result that the cardboard armour all fell to pieces). Wolf quickly sees the kind of hostility he is in for, but he is proud of his father and attributes all the trouble to 'the unforeseen blunder of a stupid assistant'. It's always others who are wrong, it seems, 'Why, nine out of ten people,' he goes on in a sop to the popular fallacy, 'call that misshapen creature of my father's experiments – Frankenstein!'

When he gets to the castle, Wolf forgets the curtness of the mayor's salutation

('We've come to meet you, not to greet you') in his delight at the architecture of the old place, now quite miraculously restored, with wood floors gleaming in the firelight. 'It's medieval – it's exciting, exhilarating!' Rathbone cries in a performance which is already, before the monster even appears, several degrees over the top. 'Here in this very study, the luminous facets of his brilliant mind conceived his theory of the course of life!' But Mrs F. is a little bemused at the curious arrangement of the master bedroom, and not comforted by the remark of a servant:

> If the house is filled with dread,
> Place the beds at head to head.

Jack Otterson's interior design of the 'castle', with its crooked open stairways and medieval bosses meeting over the dining table, is already bidding fair to be the best thing in the picture, and this is hilariously accentuated when Police Inspector Krogh comes to call (Lionel Atwill in a much parodied performance which may have been the origin of Dr Strangelove). In order to announce his arrival he has to lift a brass doorknocker almost the size of himself. Krogh, who manipulates in stiff Teutonic fashion a rather squeaky false arm, is clearly alarmed by his host's enthusiasm, which is stimulated even by a flash of lightning. ('It's magnificent. Nothing in nature is terrifying when one understands it.') Krogh politely bides his

The set everyone remembers from *Son of Frankenstein* (1939); Basil Rathbone and Josephine Hutchinson sit down to a quiet and intimate breakfast. Emma Dunn is the housekeeper, Donnie Dunagan the awful child.

SON OF FRANKENSTEIN (1939). Inspector Krogh (Lionel Atwill) and the young baron (Basil Rathbone) contemplate the portrait of the latter's father. (Colin Clive is easily recognizable, wearing evening clothes in his laboratory.)

time, but when Wolf doubts the horrors perpetrated by his father's creation, and asks Krogh whether he ever even saw it, the policeman has his moment:

> The most vivid recollection of my life. I was but a child at the time, about the age of your own son, Herr Baron. The monster had escaped and was ravaging the countryside, killing, maiming, terrorizing. One night he burst into our house. My father took a gun and fired at him. The savage brute sent him crashing into a corner. Then the brute grabbed me by the arm. One doesn't easily forget, Herr Baron, an arm torn out by the roots . . .

Next day Wolf, when exploring the old lab, has his first encounter with Ygor, the film's true villain and a heel without a soul. Seeking his own revenge against the jury which condemned him to death, Ygor has cared for the sick monster, which amazingly survived the impact of tons of masonry at the end of the previous episode, and was robbed only of its power of speech.★ But the monster has recently been struck by lightning which on this occasion has reversed its usual stimulating effect and rendered him dormant for several months, lying in the crypt next to the tomb of 'Heinrich Von Frankenstein' (though Colin Clive was never so designated in the previous stories). 'He . . . er . . . does things for me,' mutters Ygor ambiguously. 'Make him well, Frankenstein!' In two shakes Wolf has the creature hoisted up to the main floor and, with the front door firmly locked, is enthusiastically furthering his father's researches. 'I've learned from studying his electrical hookups that he attracted cosmic rays. It's unearthly!'

The monster really doesn't have much to do in this picture, even when vertical. Wolf imports some stylish machinery (first exposure for those pivoting operating tables which later became so familiar) and soon has his father's creation ambulatory again; but he fails to keep it under lock and key, so that through secret passageways it stumbles unnoticed into the house and makes friends with his awful child. This softer side to its nature does not prevent it from threatening to kill the child in revenge when Wolf shoots the treacherous Ygor, but the stunt men take over for the spectacular climax in the laboratory. The monster snaps off Krogh's false arm and is about to toss the child into the sulphur pit when Wolf swings Tarzan-like on a chain and knocks the monster in instead. It doesn't seem a lot of plot for 97 minutes, but then at least half of it was atmosphere-building.

It was Karloff's last cinematic outing as the monster:★★ he thought that in his fifties he was past it, and besides he despaired of finding the script that would provide him with the acting opportunities he had enjoyed in 1931 and 1935. In that respect he was right: the rest of the Frankenstein movies made by Universal were scaled down to the requirements of an increasingly uncritical wartime audience which saw them not even partly as tragic dramas but as a source of easy thrills and a few unintentional laughs. The monster more and more became a silent stalking killer, always in search of a fresh brain but never finding it, and usually lying

---

★ This seems to have been Karloff's own idea – he thought many of James Whale's humorous conceits were absurd – but the result here, under Lee's plodding direction, is to limit himself to a disappointing and cold performance, enlivened only by the clumsy grace of his movements.

★★ He did quite unexpectedly, in the early sixties, don the old make-up for an episode of the television series *Route 66*. It was called *Lizard's Leg and Owlet's Wing*, and also featured Lon Chaney Jnr as the Wolf Man.

dormant until the electric sparks began to fly in the final reel and he tottered out to face the fury of the stock-shot villagers with their flaming torches held high. *The Ghost of Frankenstein* (1942) at least had a few moments of stature, but despite a promising cast its invention began to flag even in the second reel, and Lon Chaney Jnr was an expressionless, unsympathetic monster with a gash for a mouth and a white face which might have been a mask. W. Scott Darling's screenplay and Erle

SON OF FRANKENSTEIN (1939). Basil Rathbone gets a good look at the villains of the piece: evil old Ygor (Bela Lugosi) and the monster (Boris Karloff). The latter as usual is more sinned against than sinning.

C. Kenton's direction were all on a par with this central performance, though an initial effort was made to take up the story where the last episode left off. The mayor of Frankenstein briskly performs the service of Shakespeare's cushion-laying officers in bringing his council up to date with facts which they must already know but which the audience may not:

> The curse of Frankenstein? This is nonsense, folks. You know as well as I do that the monster died in the sulphur pit under Frankenstein's tower. And that Ygor, his familiar, was riddled with bullets from the gun of Baron Frankenstein himself.

'Ygor does not die that easily,' intervenes a councillor. 'They hanged him and broke his neck, but he lives. Haven't I seen him beside the hardened sulphur pit, playing his weird horn?' Audience please note: the sulphur pit which has bubbled merrily for two thousand years seems to have hardened almost overnight. It must be a plot requirement. The villagers storm the castle, and scare from his hiding place an Ygor who seems physically improved since our last encounter, to the extent of a haircut and some dental treatment. He hides below the old tower in a cave, one wall of which breaks open during an explosion to reveal not only hard sulphur, but the hand of the monster groping blindly through it. A little chipping away, and the complete monster is revealed, dusty but intact. Ygor is overjoyed:

SON OF FRANKENSTEIN (1939). The awful child almost gets his just deserts and Lionel Atwill has had his arm torn out again, but we all know that bullets are of no avail when you're dealing with the Frankenstein monster.

> My friend, they didn't kill you! You lived through the pit! The sulphur was good for you, wasn't it? It preserved you! Come, my friend – now you live forever! They can't destroy you . . .

So we feared, sighed the critics. But the film does have an ace up its sleeve in the shape of a splendid moment when the somnolent monster is tickled by a flash of lightning which catches its neck electrodes and acts like a spring tonic. Ygor now has a game plan:

> The lightning – it's good for you! Your father was Frankenstein, and your mother was the lightning. She has come down to you again. We will go to Ludwig, the second son of Frankenstein. He has all the secrets of his father who created you. We will force him to harness the lightning for you. He will give you strength.

They set off to walk to Vasaria, and on the way, by some minor cinematic miracle, the monster is not only cleansed of his sulphur dust but acquires brand new shiny boots and a stark black suit which does nothing at all for his personality. Even more oddly, for a township within walking distance of Frankenstein, the Vasarians seem to have heard nothing whatever of the monster's history, and treat him as a common or garden madman – which is grossly unfair, since he was on his best behaviour, retrieving a ball for a small girl. Meanwhile, the château at the end of the village is seen to bear a striking nameplate:

LUDWIG FRANKENSTEIN M.D.
Diseases of the mind only

Young Ludwig is just completing a difficult operation, surrounded by admiring assistants (plus the grudging Dr Bohmer, played by Lionel Atwill, who thinks he could have done better). Ludwig is personified by Cedric Hardwicke in his usual cold throwaway manner:

> LUDWIG: There you are, gentlemen. Usual post-surgical treatment.
> KETTERING: Think of it! The first time the human brain has been removed from its skull, subjected to surgery, and replaced!

Well, diseases of the mind or not, regular filmgoers can all guess what Ludwig is going to be up to before the end of the film. For him there can be no rest. No sooner is he alone in his study than he receives a visit from his daughter Elsa's intended, the village prosecutor, one Erik (Ralph Bellamy kicking his heels in the kind of vague supervisory part to which he was assigned in *The Wolf Man*). Will Ludwig please come down to examine a lunatic the police have locked up in the local jail? Ludwig nods absently, but before his departure he receives another visitor who will make him realize the true situation:

> YGOR: How does it feel to face a man you thought your brother killed, doctor?
> LUDWIG: What do you want?
> YGOR: The monster is with me. He is the one in the police station. He is more dangerous than ever before. Besides a sick brain, he has a sick body. You can

make him well, Frankenstein . . . You can harness the lightning as your father did . . . pour life into his hungry veins.

Rather easily blackmailed by the threat of exposure of his family's responsibility for the monster, Ludwig allows the creature to evade police custody and traps it in a cell which luckily exists in his own basement, complete with vapour jets which can be released to render the occupant insensible. He tells Dr Bohmer, who is fascinated by the Frankenstein family history, that he will destroy the creature:

BOHMER: Destroy? But how? He is not subject to the ordinary laws of life.
LUDWIG: There is a way. It was made bit by bit. Organ by organ. It must be unmade the same way.
BOHMER: But this thing lives! It would be murder!
LUDWIG: How can you call the removal of a thing that is not human – murder?

Ludwig insists, but when alone he is visited by the spirit of his father, justifying the 'ghost' of the title. Their conversation, though stilted, is worth quoting in full as summing up the theme of the entire series:

BARON: My son, what are you about to do? Would you destroy that which I, your father, dedicated his life to creating?
LUDWIG: I must! The monster you created is in itself destruction.
BARON: Nevertheless, I was near to solving a problem that has baffled man since the beginning of time. The secret of life! Artificially created . . .
LUDWIG: But it has brought death to everything it touched.
BARON: That is because, unknowingly, I gave it a criminal brain. With your knowledge of science you can cure that.
LUDWIG: It's beyond my cure. It's a malignant brain!
BARON: What if it had another brain?

The baron's spirit fades, having made its point. Another brain! And there's a good one lying around spare, because the monster has just killed Dr Kettering. Ludwig strides into the laboratory. 'Attach the high frequency leads to the terminal electrodes,' he cries. But he has reckoned without Ygor, who does not fancy his 'friend' becoming a man of character and learning. He conspires with Dr Bohmer to furnish Frankenstein at the proper time with a brain quite different from Dr Kettering's – Ygor's own. ('You can make us one. We'll be together always. My brain in his body!') The substitution is made after Ygor has been crushed dead behind a door during a mêlée in which the monster again, improbably, abducts a small unfrightened child. Ludwig never notices, being very busy issuing such commands as 'Build up the voltage potential to its maximum!' But when the sparks have flown, the operation is over, and Ludwig, his transgressions discovered, is required to justify his actions to the prosecutor, the convalescent monster will not agree that he is harmless Dr Kettering:

MONSTER: I am not Dr Kettering. I am Ygor! I have the strength of a hundred men. I cannot die! I cannot be destroyed. I, Ygor, will live forever!
LUDWIG: I've created a hundred times the monster my father made!

Not much remains of this exclamatory dialogue, for with flaming torches at the ready the townspeople attack, the gas is turned on, and the Ygor-monster chokes Dr Bohmer when he finds that he can't see: the eager schemer never checked that both components shared the same blood group. 'The monster's blood will not feed Ygor's sensory nerves,' as Ludwig rapidly explains. Electrical explosions now expand the chaos, the house is set on fire, and the blind monster stumbles ablaze through the house and grounds until felled by ceiling timbers. There is just time for a lover's clinch (that's Erik and Elsa) on a nearby hilltop before the fade-out.

The Ghost of Frankenstein is economically set, flatly lit and dully shot, and it lacks actors who care. Hardwicke walks through his role with something like contempt, Chaney might as well be a block of wood, and even Lugosi is less impressive than before. But the old malarkey struck a responsive chord at the box office, and Universal badly wanted to make more Frankenstein stories. Alas, they only made them badly. Their contract writers had run out of variations, and almost of Frankensteins, until one day the brilliant idea was generated of combining two monsters in one story, thus doubling the drawing power but requiring less plot for each. The scheme was no doubt developed cynically, but it worked spectacularly: there are still people around who remember the queues which ringed the block when *Frankenstein Meets the Wolf Man* was premièred in

THE GHOST OF FRANKENSTEIN (1942). Ygor is at it again, but this time he crosses the friendly monster, who turns nasty. (Lon Chaney Jnr couldn't play him any other way.)

THE GHOST OF FRANKENSTEIN (1942). The monster (probably played in this shot by stunt man Eddie Parker) goes up in flames.

New York in 1943.★ The title was something of a misnomer: the only actual Frankenstein on view was young Elsa from the previous episode, now played not by Evelyn Ankers but by Ilona Massey; and although top billed she has almost nothing to do. The Wolf Man, Larry Talbot, was the principal character; and not until the halfway mark does he arrive, after a long trek from Llanwelly, at the town of Vasaria, where his mission is to learn the secrets of life and death from Dr Frankenstein's notebooks and thus to devise a permanent rest for himself.

The geography of *Frankenstein Meets the Wolf Man* is curious. Ludwig's old home was previously shown as a small château on flat ground just at the end of

★ The British censor kept it in cold storage until the war was over.

town, but it has now become a ruin on the thickly forested slope of a distant mountain. Moreover, when Talbot, having suffered an unfortunate change into his wolf-like persona, is chased by the townsfolk into it, the ruin turns out to have cellars filled with natural ice, even though down in the village it has been a summer evening with music and dancing. In the cellar the fugitive discovers behind a wall of ice the Frankenstein monster, which has had the good fortune to escape from fire by falling into water, and is quickly thawed out. If the monster seems a bit schizophrenic in this picture it is probably because, although nominally played by Bela Lugosi (which seems reasonable since his brain, or his character's, went into the giant body in the last story) all his difficult or tiresome shots are played by a stuntman named Eddie Parker, because the 62-year-old Lugosi was so frail. (A frail monster: that certainly isn't encouraging.) The alternation is all too obvious, especially because no layer of make-up, however thick, could entirely conceal Lugosi's distinctive features, and the very first shot is of Parker. Inexplicable studio cuts add further to the confusion. When we last encountered him, it will be remembered, the monster had been briefly endowed with Ygor's voice and volubility; unfortunately he had gone blind because of a mix-up over blood groups, and tottered ablaze from the house into the darkness. The new scriptwriter, Curt Siodmak, had earnestly tried to carry on from just this situation, and a scene was shot in which, Talbot having chipped the monster out of the ice, the two immortals sit before a camp fire in the icy cellar and chat about their problems:

> MONSTER: I can't see you. I'm blind, I'm sick. Once I had the strength of a hundred men. If Dr Frankenstein were alive he'd give it back to me . . . so I could live forever.
> TALBOT: Do you know what happened?
> MONSTER: I fell into the stream when the village people burned the house down. I lost consciousness. When I woke, I was frozen into the ice.
> TALBOT: Buried alive. I know, I know . . .
> MONSTER: Dr Frankenstein created my body to be immortal. His son gave me a new brain, a clever brain. I will rule the world forever if we can find the formula that can give me back my strength. I will never die.
> TALBOT: But I *want* to die. If you wanted to die, what would you do?
> MONSTER: I would look for Dr Frankenstein's diary. He knew the secret of immortality. He knew the secret of death.

In the film as released the monster is no sooner on his feet than he is leading Talbot round what's left of the Frankenstein library, mouthing further lines which have been deleted from the sound track. Talbot can't find what he wants, but a photo of Elsa gives him the idea of buying the derelict estate, at which suggestion the baroness hurries from her distant home to Vasaria and meets Dr Mannering, a bland hero who has trailed Talbot from Llanwelly. When Talbot also dallies with her at the Festival of the New Wine, the impatient monster stumbles into town and menaces a few villagers before Talbot persuades him that he's making a fool of himself (though the scene has livened up a movie which was getting rather sluggish).* Originally there was dialogue here too:

* Because the monster was originally supposed to be blind he struts around in this scene with arms outstretched, and this is the image of him which has been adopted by impressionists ever since.

TALBOT: What made you come out? You gave us away! You spoiled our last chance . . .

MONSTER: I was afraid you had left me . . .

By helping the monster to escape Talbot has blown his cover, but Dr Mannering guesses where he can be found: in the old laboratory. Luckily for the plot, the good doctor now has an attack of megalomania when he reads Dr Frankenstein's 'Secrets of Life and Death'. For a moment it looks like a solution for everybody:

DOCTOR *(reading)*: 'Matter ages because it loses energy. This artificial body I have created has been charged with superhuman power, so that . . . its lifetime will equal the lives of a hundred human beings. This my creation can never perish unless its energies are drained off artificially – by changing the poles from plus to minus.'

TALBOT: But that's the secret of life. What good does it do me? I'm not interested in life! I wasn't created artificially! I've got real blood in my veins . . . What can we do to end my life?

DOCTOR *(reading)*: 'Energy which cannot be destroyed can be transmitted.'

TALBOT: Well, if that's the case, then the energies from my body can be drained off also. Dr Frankenstein must have performed his experiments in this room – with these machines! They don't seem to have been destroyed by the fire! You must fix them! Help me be rid of this thing that keeps me alive eternally!

DOCTOR: It shouldn't be difficult to connect these wires again . . .

Elsa persuades Mannering that the monster must never rampage again, but when it comes to the point . . .

DOCTOR: I can't do it. I can't destroy Frankenstein's creation. I've got to see it at its full power . . .

He throws all the necessary switches, and the audience is treated to the electrical display it expected. But the doctor's timing is unfortunate: it's the night of the full moon. Just as the monster comes to full power – and his flashing eyes tell us, if the script doesn't, that he can see again – Talbot changes into a wolf man, ready for action, and the two monsters start their inevitable and much-publicized battle. Meanwhile the villagers, highly suspicious of all the equipment arriving at the laboratory, blow up the dam above the ruins, with the result that both monsters are washed away . . . until next time.

Frankenstein Meets the Wolf Man, despite its need to cram in two monsters and several transformations for the Wolf Man, was an enjoyable mood piece with a few genuinely chilling moments. None of these, however, was provided by the Frankenstein monster, which was clearly played out so far as Universal's writers were concerned, especially since it was to be denied dialogue by order of the front office. Henceforth, in the rest of its appearances for Universal, it would remain in its dormant state until the final reel, when, electrically impelled, it would stagger forth to be disposed of – temporarily – by the angry mob. Even the footage of its demise would be largely the same, built around stock shots from *The Ghost of Frankenstein*.

A further difficulty was that all available members of the Frankenstein family

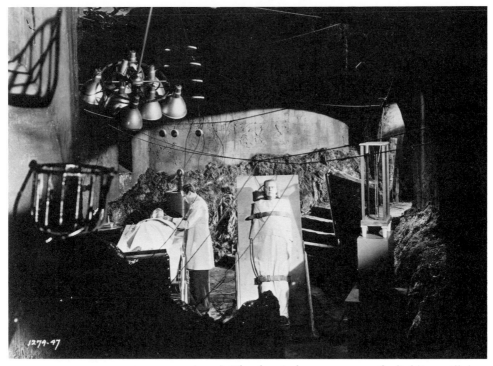

FRANKENSTEIN MEETS THE WOLF MAN (1943). The electrical apparatus goes for little in a still, but on screen it crackles effectively. Patric Knowles is attaching the wolf man's . . . rather, he's arranging for the monster to . . . well, he's doing something very scientific. But of course it won't work, or there'd be no more sequels.

had now left the scene. Only the name remained in *House of Frankenstein*, a multi-monster extravaganza which has been partly dealt with under *Dracula*. Having disposed of the vampire in three reels, the sinister Dr Niemann and his hunchback assistant Daniel, played by J. Carrol Naish, have just four reels left in which to find Frankenstein's records for their own nefarious purposes. Once more, disaster seems to have left most of the ruins still standing. 'Evidently,' says Niemann, 'the force of the flood burst through that wall and washed everything into the cave beyond . . . a glacial ice cavern.' Strange climate they have in Vasaria, but it does help the film's pace, because embedded in the ice are the bodies of both Larry Talbot and the Frankenstein monster. The latter may not be dead, but he can't do much beyond lying down, and Niemann is anxious to get the creature to his own laboratory, which it seems is also in Vasaria, 'before further changes make restoration more difficult. Desiccation of the tissues has gone further than I thought.' Soon he is busy softening the tissues with steam, 'so that the high velocity current can pass through them'. Meanwhile Talbot is pestering to be painlessly destroyed before the moon rises again, and Daniel to have his hump removed so that he can woo a gypsy girl, who inconveniently has eyes only for Talbot. Niemann evolves a complex scheme. He kidnaps an old enemy, Ullman, and explains:

HOUSE OF FRANKENSTEIN (1944). Now it's Glenn Strange under the monster make-up, and Karloff has returned to play the mad doctor, here seen at something of a disadvantage.

I'm going to give that brain of yours a new home, in the skull of the Frankenstein monster. I'm going to give *you* the brain of the wolf man, so that all your waking hours will be spent in untold agony.

The old equipment is charged up, and soon Niemann is issuing orders:

The plasma must flow at exactly that rate, no more and no less . . . if there's any change, call me . . . Turbine . . . now the generators . . . check the megavoltage . . .
– Twenty-five thousand.
– Increase to fifty. The electronic bombardment will penetrate the flesh . . .

It's all in vain, for the villagers attack right on cue, and soon the monster, brought to sluggish life, is dragging his protector away from danger . . . right into the local bog, so that the end title can be superimposed over the bubbles which are all that remain of him and Niemann.

House of Frankenstein, despite its packed plot, is a somewhat boring film, with too much footage allocated to the gypsy girl, who is clearly doomed to meet a tragic fate from one or other of her unpleasant lovers. The monster has no dialogue and comes to life only in the last five minutes of the film. He is played for the first time by Glenn Strange, a giant-sized ex-cowboy bit player, who was ignominiously billed twenty-second in the cast but by all accounts enjoyed his moment of fame, apart from the difficulty of having to pick up Boris Karloff with one hand and carry him across the fields. (The difficulty was solved by a hidden sling from his shoulder, and the substitution of a dummy for the rather sizeable horror star.) As for Karloff, in returning to the fold he brought nothing to the part of Niemann except an agreeably sepulchral whisper; but the character was weakly sketched anyway. And the doctor had been working too hard.

The picture was not too well received except by the paying customers. *Variety* reported that: 'The plot stumbles along endlessly in its top-heavy attempt to carry on its shoulders too many of yesterday's nightmares.' Yet within months Glenn Strange was again under the monster make-up for *House of Dracula*,★ in which he had even less to do, being inert until the final crackle of machinery, and then used only for continuity shots between clips from older films in the series. It seemed like the end for a star who never really was; but at least *Abbott and Costello Meet Frankenstein*★ gave him a few splendid moments: having Lou sit on his lap, chasing the comedians around the spooky house and once thrusting his fist through a door panel (and nearly braining Costello in the process).

The first Frankenstein film in the Hammer series could not have come as a greater contrast. *House of Frankenstein* and *House of Dracula* had been bland, tired action films with no more shocks than a child of six might withstand, and certainly no sense of reality. The heritage of Hammer has been briefly detailed on page 55, and its intentions were clearly signalled in the first of its new shockers. I remember all too vividly the unease with which I sat through *The Curse of Frankenstein* in a suburban cinema during the cold first month of 1957. With Universal one had always known that nothing too ghastly would assault the eye. With Hammer one was in constant danger from the sight of dripping blood, rotting corpses and bits of brain, all in vivid colour, to say nothing of well-endowed young women falling victim to the monster in various stages of undress. The only Universal film which came close to this atmosphere was the original *Frankenstein* of 1931, but there the cold chill of horror had been offset by some sharpness in the handling and by the sympathy brimming over in Karloff's portrayal. Hammer's policy was not to skate over unpleasantness but to wallow in it. One recalled Universal's doubts about colour; in *The Curse of Frankenstein* Christopher Lee's make-up was excessively nasty, as though he had been pickled for a year or two in formaldehyde; and the colour was garish in the extreme,

★ For these films see more detailed comments under *Dracula*.

ABBOTT AND COSTELLO MEET FRANKENSTEIN (1948). Glenn Strange has a slightly bigger role than usual this time, but Lenore Aubert and Bela Lugosi are worried by his sleepiness. Can it be night starvation?

seeming more so whenever the camera directed our attention to horrible details. True, the film contained an occasional suggestion of humour, but this seldom got further than a quiver on the lower lip of Peter Cushing, unless it was a steal from one of the older films, such as the baron's remark about the breakfast marmalade on the morning after a night of particularly horrendous mayhem. Lee was not enough of an actor to create anything but revulsion for this particular monster and, if he had been, the audience would have been even more upset than it was when he fell into the acid bath which had been so carefully set up for its attention. *Curse* was a film without Hollywood expertise. It set out its horrors plainly: there was no sheen of lighting, no dazzling editing, no playing with shadows, no subtlety of narrative. It simply went hammer and tongs for the most gruesome effects, hoping to collar an audience by its sheer bravura. After all, who would have expected that so outlandishly violent a film could ever come from a British studio?

The Curse of Frankenstein (which includes nothing about any curse) gives the impression of being closer to its literary original than any film before or since, but that was probably because the men's clothes were in period – Cushing in particular has a ruby smoking jacket which was much admired – and the details of the sets were convincingly European. Like the Shelley novel it begins with a flashback, but not the same one. In the Hammer version the Baron is about to be hanged, and feels that he may as well confess all to the prison priest, especially since the crime of which he was convicted was one of the few he didn't commit. He recalls his early life as a rich but lonely boy in nineteenth-century Geneva, a student capable of imbibing scientific theory as others might imbibe wine. His contemporaries think him uninterested in life, but he is. Not however in living it, but in creating it. When his parents die he is left alone in a vast house staffed by uninquiring servants, and his tutor Paul rapidly falls in with Victor's fascination with surgical research, which after several years leads to the painless killing of a dog and the regeneration of the corpse through electricity. It seems to Victor but a small step from this experiment to the creation of a man from pieces of dead tissue.

> VICTOR: A man with perfect physique. With the nature and brain of a genius. Everything planned and perfect. We can do it. Don't you see?
> PAUL: What you're saying is madness. A revolt against nature: such a thing can only end in evil.

Not for the first time Paul allows himself to be convinced, and Victor continues:

> We need the framework – the body. Whatever adaptations may be necessary, that basic material is our starting point. Last week they hanged a man in Ingolstadt. As a warning to others his body has been left on a gibbet outside the town. It'll stay there until it's rotten . . . or until it's stolen.

When the corpse has been acquired by nocturnal stealth, the head turns out to be useless: birds have been at it. It is promptly removed and dropped in the acid tank. (Sounds of someone being sick in the third row.) Victor doesn't care for the hands either: they are coarse and insensitive. So he 'borrows' some from a sculptor who has recently died. The corpse turns out to have had a defective right ankle, so to achieve balance both feet have to be replaced; and while at the charnel house Victor pauses to bargain for a pair of eyes he fancies. Finally everything is organized except the brain . . . and by now the audience is transfixed, wondering what atrocity will next be perpetrated before its eyes. Luckily for Victor, Europe's greatest living physicist comes to stay, and happens to fall downstairs – or was he pushed? – and break his neck. Hard luck for him, good luck for Frankenstein. Victor is so overjoyed by this piece of good fortune that he fails to observe that the brain has been damaged during an argument with Paul, and the hideous walking creature that results, when switched on by electric force, is possessed (as we could all have predicted) by the urge to kill. Victor finds that rather convenient when it kills his unwanted blackmailing mistress Justine (he has locked her up with it deliberately) but less so when it shows an undesirable interest in his rich cousin and bride-to-be. Even so, when Paul shoots it between the eyes, Victor digs it up and repairs the damage, with only worse results in its temper. Only when it ungratefully goes on a mad rampage at him across the roof is he impelled to throw a lantern at it. The creature goes up in flames, sharing the fate of most movie monsters, and falls through a handy skylight right into the acid bath. Alas, this means that when the corpse of Justine is discovered, Victor has nobody to blame, and the embittered Paul refuses to confirm his story about having created a murderous monster . . .

THE CURSE OF FRANKENSTEIN (1957). Peter Cushing, ever efficient as Frankenstein, has a simple method for keeping Christopher Lee out of the way when not needed.

The film manages an ironic ending, with Victor about to be hanged for the creature's crime, while tipping off the *cognoscenti* that a sequel is in the works. Indeed, no producer in his right mind would have failed to follow up such an obvious hit, a film which drew vast inquisitive audiences from lowbrows and highbrows alike. The monster may have been unsatisfactory, but he had been disposed of in the acid, and if only Frankenstein himself could be preserved he would continue to create all manner of horrors. And so, in the Hammer series, it was the Baron and not the monster who came to be immortal; and that seemed right, for Peter Cushing had presented a chilling but amusing figure, partly from his own personality but also one supposes from a consensus of writers who saw plenty to attract audiences in a prissy scientist who could not see that his actions might be morally wrong, since they were all for the advancement of science.

No matter that the *Hollywood Reporter* confessed itself 'not so much frightened as nauseated' by *The Curse of Frankenstein*; no matter that the *Monthly Film Bulletin* thought that 'immense possibilities have been sacrificed by an illmade script, poor direction and performance, and above all a preoccupation with disgusting – not horrific – charnelry.' Within eighteen months a sequel was on view, and doing as well as its predecessor. *The Revenge of Frankenstein* is really not very good: its grotesqueries lack excitement. The *Bulletin* mentioned dismissively its contrived plot, crude and pedestrian handling, and its notable lack of pace and imagination. These defects mattered not at all: the public was hooked. The little matter of the hanging at the end of *Curse* was easily explained. One of Victor's warders is Karl, a twisted dwarf who in return for a promise that he will be made handsome arranges for the unfortunate priest to be executed in Victor's stead. With the dwarf as servant, Frankenstein enrols as Dr Stein at the workhouse hospital in Carlsbruck: there he will have plenty of opportunity to collect severed organs. Gradually he builds up a perfect body and immerses it in fluid until it is ready for the operation to insert the dwarf's brain. The new Karl seems perfectly behaved in every way, apart from casually tossing his old body into a furnace, until his brain is damaged in a violent fight. Then he becomes a cannibal on the rampage, growing gradually more and more misshapen. He finally drops dead at a society party where he has identified Frankenstein as his creator; and when the news reaches the workhouse patients they tear their doctor almost limb from limb. Luckily Victor has given adequate instructions to his assistant about the use of his brain inside yet another body which waits in a nearby tank, and some time later a certain Dr Frank arrives in London to take up a Harley Street practice.

The third Hammer variation on this gruesome subject was *The Evil of Frankenstein*, made in conjunction with Universal, who had not been slow to spot the British success in their old field. Alas, *Evil* was not particularly interesting despite a considerably improved budget, and it occupies a curious narrative place in the series since Victor, having returned to his old castle, tells his assistant Hans the story of his first experiments. Unfortunately for regular viewers, it is a totally different story from anything they have heard: in this version the baron alone creates a monster, which is driven off a cliff by angry villagers. Now, years later, he and Hans find the monster frozen in an ice cave. (Where have we heard that before?) Victor brings it back to some sort of life, but needs a hypnotist to give it strength. Unfortunately the hypnotist (like Ygor many years before) uses the monster for murder missions of his own. Frankenstein himself is in danger, but eventually the monster kills the hypnotist, destroys the laboratory, and perishes in the resultant fire. The *Bulletin* commented that the film as a whole was 'sadly tatty' and that the ice containing the monster was 'all too clearly a polythene bag'.

Frankenstein Created Woman (1966) sounded like a lively departure but proved a total disappointment, especially since for some curious reason the 'creation' scene which was shot was eliminated from the release print. Baron Frankenstein in this one has spent some time in suspended animation, after a remarkable experiment involving his own death. Recovered, he is convinced that the soul can be transferred from one body to another, and has a chance to prove this when his assistant Hans is wrongly executed for murder and the boy's girl friend Christina drowns herself. By putting Hans's revengeful soul in her body, Frankenstein sends her off on a murder spree, on completion of which she drowns herself again. An abundance of tasteless detail prevented the unconvincing story from providing more than the minimum of entertainment for addicts, and the increasingly lush appearance of the Hammer product was proving small consolation for its lack of narrative interest and directorial style.

Elements of both qualities did surface in *Frankenstein Must Be Destroyed* (1969), but the tale was even more unpleasant than usual. Victor was back to brain transplants in this one, prowling the streets in a mask in search of material. He decides to kidnap a needed colleague; the man is accidentally killed, and 'awakes'

FRANKENSTEIN MUST BE DESTROYED (1969). Freddie Jones, with head sawn across and stitched together again, looks sorry that he ever accepted the role; and (right) a burglar is certainly sorry that he bothered to break into Frankenstein's laboratory.

to find that his brain has been stitched into another man's body. The resultant monster, made up of two eminent surgeons, finally picks up Frankenstein and carries him into a house which has been set ablaze. Frankenstein was virtually without redeeming qualities in this story, and that left a hole in the centre of the entertainment.

All indications were that the Hammer moguls had lost their way, and while finding it they decided to refilm the original story with a fresh Baron and a few new gory details. Ralph Bates, who had been successful as Caligula on television,

was chosen to replace Cushing, and the film when it emerged in 1970 was called *Horror of Frankenstein*. There were a few signs that it had been intended as a spoof, but Jimmy Sangster as director was no James Whale, and most audiences thought it just a poor imitation. The monster was played by stunt man Dave Prowse, and looked more muscle-bound than intimidating: once again he finished up in an acid bath. *Horror of Frankenstein* made a poor double bill with *Scars of Dracula* and was quickly forgotten; so quickly that two years later Peter Cushing was back again in his old role for what proved to be the final time; not surprisingly, since the new

film was surprisingly reminiscent of *The Revenge of Frankenstein*, now an astonishing fourteen years old. *Frankenstein and the Monster from Hell* (1973) took place
almost entirely in the unsavoury atmosphere of a nineteenth-century madhouse,
and at a hundred minutes was grossly overlong. A body-snatching young
surgeon, Helder, discovered by a policeman with a collection of eyeballs in a jar, is
committed to Carlsbruck's criminal lunatic asylum and finds that the director,
using an alias, is really Baron Frankenstein, who was thought to have died years
before but in fact only lost his hands. Since the Baron's 'collected works' have
long been Helder's bible, the two men set to with a will on the reconstruction,
using whatever spare parts fall to hand, of a brutish inmate almost killed in an
escape. The subject is given the brain of a professor, and despite the unsatisfactory
result Frankenstein plans to mate it with a mute girl inmate. When the patients
find out about this plan, they tear the monster to pieces.

Clearly this was nothing but tedious recycling, sustained only by James
Bernard's music and otherwise heavy-handed in every way. (When the eyeballs
spill across the floor, Helder sighs: 'If only you could appreciate the difficulty of
finding specimens like these . . .') Quite appropriately *The Monster from Hell*
marked the end of Hammer's variations on the Frankenstein theme, which had
become increasingly unsavoury. The *Monthly Film Bulletin* noted that 'the
characterisation of the Baron himself has now lapsed to the caricatured level of

FRANKENSTEIN AND THE MONSTER FROM HELL (1973). Dave Prowse, as a furry monster with no
redeeming features, does a spot of grave-robbing at his master's behest.

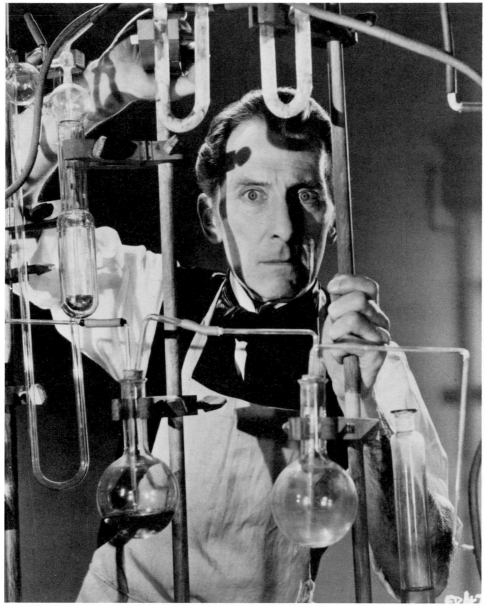

In Hammer films the monster changes, but Frankenstein remains the same. Peter Cushing was the most obsessive hero–villain the screen ever produced.

Nazi brutality', and indeed there was much to remind people of Mengele and the concentration camps, which are scarcely subjects for entertainment. Hammer had had a shockingly good run, and was wise to stop. But needless to say, its success had induced many independent producers to jump on the Frankenstein band wagon. Although there are probably more films about Dracula than about any other monster, the relatives and colleagues and disciples of Frankenstein are many and various.

★　　★　　★

Frankenstein films, obviously, could never be the sole perquisite of Universal and Hammer. Almost simultaneously with the first Hammer chapter, the inelegant American-International Pictures churned out a successor to their top-grossing cheapie *I Was a Teenage Werewolf*. It was no better; it was much the same. *I Was a Teenage Frankenstein* (1957) concerned a mad professor who restores to life, with the help of a few odd limbs from elsewhere, a teenager killed in a motor accident. The film could in fact be seen as an extension of the necrophilia which greeted the death of James Dean in 1955; AIP however cared not a whit for social comment or fine detail, and spent as little as possible on sets and make-up. Their creature looks even nastier than Christopher Lee's, with a visage apparently fashioned in white plasticine, left out in the rain and recovered after the cat has been at it. The thrust of the plot, however, is that one night on the rampage this misshapen monster kills another teenager without harming his handsome head, which the professor then transfers for his original creature's use. It seemed all very lowbrow and down-market, even in 1957, and the movie is best remembered for the ineptness of its lines, e.g. professor to monster: 'I know you've got a civil tongue in your head, I sewed it there myself!' The actor playing the monster went on to star in a television series called *Land of the Giants*, but has been little heard from since.

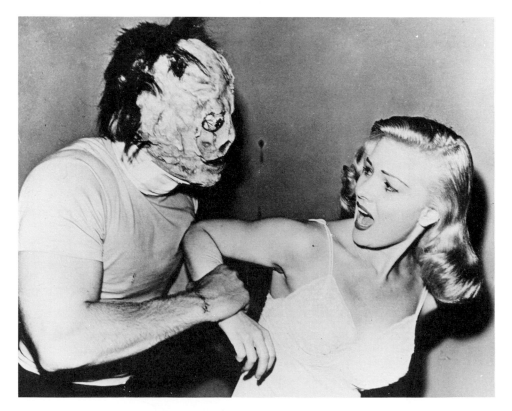

I WAS A TEENAGE FRANKENSTEIN (1957). The make-up is unpleasant without being ingenious, and it prevented Gary Conway from doing any acting; but it made the girls scream, and that was what mattered.

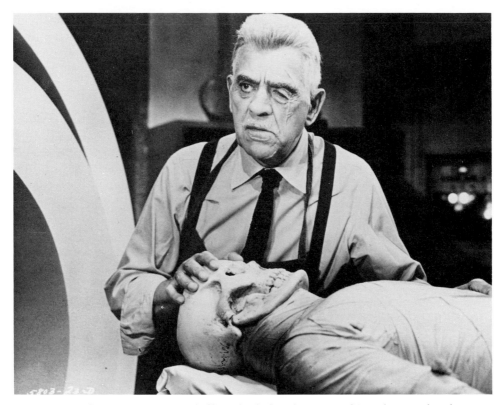

FRANKENSTEIN '70 (1958). Boris Karloff was back, but this was no fairy tale. Exactly what use the skull might be is hard to fathom.

AIP's only direct sequel to *Teenage Frankenstein* was a curious and not unamusing in-joke called *How to Make a Monster* (1958), set supposedly in the studio where AIP's cheapjack monster movies had been produced. A disgruntled make-up artist, who has been fired, mixes into the make-ups of the actors playing the werewolf and the monster enough mysterious poison to fill them with the urge to kill. And who do they kill? Why, the studio executives who have decreed that AIP shall make no more horror pictures, that's who.

Meanwhile, at another studio, Allied Artists were mixing the ingredients for *Frankenstein 1970*. This was in 1958, and the date in the title had no relevance except to set the story in the future, when presumably anything might happen. The resulting film starts rather brilliantly, with a frightening sequence about a girl being chased at night, near a lonely lake, by a horrible giant creature with huge hands. Unfortunately this turns out to be a scene being shot for a movie. The story which follows after the main titles proves on the thin side, and the mistake was made of shooting it in CinemaScope, which reduces the possibilities for mystery and terror. Allied Artists' chief coup was the engaging of Boris Karloff to play the current (or rather future) descendant of the Frankenstein family, evil of intent and hideous of visage. (We are told he has been disfigured by Nazi brutality.) Quite mad, of course, he keeps in a vault the body of the original monster, which seems intact except that its head by some curious process of deliquescence has been reduced to a grinning skull. The Baron's sole aim in life is to remedy this sad state of affairs by acquiring for his plaything a new head and assorted organs, plus an atomic reactor which will in some unspecified way fix them in position. In order to pay for the latter item he has let a film crew into his castle, and cunningly uses its members as a principal source of organ supply. The monster is promptly reactivated, its unfinished head concealed under what looks like a white bucket; only after the whole castle goes up in the predictable explosion is it revealed that this mad Frankenstein had fashioned the monster's head in his own image, or rather what used to be his image before the Nazis had a go at him.

Frankenstein 1970 lingers as a dull and vaguely unpleasant film, but it is *Gone with the Wind* compared with *Frankenstein's Daughter*, released in the same year. An independent production which seems to have emerged from a back street on Poverty Row, this concerns one Oliver Frank, an incognito descendant of the famous family. He kills a girl who resists his sexual advances, in order to restore her to life as a female monster who will be unfailingly compliant. The ghastly creature which results was allegedly played under the make-up by a male extra, but it didn't really matter: the film was unwatchable and had no *raison d'être* except to support some other monstrosity on an exploitation double bill in halls where quality was the last commodity to be required.

Six years passed, during which Hammer had the Frankenstein field to itself. Then in 1964 yet another abysmal horror saga of independent American origin was released under the title *Frankenstein Meets the Space Monster*. By now it was becoming evident that the Frankenstein story lent itself far too easily to exploitation: the sporadic brilliance of the original films shone more brightly than ever in comparison with the unutterable junk now being produced in their name. In this case Saunders, a super-monster with a remote-controlled brain, is created from corpses for the express purpose of being sent into space. Up there he encounters aliens, and a laser gunfight results in half his face being burned away, revealing his artificial brain and turning him uncontrollably savage. There is a happy ending, however, for Saunders (Christian name Frank, to partly justify the title) makes short work in space of a monster which has been causing havoc for astronauts, and in the attempt dies a hero.

In 1965 came a three-week job made by the infant Embassy Pictures to fit into a spoofy double bill with their *Billy the Kid versus Dracula*. The title may almost be guessed: it was *Jesse James Meets Frankenstein's Daughter*. If you care, she was really his granddaughter, played by one Narda Onyx, an actress since kept under wraps. The lady restores Jesse's henchman's life after a gun battle, but when Jesse rejects her amorous advances she transforms the convalescent gunman into a monster named Igor; not carefully enough, however, for he turns on her in the long run.

It was also in 1965 that Japan got into the Frankenstein act. Toho Productions, the home of Godzilla and Mothra and Rodan, co-produced with an independent American entrepreneur named Saperstein an item finally entitled *Frankenstein Conquers the World*. It presupposed that the heart of the immortal Frankenstein monster was stolen towards the end of World War Two from its resting place in Nazi Germany, and later involved in the immolation which followed the atomic

He rolled
THE SEVEN
WONDERS
OF THE
WORLD
into
ONE!

NICK ADAMS
STARRING IN
FRANKENSTEIN
CONQUERS THE WORLD
FROM AMERICAN INTERNATIONAL IN COLORscope

A TOHO CO., LTD., HENRY G. SAPERSTEIN ENTERPRISE PRODUCTION

FRANKENSTEIN CONQUERS THE WORLD (1965). Everybody wanted to get into the act . . .
even the Japanese.

bombing of Hiroshima. In some evasively unexplained way this stimulates the regeneration of an entire monster in baby form, and some years later an oddly-featured boy giant, already ten times man size, is terrorizing the countryside and shedding limbs which retain their own ghastly vitality while others grow in their place. This death-dealing monster finally becomes a hero during an earthquake, when it defeats a fire-breathing reptile escaped from the bowels of the earth, before itself being swallowed up in a further tremor. Afterwards, Frankenstein's creation joined the ghastly gallery of Toho monsters (mostly men in rubber suits) which now even included a Japanese King Kong: they met each other repeatedly and tediously, and were good only for laughing at, especially in a stupefying opus called *Destroy All Monsters* which emerged in 1968 and almost killed the genre stone dead.

After these tawdry tall tales, it was a relief in 1966 to turn to the puppet-populated *Mad Monster Party*, already mentioned under *Dracula*, especially since Boris Karloff's own sepulchral tones were used for the character of Baron Boris von Frankenstein. But the 'adult' monster extravaganzas continued more or less unabated. *Dracula vs Frankenstein* (1970) was a piece of Italian nonsense with Michael Rennie as a scientist from the planet Ummo who, apparently from mere curiosity, revives 'the four most terrible monsters in the history of mankind'. Will you be surprised to hear that three of them are the subjects of this book? In the same year a Canadian film, either contemptuously or affectionately called *Flick*, followed the troubles of one Viktor Frankenstein when he enrols at an American university. Derided on account of his family name, he takes a very personal revenge by forcing, through brain control, one student to kill several others. It is then revealed that Viktor himself is an artificially created man, the brainchild of a mad professor in charge of the university computer. Just to make life confusing, an American company then issued a second film called *Dracula vs Frankenstein*, with J. Carrol Naish as the mad doctor and Lon Chaney Jnr as his brutish assistant. The result looked as though it had been edited out of all comprehension and is distinguished only by the fact that the actor playing the 'Frankenstein' monster is more than seven feet tall.

Frankenstein films proliferated, but there was little to recommend in them. A 1971 Italian farrago, translated as *Lady Frankenstein*, had Joseph Cotten at the top of the cast, but he was soon crushed to death by his own monster and it was left to his daughter to avenge him by creating an even stronger creature, out of the body of her shepherd lover who had been smothered by her husband, and the brain of said husband who was then killed by the lady. (They would probably have called it *Lady Frankenstein's Lover*, but for fear that the D. H. Lawrence estate might sue.)

1973 set the taste buds of Frankenstein fans tingling in anticipation of a four-hour television mini-series from Universal, but despite expensive top dressing, it was a commercial disappointment, and the two-hour theatrical potted version sank without trace. Its script was by Christopher Isherwood and Don Bachardy, it boasted a distinguished cast list including James Mason, John Gielgud and Ralph Richardson, and it was called *Frankenstein: The True Story*, though to what purpose (since Frankenstein never *was* a true story) is hard indeed to conjecture. It did not even stay close to Mary Shelley's original, but in James

FRANKENSTEIN: THE TRUE STORY (1973). This TV version originally began with the famous 1816 tea party by the shores of Lake Geneva. The scene disappeared from all known prints but here, to prove its existence, are James Mason, David McCallum, Leonard Whiting and Jane Seymour.

Whale style it had (originally at least) a prologue set in 1816 during the famous Diodati holiday. Since this sequence tended to disappear in the versions released, its dialogue is worth reprinting* for comparison with that on pages 129–34:

EXTERIOR. A LAKE. SWITZERLAND. MOUNTAIN MATTE EFFECT.

Some distance from the shore, a rowboat is anchored. A picnic is in progress. Present are Lord Byron, Shelley, his wife Mary Shelley and Dr Polidori. We come close on Mary and hear her thoughts.

MARY (*unspoken thoughts*): I am Mary Shelley. Here I sit demurely beside my husband. But in my head is a story of horror, and you shall hear it.

POLIDORI (*unspoken thoughts*) (*a middle-aged man, bad humoured, wearing gloves*): Look at me, Dr John William Polidori. What am I doing here, you ask, consorting with my inferiors? I will tell you. Owing to lack of funds, I have the dubious honour to be travelling with Lord Byron – as his personal physician! They call him the greatest poet alive. Pooh! Byron's merely a journalist with a knack for rhyming. They like his verses because he's a lord, and love *him* because he's a libertine! As for Shelley and his wife, they're a pair of spoilt children.

* The original script by Christopher Isherwood and Don Bachardy is reproduced by permission of Universal Pictures.

According to Byron, Shelley's a great poet too, even greater than himself. I suspect my lord means to touch him for a loan!

BYRON *(after singing a snatch in Italian)*: Don't you admire my baritone, Mary? In me, the world lost a great Figaro.

MARY: The world should prefer you as you are, my lord. Your *verses* are *never* out of tune.

BYRON: Shelley, I hope your wife's features won't grow as sharp as her tongue!

MARY *(noting that her husband sits gazing at the lake)*: His senses are lost in the landscape. And it's useless for me to appeal to Dr Polidori for protection.

BYRON: Pollydolly, climb down off your high perch and join us!

POLIDORI *(unspoken thoughts)*: Let them sneer at me. Let them despise me! One day, I shall astound the world. Who will remember Byron or Shelley a hundred years hence? And who will not echo the name of Polidori?

BYRON: Silly fellow! He's always offended about something . . . (He regards himself, using a breadknife as a mirror.)

MARY: Surely, Byron, you need no mirror? You are reflected in the eyes of a thousand adoring females.

BYRON: But now I'm ravenous! Shelley, be a good fellow and call Dr Polly. He won't deign to listen to Mary or me.

SHELLEY: Dr Polidori! Come and join our feast!

MARY *(noting that Polidori pays no attention)*: I fear I may be the one to blame. You remember we sat up long after midnight last week, talking of ghosts and ghouls and horrors, and vowed we'd each write a story? Polidori brought me his yesterday. It was cruel of me, but I couldn't resist laughing. Such a fandango of fiends!

SHELLEY: Well, at least he wrote something. I was too lazy.

BYRON: And I got no further than page two.

SHELLEY: And you, Mary? Have you anything to offer us?

MARY: An idea, no more. But perhaps it will come to life in the telling.

BYRON: Capital. We've a treat to look forward to this evening.

MARY: My story is too horrible for darkness. I hope to frighten you quite sufficiently here and now in this bright sunshine.

BYRON: You'd deprive us of our luncheon?

MARY: I defy you to think of your stomach before I've finished. If you do, I shall have failed, and you may eat at once.

BYRON: That's fair enough. Sit down, Shelley, and let's listen.

MARY: You are not to be mere listeners, but actors as well. Shelley, you are to become Victor Frankenstein, a young doctor of medicine.

SHELLEY: Frankenstein? I'm a foreigner?

MARY: You are Swiss. But you needn't assume a foreign accent. Like many of your countrymen, you speak English perfectly.

SHELLEY: But why should I speak English? This isn't England.

MARY: Are you sure? Try to look through my eyes. Tell me what you see.

And from Shelley's point of view we see a small eighteenth-century English mansion in the middle distance, where the mountain was.

SHELLEY: Why – it's like my father's house in Sussex. It can't be real!

MARY: You'll find that water real enough. Take off your clothes. You're going for a swim.

SHELLEY: You know I can't swim!

MARY: Victor Frankenstein is an excellent swimmer. And so is his brother William.

Now 16-year-old William pops up out of the water and Mary's imagination. Shelley/Frankenstein dives in to play with him; Byron joins Polidori on a rock where they remain for the moment, spectators of the play which now begins, with Mary herself taking the role of Elizabeth, Victor's wife-to-be. Suddenly the imaginary William becomes entangled in weeds, and quickly drowns despite Victor's frantic efforts to save him. We cut to the funeral, after which the embittered Victor is already irrevocably set on the familiar Frankenstein path:

VICTOR: Death, peace, God's will. And all of us listening with pious faces! Why *God*'s will? Any fool with a sword or a gun can give death. Why can't we give life?

ELIZABETH: But we can! One day, if God blesses us, when we are man and wife . . .

VICTOR: So can a pair of animals. Life out of life – that's no miracle. Why can't I raise life out of death? Out of my brother's corpse?

ELIZABETH: That's how Satan tempted our Lord.

VICTOR: If Satan could teach me how to make William live again, I'd gladly become his pupil.

The next cut is to a desk littered with papers and anatomical diagrams. Victor is working every hour of the day, and Elizabeth is shamefully neglected. Where have we heard this before? One night Victor happens to pass the scene of a road accident, and follows the bier of an injured youth to hospital, where he is attended by Dr Henry Clerval, played by the actor who played Byron. It turns out that Clerval rather than Frankenstein is the mad genius of this story: he amputates the injured boy's arm, then takes the severed limb back to his apartments and by a process of his own invention keeps it alive, capable of gripping Victor's hand; he has even given active life to a whole dead grasshopper. Needless to say, the two men are soon working frenziedly together, and when Elizabeth eventually makes an impatient call, she is given a demonstration: a butterfly brought back to life. Shocked, she instinctively kills it with a well-aimed symbolic Bible.

Victor has no time to worry about this, for news comes through of a quarry landslide, with several men dead. Their injuries are all different, and it is easy enough for Henry, as the surgeon in charge, to collect enough sound parts to fashion a whole new man, named for the nonce after the only one whose head was not crushed. But before the ultimate is achieved, Henry dies of a heart attack, shocked by the sight of the severed arm, which though still active is growing distorted and bestial in form, a sign that his secret process has not yet been brought to perfection.

Victor is left to work alone, but as a tribute to his dead friend he transfers Henry's own brain into the multipart corpse, and goes blithely into the creation sequence almost as though it were a musical number. The result is a perfect, even a beautiful, young man; and only the audience knows what happened to Henry's severed arm. The creature speaks perfect English in a melodious voice, and is at first obedient to Victor's every whim, though quick to mature into his intellectual equal, capable of being passed off to Victor's landlady as a friend unexpectedly arrived from another country. Victor even takes his creation to the opera, where it wins all hearts. But signs of deterioration are already setting in, and Victor is eventually forced to conclude that Henry's process is reversing itself. The creature, with its sharp intellect, realizes this too, and tries to commit suicide, but finds itself indestructible: when it stabs itself, only a little purple goo slurps out, and instantly congeals. On the run, the creature terrifies a band of gypsies, then stays to befriend a welcoming blind man in his forest hut. This innocent encounter ends unintentionally in two deaths, including that of the blind man's grand-daughter Agatha, whom the creature had fancied from afar. Shattered, it runs with the corpse back to Victor's apartments, only to find in residence Dr Polidori, who as chief villain in the narrated story keeps his own name (presumably an indication of how much Byron and the Shelleys disliked him). He has already been briefly introduced as a half-mad colleague of Henry's, and has cunningly taken over Victor's apartment in the expectation that the now ugly creature will eventually return to the scene of his 'birth'. Meanwhile Victor has married his Elizabeth, but is soon blackmailed by Polidori into continuing his experiments in their joint name – Polidori being unable to operate because his impeccable white gloves conceal warped and useless hands. He even brings along the threatening and embarrassing presence of the creature, arrayed in a broad-brimmed hat and oriental mask. Victor has no choice but to accompany the ill-assorted pair to his own old apartment, where he finds under Polidori's command the severed head of Agatha – all that could be saved – and, floating in a tank, a headless female body. 'I had to send my servants out to find the rest of the material,' murmurs Polidori.

FRANKENSTEIN: THE TRUE STORY (1973). Polidori introduces young Frankenstein to some of his more outlandish experiments.

There follows another extended creation sequence. Eventually Victor cries 'She's alive!' and dismisses the male creature from view in case his presumed bride-to-be is upset by finding him the first thing she sees on her re-awakening. Satisfied with his work so far, he leaves the new woman, named Prima, in Polidori's hands and goes off on a delayed honeymoon, returning only to find that Polidori has insinuated himself with Victor's in-laws, the Fanshawes. We then discover, in a scene reminiscent of *Pygmalion*, that the smiling villain has introduced Prima into polite society: she is at that moment in the next room, reciting poetry to an attentive circle. Thoroughly enjoying himself, Polidori explains to the circle that Prima is an amnesiac whom Victor restored to health after a *grave* illness. He plans next to take her to London, and urges Victor to kill off the male creature, which has become restless and violent at being deprived of Prima, by popping him into a vat of acid prepared for the purpose. Instead, through a chapter of accidents, the whole building goes up in flames, and Victor supposes that the creature has perished inside it; but we have seen the rapidly deteriorating monster leap from the roof into an adjacent tree and run screaming off into the forest. It reappears disastrously at the Fanshawes' ball, where it savagely attacks Prima, and in a startling shot knocks her head clean off. Victor gives himself up to the police; the creature is put behind bars. Polidori talks the authorities into releasing Victor as his patient and sets off with him and Elizabeth on a sea voyage; but the creature escapes and follows, stowing away on the ship. Eventually during a storm it emerges and vengefully hoists Polidori to the top of the mast, where he is promptly struck by lightning and turned into a pile of ashes. The shock however only gives the creature renewed strength. Victor is injured and lies in a high fever; when he recovers, it is to find that the creature has set a course due north, has forced the evacuation of the entire crew, and has strangled Elizabeth. Having set sail from Edinburgh, the ship is now stranded in arctic ice; with a wail of despair Victor follows the footprints of his creation over an empty snowscape, and catches up with it under an ice cliff. The two protagonists gaze at each other more in sorrow than in anger:

> VICTOR: Are you satisfied now, monster? Am I punished enough? For giving you life? I have wronged you, I know. I disowned you. I wanted to destroy you. How can I blame you for anything you've done? Speak to me, for God's sake!
> *The creature silently hands over a pistol.*
> Poor creature, are you as weary of life as I am? I'd kill myself gladly, with a clear conscience, if only I could rid mankind of us both. I'm a weak human. I can't survive long in this terrible place. But your iron body will keep you alive against your will, for years perhaps. No bullet can help *you*! You'll be all alone. That would be too cruel . . . Is there no escape for us? Yes, perhaps we can both be free!

In a moment of inspiration Victor fires the pistol at an overhanging snow cornice, and as the reverberations build up an avalanche, the creature has time to mutter in Henry's voice 'Well done, Victor' before both figures are buried under megatons of ice.

In the original script there is an ironic fadeout which was not filmed. As the credits roll, we watch the arctic landscape transformed by the coming of summer.

An iceberg breaks away from the land and floats south. Gulls circle and land on it. Suddenly a crack appears in the ice, and through it emerge fingers . . . the creature's indestructible fingers. The hand opens as it feels the sunlight.

Followers of the Frankenstein saga will have realized from the above brief account that only in the latter stages is *Frankenstein: The True Story* even halfway true to the original novel. What Isherwood and his partner have done is to rearrange the elements of the old Universal films – especially of *The Bride of Frankenstein* – and weave them into a fresh if somewhat arbitrary pattern. Gypsies, a blind man, a female monster, a blackmailing scientist . . . one can tick off the resemblances as they appear, and smile to oneself a little, especially at the stress on the homosexual elements. It might all have been enough, given a much wittier introduction,* to be transformed by James Whale into an agreeably black horror comedy. But James Whale was no longer available, a 200-minute running time was too much, and gleaming TV movie colour provided no atmosphere except to make one purse one's lips at the all-too-visible charnel house aspects of the story. The script cried out to be reshaped and put on film by one man with a touch of vision; *Frankenstein: The True Story* is the work of a committee devoted to routine.

It was not the only TV movie version of the theme. *Dr Franken* appeared in 1979 and simply put the whole plot of the 1931 Universal film in a modern hospital setting, without even a vestige of humour. In *Prototype* (1983) Levinson and Link devised a fashionable anti-establishment fable, with Christopher Plummer stealing back the humanoid he has created when he finds that the Pentagon plans an evil purpose for it. To be fair, some TV companies did show interest in the original story, which was put on tape in England by Thames and later by Yorkshire TV, and in the US by Dan Curtis. Only occasionally in the seventies was the subject approached by theatrical movies, such as *Coma*, in which patients were put into irreversible comas so that their organs could be sold, and the French *Traitement de Choc*, in which itinerant workers are slowly killed by having their vital fluids drained off so that the idle rich can have their lives fortified and extended. In 1985 Franc Roddam made *The Bride*, an attempt to re-use the elements of *The Bride of Frankenstein* in something akin to the original Gothick setting; unfortunately, after a reasonably stimulating creation sequence, with Sting and Quentin Crisp making rather satisfactory stand-ins for Colin Clive and Ernest Thesiger, it sends both its creations off on extended voyages of discovery. The clumsy original is befriended by a know-it-all dwarf and becomes a freak in a travelling circus; the lady falls for a dashing Hussar. Eventually monster and mate have a romantic get-together in Venice, obeying the nauseous dwarf's dictum: 'Follow your heart – it's the key to everything!' Rather more palatable than these pretensions was a simultaneously released teenage frolic called *Weird Science*, in which two young computer experts need only press buttons in order to conjure up a fine female body with the brain of Einstein.

For quite a while the most interesting film treatments of the Frankenstein theme had been the spoofs. In Britain in 1966 the 'Carry On' team had a fair whack at the subject in *Carry On Screaming*, in which Kenneth Williams was the Frankenstein

---

* The gloves, the breadknife, and *Figaro*, from the introduction, are put to use in Mary's story.

CARRY ON SCREAMING (1966). Kenneth Williams as the mad scientist gets into hot water of his own making.

figure, Dr Watt ('Doctor who?' – 'No. Dr Watt. Who's my uncle.'), and his creations were labelled Oddjob I and Oddjob II. On American series television in 1964 the Frankenstein monster was typically disguised as Lurch, the butler, in *The Addams Family*, and as Herman, misshapen paterfamilias of *The Munsters*, who became a much-loved comic figure. But these pale in comparison with Mel Brooks's unusually elegant and inventive *Young Frankenstein*, which emerged in 1975 and won the hearts of all connoisseurs by being lovingly photographed in black and white, in such a way as at least to approach the visual texture of those moody-looking old Universal movies. The actual plot was more akin to *Son of Frankenstein* than anything else, with Gene Wilder returning somewhat timidly to the castle he has inherited, the scene of his grandfather's researches. 'Pardon me, boy,' he enquires, sticking his head out of a train window, 'is this the Transylvania station?' He finds at the ancestral castle a housekeeper whose maniacal laugh frightens the horses and a rolling-eyed hunchback whose hump shifts alarmingly from one side to the other. But at least his reactivated monster has better luck than usual. Though unintentionally scalded and set on fire by the blind hermit, it fortunately catapults the unfrightened little girl right back into the safety of her bed, is allowed to taste the pleasures of sex, and ends up doing a cabaret double act with its creator, in which they sing 'Puttin' On The Ritz'. *Young Frankenstein* is a parody which, apart from its over-length, James Whale would have much

appreciated. And perhaps parody was the only way to go – 1986 promises
Frankenstein's Aunt – for a theme which, when played straight, had long since
exhausted its welcome. There had been in fact no welcome at all, even from the
public, for such extremely gruesome modern variations as *Flesh for Frankenstein*,
produced in the mid-seventies under the aegis of Andy Warhol. This was

In 1964 American television had two rival Frankenstein monster derivatives, both played for laughs. In *The Addams Family* Ted Cassidy was Lurch the butler (left), in *The Munsters* Fred Gwynne was Herman (with Yvonne de Carlo as his lady wife Vampira).

fairground exploitation of the most depraved kind, invented by and for people whose perversion of mind cannot be doubted. It took the theme all too literally during an age which had become all too accustomed to human transplants and for its entertainment preferred such parodies as 1983's *The Man with Two Brains*, a Carl Reiner movie in which Steve Martin plays a surgeon excelling in cranial

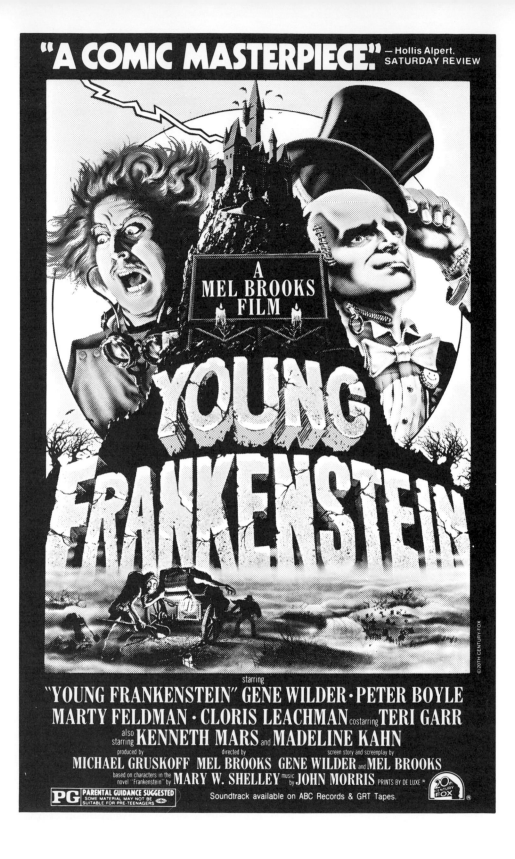

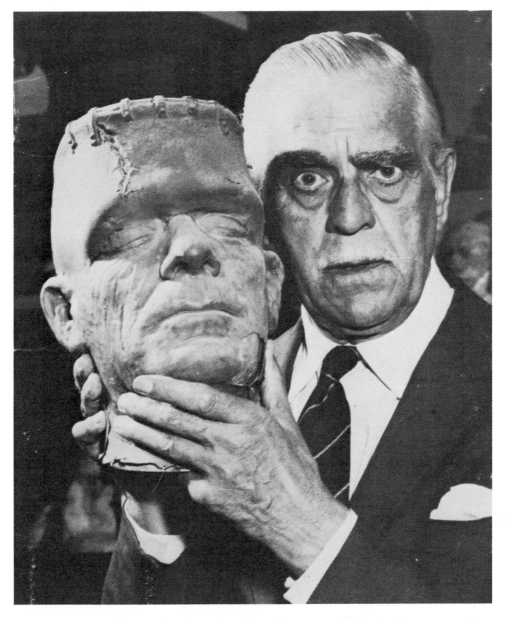

In 1960 Boris Karloff returned to the studio where thirty years earlier he had become a star by playing the Frankenstein monster. Here he radiates his gratitude for 'the best friend I ever had'.

screw-top surgery, tries to find a suitable casing for a disembodied female brain with which he has fallen in love, and fails to trap an elevator murderer who turns out to be America's talk show host Merv Griffin. We've all come a long way since Diodati. Or have we?

Like Dracula, in America at least, the Frankenstein monster has become a cuddly plaything for the younger generation. The unsuspecting visitor to the Universal Studios theme park may find himself being photographed with the monster's arm round the visitor's shoulder, and the monster's great green face grinning into the camera alongside that of the nervous visitor. Women have claimed that the still unnamed creature stimulates their mother instinct. He is known in every country of the world, in all walks of life. As early as 1967 I was offered a drink by Bob Hope at his Palm Springs home, and saw on the bar a plastic representation of the monster, about eighteen inches high. I asked its purpose. 'It's for charity,' said Hope. 'Got a quarter?' I had, and found a slot in the creature's foot. The thing whirred into life; its shoulders hunched; it took one clumsy step after another in my direction. Then, suddenly, its pants fell down and its face went red.

In accepting such ingenious jokes at their face value we should not lose sight of the moving and infinitely pathetic being created by Boris Karloff in the first two Frankenstein talkies, assisted of course by considerable subtlety of intent and accomplishment on the part of James Whale and others behind the camera. Even fifty years later, as these films unspool, any initial sniggering is quickly silenced, for in both script and performance they provide no mere cheap thrill but a dark and powerful statement on the human condition. Karloff's monster is considerably different from Mary Shelley's. But he has kept her novel in circulation (if largely unread) and he stands in his own right as one of the great creations in the history of the cinema.

Chapter 3
THE MENACE OF THE MUMMY

Boris Karloff once made some wise remarks about horror movies:

> Horror means something revolting. Anybody can show you a pailful of innards. But the object of the roles I played is not to turn your stomach, but merely to make your hair stand on end. The descriptive word should have been terror. They are bogey stories, that's all. Bogey stories with the same appeal as thrilling ghost stories or fantastic fairy tales that entertain and enthral children in spite of being so hokey.

Certainly Karloff himself brought sympathy, even tragic stature, to his mad doctors and monsters; viewers were shocked by their plight and relieved when their suffering was over. But he was set his most difficult task when Universal in 1932 decided to film *The Mummy*.

A living 4,000-year-old mummy, all earth mould and dirty bandages, is a pretty loathsome concept, not a creature which even the most ardent horror fan can readily take to his heart. Yet the fascination felt by occasional readers and fairly frequent filmgoers for the details of ancient Egyptian funeral practices is the fulfilment of an immemorial fantasy which still lingers. Sophisticated twentieth-century people, reading about how the Egyptians buried their dead 4,000 years ago, may smile at the pious beliefs involved. Not only the dead person's belongings but the body itself had to be preserved in the tomb for use in the after-life; though what use it could be is difficult to imagine, since the preservation process involved the removal of most of the essential organs, by the unceremonious method of pulling the brains out through the nostrils and everything else out through the other end. The remains were then anointed with soda and spices, the organs were separately wrapped and replaced within the body cavity or separately stored in canopic jars; the whole was wound from head to toe in fine linen bandages. The rich and powerful dead had at least three coffins, one inside the other, and the outermost one sometimes of stone. The complete package was then reverently placed in a secret rock chamber, and food and drink were left for the soul of the departed. Pharaohs were protected in enormous specially erected tombs called pyramids, the work of whole armies of slaves. There were trick entrances, passages leading to dead ends, booby traps, and guards constantly on duty, all to fend off tomb thieves. Yet every precaution was largely in vain. Over

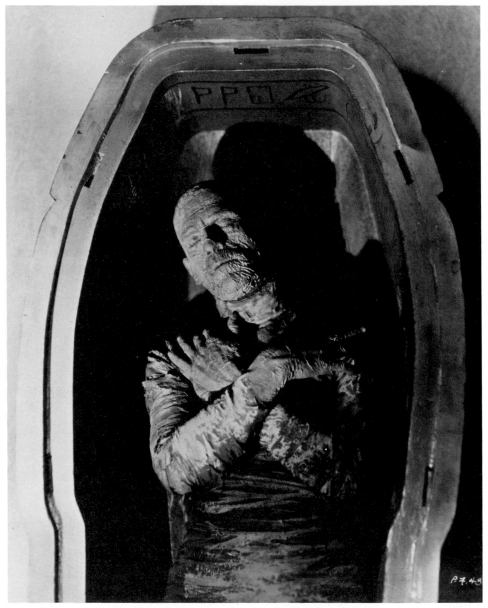

THE MUMMY (1932). The hieroglyphics may be a bit sketchy, but this is the most famous shot in all the mummy films. It is on the screen for about a second, and Karloff is unlikely to have donned the make-up more than once.

the centuries all known tombs were plundered with the exception of that of Tutankhamun, a boy king who died at the age of 18 in 1352 BC. When his relics were discovered in 1922 they sparked off a world-wide interest in Egyptology which Hollywood could not be expected to ignore.

The mummy films were never a major cycle – women generally hated them – but they certainly scared the pants off plenty of boys of my generation, boys who had usually defied the Adults Only rule to huddle in a seat near the front and shudder as the ominous music grew louder, and louder, and louder. The myth which Hollywood had developed for them naturally added a few elements to the known facts. In these films, by incantation or by the imbibing of a rare fluid, the half-preserved shell of a 4,000-year-old man was able to stagger to its feet and take violent revenge on all those who (a) plundered his tomb, (b) buried him alive, or (c) deprived him of his sweetheart. An element of reincarnation usually crept in, with the mummy seeing in a modern young woman the soul of his ancient love and wanting to carry her back with him into eternity. (This was entirely out of place historically, since reincarnation was not among the many curious beliefs of the Egyptians.) And although the mummy invariably moved as stiffly as the Tin Man before Dorothy found the oil can, no small-part actor was ever found who could move fast enough to get out of the way of this foul accumulation of rotten bandages, its one good outstretched arm ending in a clawlike fist.

Nearly a hundred years before the discovery of Tutankhamun there had been stories about mummies, inspired no doubt by the many Egyptian expeditions which brought back specimens to fill glass cases in eager museums around the world. Few will remember that Edgar Allan Poe wrote a mummy story, but he did. In subject matter it accords with his usual mood of melancholy, but 'Some Words with a Mummy' is clearly conceived as a satire. The narrator is awakened from sleep, after a fine meal of Welsh rabbit, by a message from his friend Dr Ponnonner, who invites his attendance at the official opening-up of a mummy at his house that evening at eleven o'clock. The mummy is one of a pair recently brought back from Egypt, and the museum has given its blessing. Unable to resist this remarkable invitation, Poe hastens to his friend's house to find the mummy 'extended upon the dining table'; and what follows includes a splendid technical description of the problems likely to be encountered by specialists in this subject:

> Approaching the table, I saw on it a large box, or case, nearly seven feet long, and perhaps three feet wide, by two feet and a half deep. It was oblong – not coffin-shaped. The material was at first supposed to be the wood of the sycamore (*platanus*), but upon cutting into it, we found it to be pasteboard, or, more properly, *papier-mâché*, composed of papyrus. It was thickly ornamented with paintings, representing funeral scenes, and other mournful subjects – interspersed among which, in every variety of position, were certain series of hieroglyphical characters, intended, no doubt, for the name of the departed. By good luck, Mr Gliddon formed one of our party; and he had no difficulty in translating the letters, which were simply phonetic, and represented the word, *Allamistakeo*.
>
> We had some difficulty in getting this case open without injury; but, having at length accomplished the task, we came to a second, coffin-shaped, and very considerably less in size than the exterior one, but resembling it precisely in every other respect. The interval between the two was filled with resin, which had, in some degree, defaced the colours of the interior box.
>
> Upon opening this latter (which we did quite easily) we arrived at a third case, also coffin-shaped, and varying from the second one in no particular, except in that of its material, which was cedar, and still emitted the peculiar and highly aromatic odour of that wood. Between the second and the third case there was no interval – the one fitting accurately within the other.
>
> Removing the third case, we discovered and took out the body itself. We had

expected to find it, as usual, enveloped in frequent rolls or bandages of linen; but, in place of these, we found a sort of sheath, made of papyrus, and coated with a layer of plaster, thickly gilt and painted. The paintings represented subjects connected with the various supposed duties of the soul, and its presentation to different divinities, with numerous identical human figures, intended, very probably, as portraits of the persons embalmed. Extending from head to foot, was a columnar, or perpendicular inscription, in phonetic hieroglyphics, giving again his name and titles, and the names and titles of his relations.

Around the neck thus ensheathed, was a collar of cylindrical glass beads, diverse in colour, and so arranged as to form images of deities, of the scarabæus, &c., with the winged globe. Around the small of the waist was a similar collar or belt.

Stripping off the papyrus, we found the flesh in excellent preservation, with no perceptible odour. The colour was reddish. The skin was hard, smooth, and glossy. The teeth and hair were in good condition. The eyes (it seemed) had been removed, and glass ones substituted, which were very beautiful, and wonderfully life-like, with the exception of somewhat too determined a stare. The fingers and the nails were brilliantly gilded.

Mr Gliddon was of opinion, from the redness of the epidermis, that the embalm-ment had been effected altogether by asphaltum; but, on scraping the surface with a steel instrument, and throwing into the fire some of the powder thus obtained, the flavour of camphor and other sweet-scented gums became apparent.

We searched the corpse very carefully for the usual openings through which the entrails are extracted, but, to our surprise, we could discover none. No member of the party was at that period aware that entire or unopened mummies are not unfrequently met. The brain it was customary to withdraw through the nose; the intestines through an incision in the side; the body was then shaved, washed and salted; then laid aside for several weeks, when the operation of embalming, properly so called, began.

As no trace of an opening could be found, Doctor Ponnonner was preparing his instruments for dissection, when I observed that it was then past two o'clock. Hereupon it was agreed to postpone the internal examination until the next evening; and we were about to separate for the present, when some one suggested an experiment or two with the Voltaic pile.

The application of electricity to a mummy three or four thousand years old at the least, was an idea, if not very sage, still sufficiently original, and we all caught it at once. About one-tenth in earnest and nine-tenths in jest, we arranged a battery in the doctor's study, and conveyed thither the Egyptian.

After several attempts the mummy is galvanized into life by having an electric current applied to an incision in the tip of its nose.

Morally and physically – figuratively and literally – was the effect electric. In the first place, the corpse opened its eyes, and winked very rapidly for several minutes, as does Mr Barnes in the pantomime; in the second place, it sneezed; in the third, it sat up on end; in the fourth, it shook its fist in Doctor Ponnonner's face; in the fifth, turning to Messieurs Gliddon and Buckingham, it addressed them, in very capital Egyptian, thus –

'I must say, gentlemen, that I am as much surprised as I am mortified, at your behaviour. Of Doctor Ponnonner nothing better was to be expected. He is a poor little fat fool who *knows* no better. I pity and forgive him. But you, Mr Gliddon – and you, Silk – who have travelled and resided in Egypt until one might imagine you to the manner born – you, I say, who have been so much among us that you speak Egyptian fully as well, I think, as you write your mother tongue – you, whom I have always been led to regard as the firm friend of the mummies – I really did anticipate more gentlemanly conduct from *you*. What am I to think of your standing quietly by and seeing me thus unhandsomely used? What am I to suppose by your permitting Tom, Dick, and Harry to strip me of my coffins, and my clothes, in this wretchedly cold climate? In what light (to come to the point) am I to regard your aiding and abetting that miserable little villain, Doctor Ponnonner, in pulling me by the nose?'

The consequent conversation of the scientists with the Mummy is designed to point up the superiority of ancient Egyptian civilization to that of America in the nineteenth century; but in the process it becomes clear that technically this is not a mummy at all, but a victim of the fate which Poe feared most: burial alive.

It will be readily understood that Mr Gliddon's discourse turned chiefly upon the vast benefits accruing to science from the unrolling and disembowelling of mummies; apologising, upon this score, for any disturbance that might have been occasioned *him*, in particular, the individual mummy called Allamistakeo; and concluding with a mere hint (for it could scarcely be considered more) that, as these little matters were now explained, it might be as well to proceed with the investigation intended. Here Doctor Ponnonner made ready his instruments.

In regard to the latter suggestions of the orator, it appears that Allamistakeo had certain scruples of conscience, the nature of which I did not distinctly learn; but he expressed himself satisfied with the apologies tendered, and, getting down from the table, shook hands with the company all round.

When this ceremony was at an end, we immediately busied ourselves in repairing the damages which our subject had sustained from the scalpel. We sewed up the wound in his temple, bandaged his foot, and applied a square inch of black plaster to the tip of his nose.

It was now observed that the Count (this was the title, it seems, of Allamistakeo) had a slight fit of shivering – no doubt from the cold. The doctor immediately repaired to his wardrobe, and soon returned with a black dress coat, made in Jennings' best manner, a pair of sky-blue plaid pantaloons, with straps, a pink gingham *chemise*, a flapped vest of brocade, a white sack overcoat, a walking cane with a hook, a hat with no brim, patent-leather boots, straw-coloured kid gloves, an eye-glass, a pair of whiskers, and a water-fall cravat. Owing to the disparity of size between the Count and the doctor (the proportion being as two to one), there was some little difficulty in adjusting these habiliments upon the person of the Egyptian; but when all was arranged, he might have been said to be dressed. Mr Gliddon, therefore, gave him his arm, and led him to a comfortable chair by the fire, while the doctor rang the bell upon the spot and ordered a supply of cigars and wine.

The conversation soon grew animated. Much curiosity was, of course, expressed in regard to the somewhat remarkable fact of Allamistakeo's still remaining alive.

'I should have thought,' observed Mr Buckingham, 'that it is high time you were dead.'

'Why,' replied the Count, very much astonished, 'I am little more than seven hundred years old! My father lived a thousand, and was by no means in his dotage when he died.'

Here ensued a brisk series of questions and computations, by means of which it became evident that the antiquity of the Mummy had been grossly misjudged. It had been five thousand and fifty years, and some months, since he had been consigned to the catacombs at Eleithias.

'But my remark,' resumed Mr Buckingham, 'had no reference to your age at the period of interment (I am willing to grant, in fact, that you are still a young man); and

my allusion was to the immensity of time during which, by your own showing, you
must have been done up in asphaltum.'

'In what?' said the Count.

In asphaltum,' persisted Mr B.

'Ah, yes; I have some faint notion of what you mean; it might be made to answer,
no doubt – but in my time we employed scarcely anything else than the Bichloride of
Mercury.'

'But what we are especially at a loss to understand,' said Doctor Ponnonner, 'is,
how it happens that, having been dead and buried in Egypt five thousand years ago,
you are here to-day all alive, and looking so delightfully well.'

'Had I been, as you say, *dead*,' replied the Count, 'it is more than probable that dead
I should still be; for I perceive you are yet in the infancy of galvanism, and cannot
accomplish with it what was a common thing among us in the old days. But the fact
is, I fell into catalepsy, and it was considered by my best friends that I was either dead
or should be; they accordingly embalmed me at once – I presume you are aware of the
chief principle of the embalming process?'

'Why, not altogether.'

'Ah, I perceive – a deplorable condition of ignorance! Well, I cannot enter into
details just now; but it is necessary to explain that to embalm (properly speaking) in
Egypt, was to arrest indefinitely *all* the animal functions subjected to the process. I use
the word "animal" in its widest sense, as including the physical not more than the
moral and *vital* being. I repeat that the leading principle of embalmment consisted,
with us, in the immediately arresting, and holding in perpetual abeyance, *all* the
animal functions subjected to the process. To be brief, in whatever condition the
individual was, at the period of embalmment, in that condition he remained. Now, as
it is my good fortune to be of the blood of the Scarabæus, I was embalmed *alive*, as
you see me at present.'

'Some Words with a Mummy' is not to be read for thrills. As an intellectual *jeu
d'esprit*, however, it stimulated a literary interest in the activities of mummies, one
which was taken up by Théophile Gautier (1811–72) in a once-popular story with
a more firmly defined plot. The title, 'The Mummy's Foot', may strike a chill
note. The story, however, is not one of horror, but of whimsy. The narrator buys
from an antique shop a mildly grisly object alleged to be the severed foot of the
Princess Hermonthis, daughter of an ancient Pharaoh. That night, having put the
foot to use as a paperweight, he is roused from sleep by the odour of myrrh, a
slight headache, and a feeling of expectation . . .

My eyes accidentally fell upon the desk where I had placed the foot of the Princess
Hermonthis.

Instead of remaining quiet – as behoved a foot which had been embalmed for four
thousand years – it commenced to act in a nervous manner; contracted itself, and
leaped over the papers like a startled frog. One would have imagined that it had
suddenly been brought into contact with a galvanic battery: I could distinctly hear the
dry sound made by its little heel, hard as the hoof of a gazelle.

Suddenly I saw the folds of my bed-curtain stir, and heard a bumping sound, like
that caused by some person hopping on one foot across the floor. I must confess I
became alternately hot and cold; that I felt a strange wind chill my back.

The bed-curtains opened and I beheld the strangest figure imaginable before me.

It was a young girl of a very deep coffee-brown complexion, like the bayadere
Amani, and possessing the purest Egyptian type of perfect beauty: her eyes were
almond shaped and oblique, with eyebrows so black that they seemed blue; her nose

was exquisitely chiselled, almost Greek in its delicacy of outline; and she might indeed have been taken for a Corinthian statue of bronze but for the prominence of her cheekbones and the slightly African fullness of her lips.

Her arms, slender and spindle-shaped, like those of very young girls, were encircled by a peculiar kind of metal bands and bracelets of glass beads; her hair was all twisted into little cords, and she wore upon her bosom a little idol-figure of green paste, bearing a whip with seven lashes, which proved it to be an image of Isis. Her brow was adorned with a shining plate of gold, and a few traces of paint relieved the coppery tint of her cheeks.

As for her costume, it was very odd indeed.

Fancy a *pagne* or skirt all formed of little strips of material bedizened with red and black hieroglyphics, stiffened with bitumen, and apparently belonging to a freshly unbandaged mummy.

The lady has of course come to seek her missing foot, with which she has a touching conversation.

'Princess,' I then exclaimed, 'I never retained anybody's foot unjustly; – even though you have not got the five louis which it cost me, I present it to you gladly: I should feel unutterably wretched to think that I were the cause of so amiable a person as the Princess Hermonthis being lame.'

She turned a look of deepest gratitude upon me; and her eyes shone with bluish gleams of light.

She took her foot – which surrendered itself willingly this time – like a woman about to put on her little shoe, and adjusted it to her leg with much skill.

This operation over, she took a few steps about the room, as though to assure herself that she was really no longer lame.

'Ah, how pleased my father will be! – he who was so unhappy because of my mutilation, and who from the moment of my birth set a whole nation at work to hollow me out a tomb so deep that he might preserve me intact until that last day when souls must be weighed in the balance of Amenthi! Come with me to my father; – he will receive you kindly; for you have given me back my foot.'

The princess then takes our hero on a fantastic journey by sky and sea, back to the mountain-tombs of ancient Egypt:

We traversed corridors hewn through the living rock: their walls, covered with hieroglyphics and paintings of allegorical processions, might well have occupied thousands of arms for thousands of years in their formation; – these corridors, of interminable length, opened into square chambers, in the midst of which pits had been contrived, through which we descended by cramp-irons or spiral stair-ways; – these pits again conducted us into other chambers, opening into other corridors, likewise decorated with painted sparrow-hawks, serpents coiled in circles.

At last we found ourselves in a hall so vast, so enormous, so immeasurable, that the eye could not reach its limits; files of monstrous columns stretched far out of sight on every side, between which winked livid stars of yellowish flame.

The Princess Hermonthis still held my hand, and graciously saluted the mummies of her acquaintance.

My eyes became accustomed to the dim twilight, and objects became discernible.

I beheld the kings of the subterranean races seated upon thrones – grand old men, though dry, withered, wrinkled like parchment, and blackened with naphtha and bitumen – all wearing *pshents* of gold, and breastplates and gorgets glittering with precious stones; their eyes immovably fixed like the eyes of sphinxes, and their long beards whitened by the snow of centuries. Behind them stood their peoples, in the stiff and constrained posture enjoined by Egyptian art, all eternally preserving the attitude prescribed by the hieratic code. Behind these nations, the cats, ibises, and crocodiles contemporary with them – rendered monstrous of aspect by their swathing bands – mewed, flapped their wings, or extended their jaws in a saurian giggle . . .

After permitting me to gaze upon this bewildering spectacle a few moments, the Princess Hermonthis presented me to her father Pharaoh, who favoured me with a most gracious nod.

'I have found my foot again! – I have found my foot!' cried the Princess, clapping her little hands together with every sign of frantic joy. 'It was this gentleman who restored it to me.'. . .

'By Oms, the dog of Hell, and Tmei, daughter of the Sun and of Truth! this is a brave and worthy lad!' explained Pharaoh, pointing to me with his sceptre, which was terminated with a lotus-flower. 'What recompense do you desire?'

Filled with that daring inspired by dreams in which nothing seems impossible, I asked him for the hand of the Princess Hermonthis; – the hand seemed to me a very proper antithetic recompense for the foot.

Pharaoh opened wide his great eyes of glass in astonishment at my witty request.

'What country do you come from? and what is your age?'

'I am a Frenchman; and I am twenty-seven years old, venerable Pharaoh.'

'– Twenty-seven years old! and he wishes to espouse the Princess Hermonthis who is thirty centuries old!' cried out at once all the Thrones and all the Circles of Nations.

Only Hermonthis herself did not seem to think my request unreasonable.

'If you were even only two thousand years old,' replied the ancient King, 'I would willingly give you the Princess; but the disproportion is too great; and, besides, we must give our daughters husbands who will last well; you do not know how to preserve yourselves any longer; even those who died only fifteen centuries ago are already no more than a handful of dust; – behold! my flesh is solid as basalt; my bones are bars of steel!

'I shall be present on the last day of the world, with the same body and the same features which I had during my lifetime; my daughter Hermonthis will last longer than a statue of bronze.

'Then the last particles of your dust will have been scattered abroad by the winds; and even Isis herself, who was able to find the atoms of Osiris, would scarce be able to recompose your being.

'See how vigorous I yet remain, and how mighty is my grasp,' he added, shaking my hand in the English fashion with a strength that buried my rings in the flesh of my fingers.

He squeezed me so hard that I awoke, and found my friend Alfred shaking me by the arm to make me get up.

'O you everlasting sleeper! – must I have you carried out into the middle of the street, and fireworks exploded in your ears? It is after noon; don't you recollect your promise to take me with you to see M. Aguado's Spanish pictures?'

'God! I forgot all, all about it,' I answered, dressing myself hurriedly; 'we will go there at once; I have the permit lying on my desk.'

I started to find it; – but fancy my astonishment when I beheld, instead of the mummy's foot I had purchased the evening before, the little green paste idol left in its place by the Princess Hermonthis!

This charming, scholarly story is not only interesting in itself. It also provides an early example of what in later years became a favourite Hollywood trick. A fantastic story proves to be only a dream; and yet, just as the tale is being rounded off, we are handed some piece of evidence to prove that it can't have been. The scarf in *Portrait of Jennie*, the coin in *Miracle in the Rain* are familiar examples to filmgoers.

The time was coming when mummies would be seen as figures of horror. Arthur Conan Doyle wrote short stories of many kinds. Fifty-six of them concerned Sherlock Holmes, who explained everything by scientific deduction; but Conan Doyle was always very interested in the occult, and during the 1890s he wrote two stories about mummies. 'Lot No. 249' is the less interesting of them,

Sir Arthur Conan Doyle, whose short stories may have had more to do with the mummy cult than has hitherto been suspected.

but by far the more frightening. It concerns a group of Oxford students who find it difficult to conceal their dislike of a sinister specialist in Oriental languages, one Edward Bellingham, who keeps a mummy in rooms crammed with other examples of his Egyptian interests:

In the centre of this singular chamber was a large, square table, littered with papers, bottles and the dried leaves of some graceful, palm-like plant. These varied objects had all been heaped together in order to make room for a mummy case, which had been conveyed from the wall, as was evident from the gap there, and laid across the front of the table. The mummy itself, a horrid, black, withered thing, like a charred head on a gnarled bush, was lying half out of the case, with its claw-like hand and bony forearm resting upon the table. Propped up against the sarcophagus was an old, yellow scroll of papyrus, and in front of it, in a wooden armchair, sat the owner of the room, his head thrown back, his widely opened eyes directed in a horrified stare to the crocodile above him, and his blue, thick lips puffing loudly with every expiration.

'My God! he's dying!' cried Monkhouse Lee, distractedly.

'What the deuce can have frightened him so?' I asked.

'It's the mummy.'

'The mummy? How, then?'

'I don't know. It's beastly and morbid. I wish he would drop it. It's the second fright he has given me. It was the same last winter. I found him just like this, with that horrid thing in front of him.'

'What does he want with the mummy, then?'

'Oh, he's a crank, you know. It's his hobby. He knows more about these things than any man in England. But I wish he wouldn't! Ah, he's beginning to come to.'

A faint tinge of colour had begun to steal back into Bellingham's ghastly cheeks, and his eyelids shivered like a sail after a calm. He clasped and unclasped his hands, drew a long, thin breath between his teeth, and suddenly jerking up his head, threw a glance of recognition around him. As his eyes fell upon the mummy, he sprang off the sofa, seized the roll of papyrus, thrust it into a drawer, turned the key, and then staggered back on to the sofa.

'What's up?' he asked. 'What do you chaps want?'

'You've been shrieking out and making no end of a fuss,' said Monkhouse Lee. 'If our neighbour here from above hadn't come down, I'm sure I don't know what I should have done with you.'. . .

'How long was it from the time you ran down, until I came to my senses?'

'Not long. Some four or five minutes.'

'I thought it could not be very long,' said Bellingham, drawing a long breath. 'But what a strange thing unconsciousness is! There is no measurement to it. I could not tell from my own sensations if it were seconds or weeks. Now that gentleman on the table was packed up in the days of the eleventh dynasty, some forty centuries ago, and yet if he could find his tongue, he would tell us that this lapse of time has been but a closing of the eyes and a reopening of them. He is a singularly fine mummy, Smith.'

Smith stepped over to the table and looked down with a professional eye at the black and twisted form in front of him. The features, though horribly discoloured, were perfect, and two little nut-like eyes still lurked in the depths of the black, hollow sockets. The blotched skin was drawn tightly from bone to bone, and a tangled wrap of black, coarse hair fell over the ears. Two thin teeth, like those of a rat, overlay the shrivelled lower lip. In its crouching position, with bent joints and craned head, there was a suggestion of energy about the horrid thing which made Smith's gorge rise. The gaunt ribs, with their parchment-like covering, were exposed, and the sunken, leaden-hued abdomen, with the long slit where the embalmer had left his mark; but the lower limbs were wrapped round with coarse, yellow bandages. A number of little clove-like pieces of myrrh and of cassia were sprinkled over the body, and lay scattered on the inside of the case.

'I don't know his name,' said Bellingham, passing his hand over the shrivelled head. 'You see the outer sarcophagus with the inscriptions is missing. Lot 249 is all the title he has now. You see it printed on his case. That was his number in the auction at which I picked him up.'

'He has been a very pretty sort of fellow in his day,' remarked Abercrombie Smith.

'He has been a giant. His mummy is six feet seven in length, and that would be a giant over there, they were never a very robust race. Feel these great, knotted bones, too. He would be a nasty fellow to tackle.'

'Perhaps these very hands helped to build the stones into the pyramids,' suggested Monkhouse Lee, looking down with disgust in his eyes at the crooked, unclean talons.

'No fear. This fellow has been pickled in natron, and looked after in the most approved style. They did not serve hodsmen in that fashion. Salt or bitumen was enough for them. It has been calculated that this sort of thing cost about seven hundred and thirty pounds in our money. Our friend was a noble at the least. What do you make of that small inscription near his feet, Smith?'

'I told you that I know no Eastern tongue.'

'Ah, so you did. It is the name of the embalmer, I take it. A very conscientious worker he must have been. I wonder how many modern works will survive four thousand years?'

Subsequently, strange things begin to happen. Lee is found in the river half-drowned, having been picked up and thrown in by some strange giant which he can barely describe. Smith, who has been astonished when calling on Bellingham to find the mummy out of its case and missing, but back in place a few moments later, has an equally unnerving experience one evening when striding down a dark country lane to call on a friend:

It was a lonely and little-frequented road which led to his friend's house. Early as it was, Smith did not meet a single soul upon his way. He walked briskly along until he came to the avenue gate, which opened into the long, gravel drive leading up to Farlingford. In front of him he could see the cosy, red light of the windows glimmering through the foliage. He stood with his hand upon the iron latch of the swinging gate, and he glanced back at the road along which he had come. Something was coming swiftly down it.

It moved in the shadow of the hedge, silently and furtively, a dark, crouching figure, dimly visible against the black background. Even as he gazed back at it, it had lessened its distance by twenty paces, and was fast closing upon him. Out of the darkness he had a glimpse of a scraggy neck, and of two eyes that will ever haunt him in his dreams. He turned, and with a cry of terror he ran for his life up the avenue. There were the red lights, the signals of safety, almost within a stone's-throw of him. He was a famous runner, but never had he run as he ran that night.

The heavy gate had swung into place behind him but he heard it dash open again before his pursuer. As he rushed madly and wildly through the night, he could hear a swift, dry patter behind him, and could see, as he threw back a glance, that this horror was bounding like a tiger at his heels, with blazing eyes and one stringy arm out-thrown. Thank God, the door was ajar. He could see the thin bar of light which shot from the lamp in the hall. Nearer yet sounded the clatter from behind. He heard a hoarse gurgling at his very shoulder. With a shriek he flung himself against the door, slammed and bolted it behind him, and sank half-fainting on to the hall chair.

Even from the room in which his friend's party is held the mummy can be seen: 'a man rather thin, apparently, and very very tall.' And after a glass of wine Smith is able to give his view as to what has been happening:

'Well, it must be a little vague in detail, but the main points seem to me to be clear enough. This fellow Bellingham, in his Eastern studies, has got hold of some infernal secret by which a mummy – or possibly only this particular mummy – can be temporarily brought to life. He was trying this disgusting business on the night when he fainted. No doubt the sight of the creature moving had shaken his nerve, even though he had expected it. You remember that almost the first words he said were to call out upon himself as a fool. Well, he got more hardened afterwards, and carried the matter through without fainting. The vitality which he could put into it was evidently only a passing thing, for I have seen it continually in its case as dead as this table. He has some elaborate process, I fancy, by which he brings the thing to pass. Having done it, he naturally bethought him that he might use the creature as an agent. It has intelligence and it has strength. For some purpose he took Lee into his confidence; but Lee, like a decent Christian, would have nothing to do with such a business. Then they had a row, and Lee vowed that he would tell his sister of Bellingham's true character. Bellingham's game was to prevent him, and he nearly managed it, by setting this creature of his on his track. He had already tried its powers upon another man – Norton – towards whom he had a grudge. It is the merest chance that he has not two murders upon his soul. Then, when I taxed him with the matter, he had the strongest reasons for wishing to get me out of the way before I could convey my knowledge to anyone else. He got his chance when I went out, for he knew my habits and where I was bound for. I have had a narrow shave, Peterson, and it is mere luck you didn't find me on your doorstep in the morning. I'm not a nervous man as a rule, and I never thought to have the fear of death put upon me as it was to-night.'

Smith is a man for direct action, and just as soon as he feels recovered, he goes to call on Bellingham:

Smith ascended the stairs, opened Bellingham's door and stepped in. Bellingham was seated behind his table, writing. Beside him, among his litter of strange possessions, towered the mummy case, with its sale number 249 still stuck upon its front, and its hideous occupant stiff and stark within it. Smith looked very deliberately round him, closed the door, and then, stepping across to the fireplace, struck a match and set the fire alight. Bellingham sat staring, with amazement and rage upon his bloated face.
    'Well, really now, you make yourself at home,' he gasped.
    Smith sat himself deliberately down, placing his watch upon the table, drew out his pistol, cocked it, and laid it in his lap. Then he took the long amputating knife from his bosom, and threw it down in front of Bellingham.
    'Now, then,' said he, 'just get to work and cut up that mummy.' . . .
    'Why should I destroy my own property? It is a valuable mummy.'
    'You must cut it up, and you must burn it.'
    'I will do no such thing.'
    'Four minutes are gone.'
    Smith took up the pistol and he looked towards Bellingham with an inexorable face. As the second-hand stole round, he raised his hand, and the finger twitched upon the trigger.
    'There! there! I'll do it!' screamed Bellingham.
    In frantic haste he caught up the knife and hacked at the figure of the mummy, ever

glancing round to see the eye and the weapon of his terrible visitor bent upon him. The creature crackled and snapped under every stab of the keen blade. A thick, yellow dust rose up from it. Spices and dried essences rained down upon the floor. Suddenly, with a rending crack, its backbone snapped asunder, and it fell, a brown heap of sprawling limbs, upon the floor.

'Now into the fire!' said Smith.

The flames leaped and roared as the dried and tinder-like debris was piled upon it. The little room was like the stoke-hole of a steamer and the sweat ran down the faces of the two men; but still the one stooped and worked, while the other sat watching him with a set face. A thick, fat smoke oozed out from the fire, and a heavy smell of burned resin and singed hair filled the air. In a quarter of an hour a few charred and brittle sticks were all that was left of Lot No. 249.

Not a particularly good story: as in some of the mummy films which followed, the monster is insufficiently active: and, as the author admits, the details of its revivification are vague indeed. Still, Conan Doyle had formulated the idea of a silently avenging mummy under someone else's control, and that was to prove very useful indeed. ★ Meanwhile, in the same year, he produced most of the other elements of the modern myth in 'The Ring of Thoth', a story which bears such a strong relationship to the 1932 film that its lack of a credit is quite shameful.

'The Ring of Thoth' is the story of John Vansittart Smith, an Egyptologist, who one evening in the Louvre museum in Paris is struck by the unusual appearance of one of the attendants:

The regular statuesque features, broad brow, well-rounded chin, and dusky complexion were the exact counterpart of the innumerable statues, mummy-cases, and pictures which adorned the walls of the apartment. The thing was beyond all coincidence. The man must be an Egyptian. The national angularity of the shoulders and narrowness of the hips were alone sufficient to identify him.

John Vansittart Smith shuffled towards the attendant with some intention of addressing him. He was not light of touch in conversation, and found it difficult to strike the happy mean between the brusqueness of the superior and the geniality of the equal. As he came nearer, the man presented his side face to him, but kept his gaze still bent upon his work. Vansittart Smith, fixing his eyes upon the fellow's skin, was conscious of a sudden impression that there was something inhuman and preternatural about its appearance. Over the temple and cheek-bone it was as glazed and as shiny as varnished parchment. There was no suggestion of pores. One could not fancy a drop of moisture upon that arid surface. From brow to chin, however, it was cross-hatched by a million delicate wrinkles, which shot and interlaced as though Nature in some Maori mood had tried how wild and intricate a pattern she could devise.

'Où est la collection de Memphis?' asked the student, with the awkward air of a man who is devising a question merely for the purpose of opening a conversation.

'C'est là,' replied the man brusquely, nodding his head at the other side of the room.

'Vous êtes un Egyptien, n'est-ce pas?' asked the Englishman.

The attendant looked up and turned his strange dark eyes upon his questioner. They were vitreous, with a misty dry shininess, such as Smith had never seen in a human head before. As he gazed into them he saw some strong emotion gather in their depths, which rose and deepened until it broke into a look of something akin both to horror and to hatred.

★ However, a *running* mummy was a concept quickly discarded.

Sitting quietly in a corner as he furthers his studies, Vansittart Smith falls asleep among the mummies, and his presence is not noticed at closing time. Only the chimes of midnight from Notre Dame rouse him; he chuckles at the realization of his curious misfortune. And then, down the long vista of rooms, his eyes fall upon the yellow glare of a distant lamp.

John Vansittart Smith sat up on his chair with his nerves all on edge. The light was advancing slowly towards him, pausing from time to time, and then coming jerkily onwards. The bearer moved noiselessly. In the utter silence there was no suspicion of the pat of a footfall. An idea of robbers entered the Englishman's head. He snuggled up farther into the corner. The light was two rooms off. Now it was in the next chamber, and still there was no sound. With something approaching to a thrill of fear the student observed a face, floating in the air as it were, behind the flare of the lamp. The figure was wrapped in shadow, but the light fell full upon the strange, eager face. There was no mistaking the metallic, glistening eyes and the cadaverous skin. It was the attendant with whom he had conversed.

Vansittart Smith's first impulse was to come forward and address him. A few words of explanation would set the matter clear, and lead doubtless to his being conducted to some side-door from which he might make his way to his hotel. As the man entered the chamber, however, there was something so stealthy in his movements, and so furtive in his expression, that the Englishman altered his intention. This was clearly no ordinary official walking the rounds. The fellow wore felt-soled slippers, stepped with a rising chest, and glanced quickly from left to right, while his hurried, gasping breathing thrilled the flame of his lamp. Vansittart Smith crouched silently back into the corner and watched him keenly, convinced that his errand was one of secret and probably sinister import.

There was no hesitation in the other's movements. He stepped lightly and swiftly across to one of the great cases, and, drawing a key from his pocket, he unlocked it. From the upper shelf he pulled down a mummy, which he bore away with him, and laid it with much care and solicitude upon the ground. By it he placed his lamp, and then squatting down beside it in Eastern fashion he began with long, quivering fingers to undo the cerecloths and bandages which girt it round. As the crackling rolls of linen peeled off one after the other, a strong aromatic odour filled the chamber, and fragments of scented wood and of spices pattered down upon the marble floor.

It was clear to John Vansittart Smith that this mummy had never been unswathed before. The operation interested him keenly. He thrilled all over with curiosity, and his bird-like head protruded farther and farther from behind the door. When, however, the last roll had been removed from the four-thousand-year-old head, it was all that he could do to stifle an outcry of amazement. First, a cascade of long, black, glossy tresses poured over the workman's hands and arms. A second turn of the bandage revealed a low, white forehead, with a pair of delicately arched eyebrows. A third uncovered a pair of bright, deeply fringed eyes, and a straight, well-cut nose, while a fourth and last showed a sweet, full, sensitive mouth, and a beautifully curved chin. The whole face was one of extraordinary loveliness, save for the one blemish that in the centre of the forehead there was a single irregular, coffee-coloured splotch. It was a triumph of the embalmer's art. Vansittart Smith's eyes grew larger and larger as he gazed upon it, and he chirruped in his throat with satisfaction.

Its effect upon the Egyptologist was as nothing, however, compared with that which it produced upon the strange attendant. He threw his hands up into the air, burst into a harsh clatter of words, and then, hurling himself down upon the ground beside the mummy, he threw his arms round her, and kissed her repeatedly upon the lips and brow. 'Ma petite!' he groaned in French. 'Ma pauvre petite!' His voice broke with emotion, and his innumerable wrinkles quivered and writhed, but the student observed in the lamp-light that his shining eyes were still dry and tearless as two beads of steel. For some minutes he lay, with a twitching face, crooning and moaning over the beautiful head. Then he broke into a sudden smile, said some words in an unknown tongue, and sprang to his feet with the vigorous air of one who has braced himself for an effort.

In the centre of the room there was a large, circular case which contained, as the student had frequently remarked, a magnificent collection of early Egyptian rings and precious stones. To this the attendant strode, and, unlocking it, threw it open. On the ledge at the side he placed his lamp, and beside it a small, earthenware jar which he had drawn from his pocket. He then took a handful of rings from the case, and with a most serious and anxious face he proceeded to smear each in turn with some liquid substance from the earthen pot, holding them to the light as he did so. He was clearly disappointed with the first lot, for he threw them petulantly back into the case and drew out some more. One of these, a massive ring with a large crystal set in it, he seized and eagerly tested with the contents of the jar. Instantly he uttered a cry of joy, and threw out his arms in a wild gesture which upset the pot and set the liquid streaming across the floor to the very feet of the Englishman. The attendant drew a red handkerchief from his bosom, and, mopping up the mess, he followed it into the corner, where in a moment he found himself face to face with his observer.

'Excuse me,' said John Vansittart Smith, with all imaginable politeness; 'I have been unfortunate enough to fall asleep behind this door.'

'And you have been watching me?' the other asked in English, with a most venomous look on his corpse-like face.

The student was a man of veracity. 'I confess,' said he, 'that I have noticed your movements, and that they have aroused my curiosity and interest in the highest degree.'

The man drew a long, flamboyant-bladed knife from his bosom. 'You have had a very narrow escape,' he said; 'had I seen you ten minutes ago, I should have driven this through your heart. As it is, if you touch me or interfere with me in any way you are a dead man.'

'I have no wish to interfere with you,' the student answered. 'My presence here is entirely accidental. All I ask is that you will have the extreme kindness to show me out through some side-door.' He spoke with great suavity, for the man was still pressing the tip of his dagger against the palm of his left hand, as though to assure himself of its sharpness, while his face preserved its malignant expression.

'If I thought –' said he. 'But no, perhaps it is as well. What is your name?'

The Englishman gave it.

'Vansittart Smith,' the other repeated. 'Are you the same Vansittart Smith who gave a paper in London upon El Kab? I saw a report of it. Your knowledge of the subject is contemptible.'

'Sir!' cried the Egyptologist.

'Yet it is superior to that of many who make even greater pretensions. The whole keystone of our old life in Egypt was not the inscriptions or monuments of which you make so much, but was our hermetic philosophy and mystic knowledge of which you say little or nothing.'

'Our old life!' repeated the scholar, wide-eyed; and then suddenly, 'Good God, look at the mummy's face!'

The strange man turned and flashed his light upon the dead woman, uttering a long, doleful cry as he did so. The action of the air had already undone all the art of the embalmer. The skin had fallen away, the eyes had sunk inwards, the discoloured lips had writhed away from the yellow teeth, and the broken mark upon the forehead alone showed that it was indeed the same face which had shown such youth and beauty a few short minutes before.

Faced with this catastrophe, the strange attendant becomes more amenable and confesses all.

'There may be design in this,' he said, still speaking excellent English. 'It may be decreed that I should leave some account behind as a warning to all rash mortals who would set their wits up against workings of Nature. I leave it with you. Make such use as you will of it. I speak to you now with my feet upon the threshold of the other world.

'I am, as you surmised, an Egyptian – not one of the down-trodden race of slaves who now inhabit the Delta of the Nile, but a survivor of that fiercer and harder people who tamed the Hebrew, drove the Ethiopian back into the southern deserts, and built those mighty works which have been the envy and the wonder of all after generations. It was in the reign of Tuthmosis, sixteen hundred years before the birth of Christ, that I first saw the light. You shrink away from me. Wait, and you will see that I am more to be pitied than to be feared.

His name, he says, is Sosra, and he was trained in mystic arts as well as medicine.

It is useless that I should recount my researches. You would scarce comprehend them if I did. They were carried out partly upon animals, partly upon slaves, and partly on myself. Suffice it that their result was to furnish me with a substance which, when injected into the blood, would endow the body with strength to resist the effects of time, of violence, or of disease. It would not indeed confer immortality, but its potency would endure for many thousands of years. I used it upon a cat, and afterwards drugged the creature with the most deadly poisons. That cat is alive in Lower Egypt at the present moment.

Sosra falls passionately in love with the governor's daughter, who falls ill and dies of the plague. Sosra would like nothing better than to join her, but unfortunately he has taken his own elixir and will live indefinitely. So has his colleague Parmes, Prince of Thoth, his rival for the princess's hand; but Parmes has discovered an antidote. It is concealed within his ring, and contains a secret ingredient he thinks Sosra will never discover. Parmes takes the antidote and dies; the frantic Sosra spends the next four centuries searching for the mystic ring. Eventually he discovers that Parmes had buried it with his beloved. He traces the princess's mummy to Paris and takes the job of attendant . . .

'Such is my story, Mr Vansittart Smith. I need not say more to a man of your perception. By a strange chance you have this night looked upon the face of the woman whom I loved in those far-off days. There were many rings with crystals in the case, and I had to test for the platinum to be sure of the one which I wanted. A glance at the crystal has shown me that the liquid is indeed within it, and that I shall at last be able to shake off that accursed health which has been worse to me than the foulest disease. I have nothing more to say to you. I have unburdened myself. You may tell my story or you may withhold it at your pleasure. The choice rests with you. I owe you some amends, for you have had a narrow escape of your life this night. I was a desperate man, and not to be baulked in my purpose. Had I seen you before the thing was done, I might have put it beyond your power to oppose me or to raise an alarm. This is the door. It leads into the Rue de Rivoli. Good night.'

The Englishman glanced back. For a moment the lean figure of Sosra the Egyptian stood framed in the narrow doorway. The next the door had slammed, and the heavy rasping of a bolt broke on the silent night.

It was on the second day after his return to London that Mr John Vansittart Smith saw the following concise narrative in the Paris correspondence of *The Times*:—

Curious Occurrence in the Louvre. – Yesterday morning a strange discovery was made in the principal Eastern chamber. The *ouvriers* who are employed to clean out the rooms in the morning found one of the attendants lying dead upon the floor with his arms round one of the mummies. So close was his embrace that it was only with the utmost difficulty that they were separated. One of the cases containing valuable rings had been opened and rifled. The authorities are of opinion that the man was bearing away the mummy with some idea of selling it to a private collector, but that he was struck down in the very act by long-standing disease of the heart. It is said that he was a man of uncertain age and eccentric habits, without any living relations to mourn over his dramatic and untimely end.

If 'The Ring of Thoth', with its theme of love across the centuries, was indeed plagiarized for Universal's film *The Mummy*, the process took forty years. Meanwhile mummies had appeared occasionally in films right from the turn of the century. A couple of the trick films of George Méliès involved sarcophagi. In 1912 a sensational thriller called *The Vengeance of Egypt* apparently struck the note which was to keep mummies in gainful employment, and this was followed in 1915 by *The Avenging Hand*. Both are now lost. Ernst Lubitsch's 1918 German film, *The Eyes of the Mummy*, is however a rather different proposition. Neither typical Lubitsch nor genuine mummy, it creakily introduces us to a young English painter in Egypt who is taken to a 'haunted tomb' and shown a mummy's eyes apparently blinking. The eyes actually belong to a young girl forced by her mad guardian (Emil Jannings) to perform the trick so that inquisitive visitors will stay away and leave them to what he regards as a romantic idyll. True love however will find a way. She elopes with the painter; the guardian pursues, and later turns up in her life like a vengeful Svengali. When she drops dead from his harassment, he stabs himself.

The mainstream cinema public had not flocked to see any of these essays in Egyptology. They were treated as kiddie-scarers, fit for a Saturday morning or perhaps a Bank Holiday. But the Tutankhamun business of 1922, first the discovery and then the curse which seemed to follow, hit the headlines of newspapers around the world, and you could scarcely sit at a bar without talking to somebody who had an opinion about it, though none could explain why Howard Carter, leader of the expedition and presumably chief desecrator of the tomb, remained free of all the maladies and died a normal death in 1939 at the age of 66. Robert Graves and Alan Hodge, in their invaluable study of the years between the wars *The Long Weekend*, explain the public fascination by the fact that Tutankhamun died so young and seemed somehow to embody the modernist spirit. One suspects also that greed had something to do with it, greed at the sight of so much treasure preserved from human eyes throughout four millennia. London at any rate went Tutankhamun-mad. To quote Graves and Hodge:

Ancient Egypt suddenly became the vogue. In March 1923 the veteran professor Flinders Petrie lectured on Egypt to an entranced Mayfair gathering. Replicas of the

The Tutankhamun expedition of 1922: Howard Carter in the foreground. (Courtesy BBC Hulton Picture Library.)

jewellery found in the tomb, and hieroglyphic embroideries copied from its walls, were worn on dresses; lotus-flower, scarab and serpent ornaments in vivid colours appeared on hats. Sandy tints were popular, and gowns began to fall stiffly in the Egyptian style. Even the new model Singer sewing machine of that year went Pharaonic, and it was seriously proposed that the new underground extension from Morden to Edgware, then under construction, should be called Tootancamden, because it passed through Tooting and Camden Town.

In the midst of all this excitement Lord Caernarvon died. Near the entrance of the tomb a mosquito had bitten him, and the bite had turned poisonous. It must be the curse! declared the press, though the curse was largely a press invention in the first place. Well-known Egyptologists seemed to concur in the possibility that a long-dead Pharaoh might be angry at having his rest disturbed, and Conan Doyle, thirty years after writing 'The Ring of Thoth', was interviewed on the subject as he crossed to America on the *Queen Mary*. By now a confirmed spiritualist, and a bit silly with it, Sir Arthur remarked:

> An evil elemental may have caused Lord Caernarvon's fatal illness. One does not know what elementals existed in those days, nor what their power might be. The Egyptians knew a great deal more about those things than we do.

The press now began to remember curious events which followed previous expeditions to the Valley of the Kings, notably that of 1909, when perplexing setbacks confronted Joseph Lindon Smith and his wife in their attempts to stage in the valley a play based on the life of the Pharaoh Akhnaton, who was supposed himself to have been plagued by the curse of Amon-Ra. Sudden and unpredicted storms swept through both rehearsal and performance, and during the following night both leading ladies were troubled by identical dreams in which they were violently attacked by a statue of Rameses II. Nervous breakdowns, jaundice, near-blindness and stomach cramps then afflicted various members of the party, and the expedition had to be totally abandoned. The stories were released but failed entirely to catch the public imagination; wise men remarked that only a damn fool would go to Egypt and *not* expect to catch anything. It was all good fodder for the papers now, as was the serialization of a forgotten 1917 American novel called *A King in Babylon*, by Burton Stevenson. Its weird plot, treated almost on pulp level, concerned a film company which, while filming in Egypt, found itself persistently haunted by 'something dark and shadowy, something with the unmistakable odour of grave clothes'. (Does everyone know how grave clothes smell?) The hero and heroine of the film subsequently discover themselves to be reincarnations of the long-dead mummies in the tomb near which shooting proceeds, ancient lovers whose roles (by a remarkable coincidence) they are now playing in the film.

What is astonishing is that there were no mummy films during the rest of the twenties. Surely Lon Chaney Snr would have relished the challenge of adding 4,000 years to his age and another image to his gallery of monsters and madmen? But no; interest in the subject was preserved chiefly through stories contributed to popular American magazines. One vivid example is 'A Visitor from Egypt' by Frank Belknap Long Jnr. It begins as follows:

On a dismal rainy afternoon in August a tall, very thin gentleman tapped timidly on the frosted glass window of the curator's office in a certain New England museum. He wore a dark blue chinchilla overcoat, olive-green Homburg hat with high tapering crown, yellow gloves, and spats. A blue silk muffler with white dots encircled his neck and entirely concealed the lower portion of his face and virtually all of his nose. Only a small expanse of pink and very wrinkled flesh was visible above the muffler and below his forehead, but as this exposed portion of his physiognomy contained his eyes it was as arresting as it was meagre.

Those who find the beginning reminiscent of H. G. Wells's *The Invisible Man* may not be deceiving themselves – it also has an air or two of M. R. James's 'The Tractate Middoth' – but we are not here to reprimand plagiarism, and the visitor in the homburg is not invisible, nor is he a ghost. He is, or says he is, Sir Richard (no surname given), a famous Englishman come to see Mr Buzzby's proudly assembled Luxor exhibition. He is welcomed, yet when they meet, the two enthusiasts, who should think as one, are drawn into an argument about the human remains on show – predynastic human bones, tinted blue and red:

> Mr Buzzby smiled. 'I have always considered it pathetic, Sir Richard. Infinitely amusing, but pathetic. They thought that by painting the bones they could preserve the vitality of the corruptible body. Corruption putting on incorruption, as it were.'
> 'It was blasphemous!' Sir Richard had risen from his chair. His face, above the muffler, was curiously white, and there was a hard, metallic glitter in his small dark eyes. 'They sought to cheat Osiris! They had no conception of hyper-physical realities!'

In addition to being shocked by the suggestion that Osiris might consent to restore life to supplicants who confront him in the afterworld, Sir Richard believes that the *Book of the Dead*, in which the god appears to promise to do so, is a forgery:

> 'Parts of it are undoubtedly predynastic, but I believe that the Judgment of the Dead, which defines the judicial prerogatives of Osiris, was inserted by some meddling priest as late as the historical period. It is a deliberate attempt to modify the relentless character of Egypt's supreme deity. Osiris does not judge, he *takes*.'
> 'He takes, Sir Richard?'
> 'Precisely. Do you imagine any one can ever cheat death? Do you imagine that, Mr Buzzby? Do you imagine for one moment that Osiris would restore to life the fools that returned to him?'
> Mr Buzzby coloured. It was difficult to believe that Sir Richard was really in earnest. 'Then you honestly believe that the character of Osiris as we know it is –'
> 'A myth, yes. A deliberate and childish evasion. No man can ever comprehend the character of Osiris. He is the Dark God. *But he treasures his own.*'
> 'Eh?' Mr Buzzby was genuinely startled by the tone of ferocity in which the last remark was uttered. 'What did you say, Sir Richard?'

But Sir Richard has changed the subject, still covering the lower part of his face with a muffler; he explains this as covering the results of a nasty accident to his face on board ship: 'It's in a positively unpresentable condition.' He takes from a shelf a modern work of fiction about Osiris, and Mr Buzzby is surprised to hear that he approves of it. Sir Richard reads a portion with relish:

It is beyond dispute that Osiris made his worshippers dream strange things of him, and that he possessed their bodies and souls for ever. There is a devilish wrath against mankind with which Osiris was for Death's sake inspired. In the cool of the evening he walked among men, and upon his head was the Crown of Upper Egypt, and his cheeks were inflated with a wind that slew. His face was veiled so that no man could see it, but assuredly it was an old face, very old and dead and dry, for the world was young when tall Osiris died.

Sir Richard goes on to talk what Mr Buzzby privately considers rot, stuff about the transfiguration of a God into mortal flesh and back again.

'It would be dreadful,' continued Sir Richard, 'if the god had no control over his transfiguration; if the change occurred frequently and unexpectedly; if he shared, as it were, the ghastly fate of Dr Jekyll and Mr Hyde.'
    Sir Richard was advancing towards the door. He moved with a curious, shuffling gait and his shoes scraped peculiarly upon the floor . . .

Sir Richard makes for the lavatory on the excuse of a dry throat, and moments later from that direction comes fire and smoke, with a smell 'like dinosaur eggs'. Then –

'Fool!' A muffled form emerged from the lavatory and ponderously ascended the stairs. 'Fool! You have sinned irretrievably!' . . .

The form passes by Mr Buzzby, and there follows the sound of smashing glass. The Luxor exhibits! Mr Buzzby leaps into action, but . . .

    Suddenly he stopped, and stared. At the very entrance to the Hall lay an assortment of garments which he instantly recognised. There was the blue chinchilla coat and the Alpine homburg with its high tapering crown, and the blue silk muffler that had concealed so effectively the face of his visitor. And on the very top of the heap lay a pair of yellow suede gloves.
    'Good God!' muttered Mr Buzzby. 'The man has shed all of his clothes!'
    He stood there for a moment staring in utter bewilderment and then with long, hysterical strides he advanced into the hall. 'A hopeless maniac,' he muttered, under his breath. 'A sheer, raving lunatic. Why did I not –'
    Then, abruptly, he ceased to reproach himself. He forgot entirely his folly, the heap of clothes, and the smashed case. Everything that had up to that moment occupied his mind was instantly extruded and he shrivelled and shrank with fear. Never had the unwilling gaze of Mr Buzzby encountered such a sight.
    Mr Buzzby's visitor was bending over the shattered case and only his back was visible. But it was not an ordinary back. In a lucid, unemotional moment, Mr Buzzby would have called it a nasty, malignant back, but in juxtaposition with the crown that topped it there is no Aryan polysyllable suggestive enough to describe it. For the crown was very tall and ponderous with jewels and unspeakably luminous, and it accentuated the vileness of the back. It was a green back. *Sapless* was the word that ran through Mr Buzzby's mind as he stood and stared at it. And it was wrinkled, too, horribly wrinkled, all criss-crossed with centuried grooves.
    Mr Buzzby did not even notice his visitor's neck, which glistened and was as thin as a bean-pole, nor the small round scaly head that bobbed and nodded ominously. He saw only the hideous back, and the unbelievably awesome crown. The crown shed a

fiery radiance upon the reddish tiles of the dim, vast hall, and the starkly nude body twisted and turned and writhed shockingly.

Black horror clutched at Mr Buzzby's throat, and his lips trembled as though he were about to cry out. But he spoke no word. He had staggered back against the wall and was making curious futile gestures with his arms, as though he sought to embrace the darkness, to wrap the darkness in the hall about him, to make himself as inconspicuous as possible and invisible to the thing that was bending over the case. But apparently he soon found to his infinite dismay that the thing was aware of his presence, and as it turned slowly toward him he made no further attempt to obliterate himself, but went down on his knees and screamed and screamed and screamed.

Silently the figure advanced toward him. It seemed to glide rather than to walk, and in its terribly lean arms it held a queer assortment of brilliant scarlet bones. And it cackled loathsomely as it advanced.

And then it was that Mr Buzzby's sanity departed utterly. He grovelled and gibbered and dragged himself along the floor like a man in the grip of an instantaneous catalepsy. And all the while he murmured incoherently about how spotless he was and would Osiris spare him and how he longed to reconcile himself with Osiris.

But the figure, when it got to him, merely stooped and breathed on him. Three times it breathed on his ashen face and one could almost see the face shrivel and blacken beneath its warm breath. For some time it remained in a stooping posture, glaring glassily, and when it arose Mr Buzzby made no effort to detain it. Holding the scarlet bones very firmly in its horribly thin arms it glided rapidly away in the direction of the stairs. The attendants did not see it descend. No one ever saw it again.

And when the coroner, arriving in response to the tardy summons of an attendant, examined Mr Buzzby's body, the conclusion was unavoidable that the curator had been dead for a long, long time.

A curious item, rather muddled but with the power to frighten, and adding to our stock of pseudo-myth the tendency of Osiris to shrivel people when affronted. Over in Hollywood, someone was at last reading and noting and storing, and when in 1932 Boris Karloff needed another piece of grotesquerie to follow *Frankenstein* and *The Old Dark House*, a mummy came at last to the talking screen to spawn at least two generations of monster movies of like kind. As so often, the first was the best, though in this case very different from the others, a macabre romance rather than a thriller. When Carl Laemmle first saw the rough cut, he must have wondered whether to release it. He did, with cuts, but its very moderate box-office results temporarily halted Boris Karloff's Hollywood career. Fifty years later, *The Mummy* seems to contain its star's subtlest performance.

Although Universal had ordered a shocker, and despite the publicity stories about the long ordeal suffered by Boris Karloff whenever he had to don the mummy make-up, the mummy itself puts in only the briefest of appearances. In essence this was not even a thriller at all, more a thoughtful essay about the possibilities of reincarnation; which may be why an old American advertisement for it bears the following note: 'This picture is highly recommended and endorsed by the Rosicrucian Order (AMORC) which recommends that all members in this community attend this unusual picture.'

Although the main titles credit a story by Nina Wilcox Putman and Richard Schayer, there seems little doubt that the real author was the recently deceased Sir Arthur Conan Doyle, as all the principal elements and attitudes of 'The Ring of

Thoth' are present, except that the ring itself has become a scroll. The story is set in and around a rather convincing modern Cairo at a time when the streets were less crowded than they are today, and the English had the upper hand. Enervating heat is carefully suggested, and about the whole film as directed by Karl Freund there hangs a romantic languor which is entirely suited to its offbeat approach and tends to be remembered after the details of the absurdly unconvincing plot escape one, save for the idea of a male mummy which can rejuvenate itself as a modern man speaking perfect English.

A lengthy flashback in the second half of the picture reveals the supposed facts. Imhotep, a high priest of the temple of the sun at Karnak, was condemned to living death for using the scroll of Thoth in an effort to revive his dead love, the Princess Anck-es-en-Amon. As he tells her modern reincarnation 3,700 years later,

> I dared the gods' anger . . . I stole back to thy tomb to bring thee back to life . . . I murmured the spell that raises the dead, but they broke in upon me, and found me doing an unholy thing . . . thy father condemned me to a nameless death, and the scroll was buried with me so that no such sacrilege might disturb Egypt again. A nameless grave . . . the servants were killed so that none should know, and the soldiers who killed them were also slain, so that no friend could make offerings for my condemned spirit. Anck-es-en-Amon . . . my love has lasted longer than the temples of our gods. No man ever suffered as I did for you, but the rest you may not know – not until you are about to pass through the great night of terror and triumph – until you are ready to face moments of horror for an eternity of love. Until I send back your spirit that has wandered through so many forms and so many ages.

In fact Imhotep has already shown the bewildered Helen Grosvenor, an Anglo-Egyptian and daughter of an archaeologist, visions of her previous incarnations in Roman, Saxon and medieval times (though these were cut from release prints because they seemed to slow up what action there was). While she abstractedly ponders Imhotep's urgent request that as a first step towards their eternal happiness she be killed by knife on the sacrificial altar, let us revert to the beginning of the film and discover how this situation came about. A sign in the desert reads:

FIELD EXPEDITION
SEASON 1921
BRITISH MUSEUM

Inside a nearby cave two old archaeologists and a young novice, Norton, are going over their finds of the day, chief among which is a male mummy, now propped upright against the wall in its open sarcophagus, hands folded across its chest, eyes closed as though in eternal rest. The viscera have never been removed, discover the researchers: at least, the usual scar is not there.

> NORTON: It looks as though he'd died in some sensationally unpleasant manner.
> MULLER: The contorted muscles show that he struggled in the bandages.
> NORTON: Buried alive! Poor old fellow. Now, what could you have done to make 'em treat you like that?

THE MUMMY (1932). When Bramwell Fletcher reads aloud from the scroll of Thoth, the mummy comes to life and takes it: an effective shot for which in the film you will search in vain.

>MULLER: The sacred spells which protect the soul on its journey to the underworld have been chipped off the coffin. So Imhotep was sentenced to death not only in this world but in the next.
>NORTON: Maybe he got too gay with the vestal virgins in the temple.

After that line Norton deserves what he gets. Left alone with the mummy, he begins to decipher aloud the scroll of Thoth which was found in the coffin. Only the audience sees the mummy's eyelid flicker; then one folded arm begins to move.★ These shots are all one is given of the famous character make-up, for the scene marks a skilful use of discretion at a time when Hollywood was not noted for that quality. The young man is still absorbed in his research when the mummy's shadow falls across his rough desk. He looks up and understandably cannot believe what he sees. We are shown nothing but a bandaged hand, with a bit of dirt hanging from one of the fingers, as it reaches into the frame for the scroll. Norton starts back in horror and begins to scream; the scroll is removed and the mummy makes off with it, though all we see is a loose bandage trailing across the earth floor as the creature makes its exit. Young Norton (it is Bramwell

★ It is remarkable that an ancient Egyptian could be so easily revived even by the words of a magic scroll, when it is read aloud in *English*.

Fletcher's moment of glory) is laughing insanely when the others hurry back into the room and ask what on earth happened to the mummy. 'It went for a little walk,' he gasps between his hysterics.

Another sign for another expedition establishes that we have moved on to 1932. Sir Joseph Whemple and his son Frank, and Professor Pearson, are now our leaders, and they make reference to poor old Norton, who has died in an insane asylum. As for the mummy . . . well, somebody stole it, they suppose. They will be more careful with the mummy of Princess Anck-es-en-Amon, if they find her. At that moment they have an unexpected, unknown visitor, a reserved and wrinkled Egyptian in a fez and a shift. He says that his name is Ardath Bey, but we know Boris Karloff when we see him. Are we supposed to assume that he is a miraculously cleaned-up and de-bandaged version of the mummy who disappeared, now speaking perfect English? We are, but how this miracle was accomplished the film does not venture to state. 'Permit me,' remarks the incognito Imhotep, 'to present you with the most sensational find since that of Tutankhamun.' The archaeologists are surprised at his open-handedness, and he smiles. 'We Egyptians are not allowed to dig up our ancient dead – only foreign museums.' He disappears before the validity of his instructions can be proved, but proved it is, and before long the mummy of the princess is on show in the Cairo Museum, which is where Imhotep wanted it. He now reappears in society, a man forbidding, polite, reluctant to be touched. ('I regret I am too occupied to accept invitations.') Superficially he has the behaviour of a patrician, but it is tinged with some ancient guilt. When he is introduced to Helen Grosvenor, having failed to awaken his princess, he realizes intuitively that Helen is the current custodian of the soul of his loved one, and from that moment on she is under his spell, a split personality. When she mutters strange words and faints on Sir Joseph's carpet, light begins dimly to dawn in the mind of the archaeologist:

> FRANK: What language is that?
> SIR JOSEPH: The language of ancient Egypt – not heard on this earth for two thousand years – and the name of a man unspoken since before the siege of Troy!

Now Dr Muller, an occultist in his spare time, returns to Cairo in time to realize what has happened. Edward Van Sloan in the role is clearly reprising his Van Helsing, and Imhotep is Dracula in another form, a monster received in the drawing rooms of those who wish to cause his downfall. As we have seen, he is able to spirit Helen away to his palatial if funereal chambers, and the denouement is a matter simply of whether or not Frank will get there before it is too late. (Of course he will.) Dramatically Imhotep drags the soulless mummy of his beloved from its sarcophagus (which he has stolen from the museum) and sets fire to it, declaiming his mad plan the while:

> It's safe to destroy this lifeless thing, my love, but for a few moments you must take its place, and then you will be able to rise again and be free of death forever, as I have freed myself. Come to the altar of Anubis – the time has come for the final prayers.

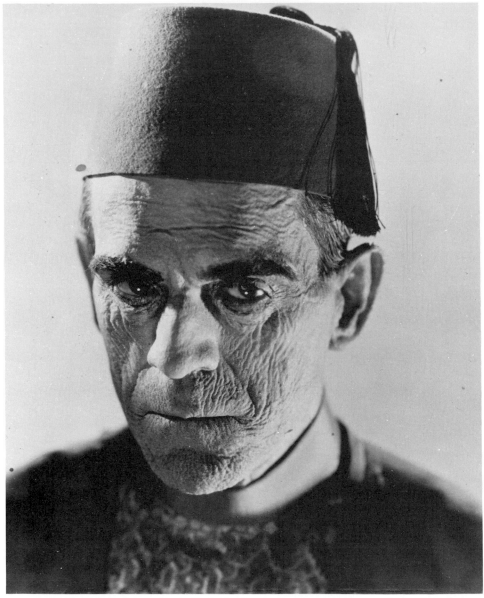

THE MUMMY (1932). Imhotep (Boris Karloff) after the magic scroll has transformed him into a modern man (well, almost).

Imhotep's Nubian slave pauses from stirring his bath of natron and lifts Helen to the level of sacrifice. But in the nick of time she remembers from her previous incarnation how to pray to the giant statue* which dominates the room:

> O Isis, holy maiden, I was thy consecrated vestal . . . teach me the ancient summons of the holy spell to succour me in this my hour of need . . .

* The figure later served us under another alias as the planet god in the Flash Gordon serials.

THE MUMMY (1932). Imhotep, in polite society, recognizes the reincarnation of his ancient love. Arthur Byron, Edward Van Sloan, Zita Johann, Karloff, David Manners.

More strange words tumble from her lips: SEHOTPE IBRE MEN-MOSUT SIT-SEKHEM! And the arm of the statue rises to point the *crux ansata* at the already stricken Imhotep. By the time the rescuers arrive he is no more than a heap of dust and powdered bone, his eternity terminated by his own arrogance in assuming the powers of a god. At least, that's one way of interpreting the mumbo-jumbo of John Balderston's script. In performance it works well enough in terms of mood: you don't have to understand the details, just to know that good is pitted against evil, right against wrong, and youth against age. We can all predict which trio from that selection will survive in Hollywood.

Eight years went by before a sequel was envisaged to what had proved an only barely profitable grotesquerie, and even then one of the chief considerations was to re-use some of the expensive sets from the recently completed jungle melodrama *Green Hell*. Also re-used was much of the flashback to Ancient Egypt from *The Mummy*: when the mists of time clear, the long shots are all of Karloff. Alas, since Karloff was either uninterested, or simply too old for the rags-and-tatters routine, a lookalike was sought for the close-ups, and found among the ranks of the second feature cowboy stars which every Hollywood studio kept on its backlot. Tom Tyler was in fact branching out – he had recently played a small part in *Gone with the Wind* and was the villain shot down by John Wayne at the end of

THE MUMMY'S HAND (1940). Tom Tyler looks frightening enough in photographic close-up. In the movie they also black out his eyeballs.

Stagecoach – but even at the age of 37 he was becoming a victim to arthritis, which seemed to clinch matters, for all he had to do was exaggerate his infirmity a little and he had the mummy's shambling walk down to a T.

Gone this time was any pretence at seriousness, any mood of sombre romance. *The Mummy's Hand* was a B-thriller, 67 minutes long, with comic-strip dialogue, the standard eerie music quickening as the mummy lurches in for the kill, and a heroine in a silk nightdress who screams and then faints as she is carried away in the monster's arms. The odd thing was that it worked, and many people remember it as the most frightening film they have ever seen, even though the British censor saw no reason to give it anything stronger than an 'A' certificate, which meant that children of any age could get in to see it if accompanied. (American kids suffered no prohibition whatever, but then they have always been built from sterner stuff.) On examination, the first two-thirds of the picture will turn out to consist of innocent banter. It is during the last twenty-five minutes that the crunch comes, with unlimited shrieks in the night around the archaeologists' camp near the Hill of the Seven Jackals. So far as the marauding mummy is concerned, the sinister cavortings are intensified by the fact that the editor ingeniously blacked out its eyeballs after each scene had been shot, making them look like bottomless pools of quivering black jelly.

Though Tyler had been born Vincent Marko, a name eminently suitable for a horror star, *The Mummy's Hand* was the only film he made in the genre, and that may well have been because of the uncomfortable make-up sessions he had to endure. Universal's expert in these matters, Jack Pierce, covered his face with thin strips of cotton soaked in spirit gum, so that the surface dried tight and wrinkled. Grey paint mixed with clay was then applied, sprayed before it dried with brown dust. Clay mixed with glue was also brushed into the hair. And getting all this stuff off was worse than getting it on.

The basis of the plot is that an ancient Egyptian sect has kept alive for 4,000 years the half-mummified corpse of a prince who was buried alive for stealing the sacred tana leaves which might revive his dead love, the Princess Ananka. Now the High Priest of Karnak (Eduardo Ciannelli with a severe case of the shakes) is passing on the responsibility for the care of Kharis the mummy to a new disciple, Andoheb, who conveniently happens to be curator of the Cairo Museum. George Zucco's performance in this role is almost more sinister than that of Tom Tyler as the mummy: even while in total repose his eyes seem to be flashing evil messages, and his voice makes the audience shiver if he is only saying 'Thank you'. The film in fact has two splendid villains, both Zucco and Tyler devoting their best efforts to it and never for a moment seeming to send themselves up.

The High Priest, gazing into the smoking waters which for him replace the gypsy's crystal ball, tells a tale which for viewers of the ensuing series will become so familiar that by the end they can recite it right along with him:

THE MUMMY'S HAND (1940). Villainous George Zucco (left) masterminds a moment of mummy mayhem in a scene which, though obviously shot, has mysteriously disappeared from the film.

Who shall defile the temples of the ancient gods, a cruel and violent death shall be his fate, and never shall his soul find rest until eternity. Such is the curse of Amon–Ra, king of the gods . . . Daring the anger of the ancient gods, Kharis stole the forbidden tana leaves . . . now he waits, asleep, to bring death to those who defile Ananka's tomb . . . three of the leaves will make enough fluid to keep his heart beating . . . once every night during the cycle of the full moon . . . nine leaves to bring life and movement . . . but never for any reason must you brew more than nine . . . he would become an uncontrollable monster, a soulless demon with the desire to kill, and kill . . . and kill . . .

All very puzzling. Kharis was buried alive for stealing the tana leaves in order to restore Princess Ananka, but now it's OK for priests who serve the same gods to keep *him* alive on the fluid. Who were the tana leaves for, anyway, if they couldn't be used on a princess? Ah well, at Universal it was always unwise to ask too many questions. The legend has been redefined, as it had to be since Karloff ended up in the last episode as a pile of dust; Imhotep has simply been written out of history, and Kharis takes his place.

Now we meet our heroes Steve and Babe, an unlikely pair of archaeologists as played by Dick Foran and Wallace Ford, though when they find an intriguing vase on a junk stall they do have the sense to take it along to Dr Petrie (Flinders Petrie?) at the museum. He of course confirms that it may lead to the tomb of Ananka, and takes it along in great excitement to show to our old friend Andoheb, who suavely

THE MUMMY'S HAND (1940). Kharis is about to be revealed, and some of the onlookers may not survive his coming. Charles Trowbridge, Dick Foran, Wallace Ford, Cecil Kellaway, Peggy Moran.

conceals his fury with remarks like: 'The Cairo bazaar does a thriving business for tourists. The desert is paved with the good intentions of many enthusiastic but mistaken archaeologists.' When he can't dissuade them, he clumsily drops the vase, but Steve simply puts it together again and mounts an expedition with the financial help of a drunken magician called the Great Solvani (Cecil Kellaway, always welcome) who just happens to have a beautiful daughter Marta. The expedition is unlucky at first, but eventually the dynamiting of a slope uncovers the cave in which Kharis lies dormant in his sarcophagus. Alone one night, Dr Petrie is examining the mummy when Andoheb appears from nowhere (there is a passage from the cave to his temple) and points out that the mummy has a pulse. 'Absurd . . . fantastic!' says Petrie, feeling the beat but unable to believe his own senses. They are almost his last words. Andoheb further demonstrates the effect of the tana juice. The mummy stirs, sits up, and grabs Petrie by the neck. One down, several to go. Kharis has a withered arm and leg, and Andoheb tells him that only tana juice will cure him, and that where he finds it he must kill. The mummy shuffles off into the desert night, and Andoheb hastens to secrete vials of juice where they will do most good. This part of the film tends to consist of nothing but mummy-stranglings in close-up, to suitable music backing; but before he gets to the principals, Andoheb has a change of plan. He falls for Marta, and decides that she shall be his bride throughout eternity, fortified and preserved by the tana juice. He doesn't seem to have thought about who will administer it every full moon if they are both dormant along with Kharis; but let's not niggle. He sends Kharis off to kidnap Marta and bring her to the temple, where she is strapped to the sacrificial altar from *Green Hell*. But our heroes can't take this lying down. Babe confronts Andoheb and shoots him when he proves treacherous. Steve is just unfastening Marta when Kharis lurches in, intent on the central supply of tana juice which is bubbling away on a brazier. Bullets don't stop him, but flame apparently does, for when Steve tips the brazier on him he goes up in a pool of fire.

The Mummy's Hand may not sound like much, but innumerable audiences have breathed sighs of relief at the approach of the happy ending. Alas, the same cannot be said of the three faint copies which Universal extracted from the theme to fill double bills for wartime audiences. They all starred Lon Chaney Jnr, who after *The Wolf Man* and *Son of Dracula* was being promoted as 'the screen's master character actor'; but it could have been almost anybody inside the bandages, and he was far less impressive than Tom Tyler because there was absolutely no expression in his face (not that Chaney could have given much anyway). Pierce had devised a time-saving mask: it revealed nothing of Chaney but a single eye, and was most unconvincing. Scripts and production were alike hasty and uninventive, with flat acting and plots which, sometimes hilariously, exemplified the old Hollywood adage, 'If you find something goes pretty well the first time, why not do it again?' The trouble was that with such scant attention to detail or logic, only the familiar horror music could now squeeze any suspense out of situations on which the audience was way ahead of the actors.

The only thing to be said for the arrant potboiler called *The Mummy's Tomb* (1942) is that it made a surprising amount of money and so kept the monster

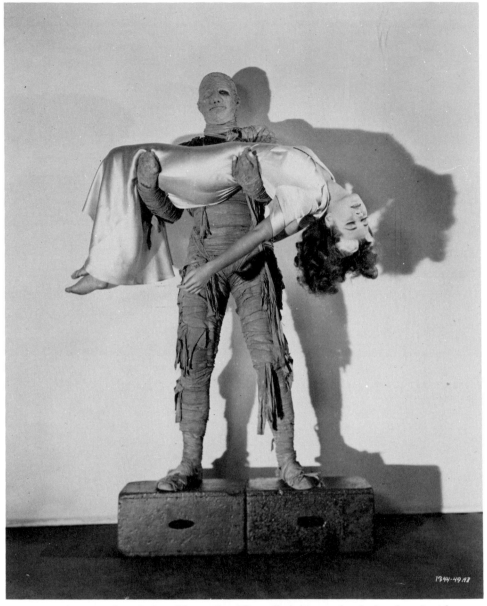

THE MUMMY'S GHOST (1944). Lon Chaney Jnr (if it really is him under the bandages) with Ramsay Ames in a truly absurd publicity pose. Photo editors were supposed to obscure the boxes.

stalking for two further films of diminishing plausibility. Curiously, it kills off the two heroes of *The Mummy's Hand,* who have apparently survived no fewer than forty years of peace and modest fame when George Zucco, only somewhat more ancient and palsied than in the previous film, calls a new young priest to his cell inside the Hill of the Seven Jackals, and explains that he was not after all so badly hurt in the previous fracas: 'The bullet he fired into me only crushed my arm. The fire they thought consumed Kharis only seared and twisted his leg.' Funny, when we last saw Kharis he was flat on his face in a pool of flaming oil. And Andoheb was not only shot full of holes but fell down a long flight of stone steps. But no matter: 'Kharis still lives. Lives for the moment he will carry death and destruction to all those who dared violate the tomb of Ananka . . .' That moment has clearly now arrived, though why Andoheb has waited forty years for it is hard to say. Luckily everyone in the audience is well versed in the story, whether or not they saw the first film, for Steve Banning (Dick Foran with grey hair) has spent the first two reels of this one telling it to guests in his cosy New England mansion. His narration has been spiced with a second repeat of judiciously edited flashbacks from *The Mummy*, omitting only the references to reincarnation, for this episode is to concern itself not with love across the centuries but with revenge.

Andoheb has been thorough, as is demonstrated by his instructions to his new acolyte:

> I place in your hands the curse of Amon-Ra, and the destiny of Kharis. Preparations are complete to the last detail. The position as caretaker of the little cemetery at Mapleton has been arranged. Now, swear by the sacred gods of Egypt that you will never rest until the last remaining member of the Banning family has been destroyed.

A smart editor gets Mehemet (his sarcophagus with its curious contents presumably cleared with no difficulty through several sets of customs) conveniently established within a minute in the little New England town. The mummy case is propped up in the cemetery mausoleum, apparently bringing no objection from the white Anglo-Saxon Protestants of Mapleton, and soon Mehemet is about his deadly work: 'The moonlight is high in the sky tonight, Kharis. There is death in the night air. Your work begins.'

The juice of a few tana leaves sends Kharis shambling off through the undergrowth, and within seconds our erstwhile hero Steve Banning has gone the way we have come to expect. His friend Babe hurries in to investigate, but he doesn't last long either. Since the marauding mummy contrives to be seen by nobody, police and reporters are equally baffled; one of the latter, in a topical note, wonders why he chose to cover the activities of the 'Mapleton fiend killer' when he could have been sent to the Russian front. It is a Professor Norman who first suspects the truth after examining pieces of linen which Kharis has carelessly shed at the scene of each crime:

> There is a distinct smell common to both of them. It is undoubtedly the odour of myrrh. It comes from a tree known as the Commethora Abyssenica which grows only in parts of Africa. It was used for embalming . . . whether you are ready to accept it or not, we are in the presence of the living dead . . .

The fly in the ointment from Kharis's point of view is that you can never trust a priest of Karnak. Like Andoheb before him, Mehemet has taken a fancy to a young white girl, in this case the one who would have been Steve's daughter-in-law. He tells the expressionless Kharis all about it:

> I am going to take unto myself a wife, Kharis, a wife . . . the one who is supposed to
> be the bride of the last of the Bannings. The one who it was ordained I should find!
> Together we three shall stand, until the world crumbles and there is no longer a stone
> or a rock or a tree or a blade of grass. That is my will, Kharis, and you shall obey it.

Kharis's initial reaction is the nearest a bandaged-up mummy can give to a shrug, and he loses no time in abducting the white-draped heroine for his master. The villagers spot him on this occasion, and they in their turn lose no time in getting out the blazing torches left for so long in the Frankenstein store room: scenes are even cut in from *The Ghost of Frankenstein* as the mummy with its glamorous burden stalks off into the dark woods.

Isobel wakes up in the mausoleum with Mehemet bending over her, and screams at the memory of the monster who abducted her. Mehemet means to be reassuring:

> You have nothing to fear from Kharis. He has brought you here because it is your
> destiny to achieve the highest honour that can come to a woman. You will be the
> bride of a high priest of Karnak. You will bear me a son and he will be brought up in
> the confines of the tombs of Egypt, as I was myself . . . a new priest of Karnak, who
> will carry on the ancient and honourable line.

But the posse approaches, and Kharis has to set off on his travels with Isobel once more. For some inscrutable reason he makes for the Banning house and climbs up the rose trellis with her in his arms, a pretty remarkable feat for a creature which has only one good arm and one good leg. There is just time for a fight with the only hero left before the house goes up in flames and Kharis apparently with it. We never do find out what happened to Mehemet, but a Banning wedding is taking place as the credits roll.

The Mummy's Tomb was stitched together with no thought at all, and only proved that you don't need thought to make money. It was Universal's most profitable film of the year, and nobody even complained about the poor matching between the gaunt Kharis of Tom Tyler in the flashbacks and the portly one played by Lon Chaney in the main story. And though Chaney claims to have complained bitterly about his limited role, a contract is a contract; he played Kharis twice more before all concerned lost interest.

The Mummy's Ghost (1944) maintains the location of Mapleton, and seems to follow straight on. At any rate, in the inevitable flashback opening, Andoheb (a still undaunted but now super-aged George Zucco, using the same misty sequences from the previous films but mentioning this time Kharis's ancient love for his dead Ananka) recounts to a new disciple played by John Carradine a history which he must surely have known already. The narrative is taken over, by courtesy of a cinematic dissolve, by a Mapleton professor telling his students that 'every live member of the party who had dared set foot in that faraway tomb, died by the mummy's hands. The monster itself was later consumed in the flames of the Banning house.' Unless, of course, someone knows better, and at least three people do. Professor Norman is conducting potentially dangerous experiments with tana leaves; a local girl named Amina has bad dreams, and tells a friend that 'something happens to me when I think of Egypt'; besides, Lon Chaney has to be found something to do in the picture, since he's top-billed. Meanwhile Andoheb is still nattering on: 'Once each night, during the cycle of the full moon, you will brew nine tana leaves. Kharis will know – and come for the fluid that preserves him!' That's a new twist, magnetic fluid; and incidentally, just how *did* Kharis escape from the fire? Yousef Bey asks no such awkward questions, but stands to attention and takes the oath of allegiance:

> By the mighty power of Amon-Ra, whose anger shall shatter the world, and by the dread horror of Set, I swear that I shall never forsake my trust as a priest of Arkam, nor shall I rest until the princess Ananka and Kharis are safe once more in the hills of Arkam.

Why Karnak has become Arkam is not explained – perhaps there was a real sect of Karnak which sued. And Dennis Wheatley fans may be amused to recall that in *The Devil Rides Out*, the dread horror of Set turned out to be a mummified penis. But no matter. For Yousef Bey the problem at hand is to get hold of the mummy of Ananka, which has mysteriously become 'one of the choice possessions of the Scripps museum'.

Time passes – not too much, for in a 61-minute film, if audience interest is to be maintained, the mummy must strike no later than reel two – and the professor late one night has discovered the secret of the hieroglyph which mentions tana leaves. Nine, that's it; nine each night during the cycle of the full moon. When his wife demurs, he shrugs rather unscientifically: 'It does sound ridiculous, doesn't it? But how are we to be certain? The moon affects the tides. It may have the power to affect these tana leaves as well. I don't know.' He suffers mightily for his ignorance, for the moon turns full while he is still tut-tutting at his desk, and in from nowhere stalks Kharis to strangle him. Rather splendid newspaper headlines now fill the screen:

MUMMY BELIEVED TO BE BACK IN NEW ENGLAND

MAPLETON MONSTER, THOUGHT DESTROYED, IS BLAMED FOR NEW ATROCITY

ALL ABLE-BODIED MEN ASKED TO CONTRIBUTE PART OF TIME TO PATROL STREETS FROM SUNDOWN TO SUN-UP. REGISTER AT SHERIFF'S OFFICE.

These precautions do not prevent Kharis from loping into view roughly every five minutes for the remainder of the picture, to strangle anyone foolish enough to stand in his way, which is just about everybody except the hero and heroine. Meanwhile the garrulous Yousef Bey, having established a secret hiding place, steals the mummy of Ananka and makes speeches to it:

> Forgive us, priests of Arkam, who have been powerless to prevent the gaze of heretics from resting upon her. May the reclamation of her body absolve us for any laxity which may have been ours. The hour of fulfilment is at hand. Behold her, Kharis. Ananka, the princess of your forbidden love. The gods have been kind. Beneath the

sheltering wings of their protection we have come to the end of our quest. Kharis, the
tombs of Arkam are waiting to claim their own!

Alas, no doubt from boredom at such verbosity, the mummy of Ananka
crumbles into dust, just as Kharis stiffly bends over to embrace it. At this
development Kharis is even more silent than usual, and clearly none too pleased,
but Yousef thinks of a quick alibi to satisfy him: 'Amon-Ra, almighty god, thy
wrath is far-reaching. By thy will her soul has entered into another form!' It seems
a pity that Amon-Ra did not perform the same function for the excessively ugly
Kharis. But Yousef's point is proved for the audience by a shot of our briefly met
Amina sitting up in bed and screaming, sobbing that she can feel someone in the
room touching her; and so the audience has to accept her, with no further

THE MUMMY'S GHOST (1944). Lon Chaney Jnr in close-up. The plaster mask removed both the
possibility of acting and the need for it. Only the eye was real.

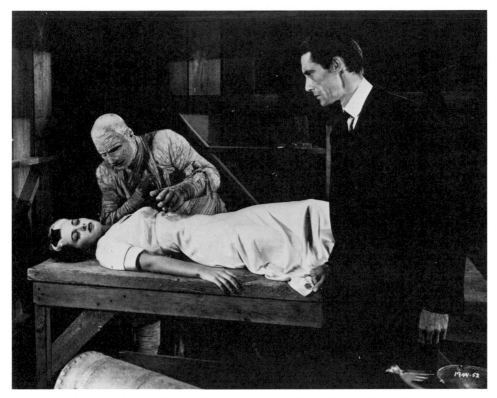

THE MUMMY'S GHOST (1944). The mask shows up in a darker colour as Kharis bends over the defenceless heroine. As a change from two Draculas in the same year, John Carradine plays the high priest.

explanation, as the reincarnation of Ananka. The burden of the rest of the movie is how Kharis finds her and carries her off. He does so somewhat inexplicably with the help of light from a mystic talisman, but when she wakes from her under-standable faint Amina is far from impressed by the fiancé who has been imposed on her. Perhaps sensing this, Yousef discovers that he rather fancies her himself, and despite his prayers to be saved from his own weakness ('O mighty Isis, protect me in this my hour of temptation') he arouses his mummy's worst suspicions when he proposes that he as well as Amina shall drink the tana fluid. Steal my girl, would you, Kharis seems to say as he lumbers menacingly towards Yousef and the ominous music starts up. 'Kharis, stop!' cries Yousef. 'I'll take her back . . . together we'll go to Arkam, the three of us, I swear it.' Not exactly Noël Coward's design for living, and in any case Kharis doesn't seem to fancy a *ménage à trois*: he can't see it working. So he pushes Yousef from a high window and lopes off with the girl. The posse is soon at the scene of the crime: 'Somebody else has been messing about with tana leaves,' notes the sheriff. But when it comes to catching fugitives he's really no fool. Within minutes the mummy is surrounded and has no option but to walk into the swamp (there are swamps in New England?) until he and his beloved are represented by nothing but a few surface bubbles. The last we see of the unfortunate Amina, her face has become shrivelled and ancient, for no very logical reason except, we suspect, that the screenwriters once saw *Lost Horizon*.

The Mummy's Curse, which was shot almost consecutively, also runs a scant 61 minutes, and were it not for different writing credits one might imagine that it was originally conceived as a conclusion to *The Mummy's Ghost*, for without the latter to back it up *Curse* has too great a lapse of the logic required even from a low-budget horror series on its last legs.

It starts like a musical, of sorts. In a workmen's café in French Louisiana an ample proprietress named Tante Berthe is giving out with song while she flirts with a character called Cajun Joe, played by Kurt Katch, who became as indispensable to the latter Universal horrors as Dwight Frye had been to the earlier ones. 'You gotta be a reech man,' she tells him, 'working as foreman in ze swamp clearing.' Ah yes, the swamp, murmurs the audience to itself; but wasn't that in New England? Apparently not, for Joe's friend Achilles tells her 'Nobody is so crazy to work in ze swamp any more – because on ze night when ze moon is so high in ze heavens, the mummy and his princess – zey walk.' Ah, so it *is* our Kharis after all. Cajun Joe shrugs: 'Long ago zere was a mummy as you say. And he take a girl in ze swamp. But that been twenty five year past.' Okay, so the swamp has moved, with the tide perhaps, from New England to Lousiana. But since *Tomb* was stated to take place forty years after *Hand*, it is now at least sixty-five years since Kharis was first brought back to the light of day.

No further explanations are given, but on the next morning a stalwart young man arrives at the worksite and announces himself as Dr Halsey from the Scripps Museum, come to recover the bodies of Kharis and Princess Ananka, believed to be buried in the swamps. Without explaining why the Museum waited a quarter of a century, he introduces his befezzed colleague Dr Ilzor Zandaab. This gentleman is marked by the fez alone as chief villain; and in his name I smell a writer's joke, for many a waiter in a Californian fish restaurant must have nominated his *plats du jour* as 'eels or sand-dab'.

The scholars are welcomed only grudgingly by a foreman scornful of their story, despite Halsey's assurance that 'a small group in Egypt harboured the mummy through the centuries, and he has been traced right here to this country.' To this, friend Zandaab can only add epigrammatically: 'In the dicta of the fathers it is written: Truth will flourish in fantasy, only to wither and die in what you are pleased to call reality.' (Yes, yes, dicta means spoken words, not written ones, but this is Universal, where many apparent truths flourish for the duration of the movie, but wither as soon as the lights go up.)

At this very moment the obligatory frightened black rushes in to declare in Sam Scram fashion: 'Boss, boss, somethin' terrible's happened. It's Antoine . . . dey just found him daid . . . at de edge of de pit on de other side of de swamp . . .' It can hardly be the mummy that killed Antoine, for the unfortunate fellow has a knife in his back, and Kharis only strangles; but Antoine's hands are clutching a piece of cloth which could just possibly be mummy wrapping – in Dr Halsey's opinion. And a few steps away is a neatly edged, irregular-shaped hole in the ground which might have contained a big man's body . . . 'Not an ordinary man,' insists Dr Halsey; 'unless I'm very much mistaken, a mummy was buried here.' Well, he looks like the sort of man who *could* be very much mistaken, but not in a 61-minute film called *The Mummy's Curse*.

The facts are soon revealed to the audience. Ilzor is the master mummy fancier, our old friend Andoheb having finally given up the ghost, and it is his assistant Ragheb who has found Kharis in the mud and led him off to hide in the old derelict monastery atop a distant hill. Within this ruin Kharis now lies dormant in his sarcophagus, remarkably clean considering his long interment in mud; but having been allowed a peep we are obliged to pause for the best part of a reel while Ilzor pads out the script by telling Ragheb a great many things which can't be entirely new to him. The image goes misty at the edges, and once again we are back to Karloff in the long shots while Ilzor drones on about the tana leaves, the copper box, the death of Ananka, the daring of Kharis, the wrath of the gods, and the burying alive of our ancient hero, who really must have been confused as to whether the gods were for him or against him, since after condemning him to living death they are now said to have arranged that his heart shall beat throughout eternity so that he can guard the tomb of the princess he loved. After 4,000 years, Kharis is clearly fed up with all the alarums and excursions: all he wants now is to be taken back with his princess to the Hill of the Seven Jackals. Of course, if he has to kill to get her, that will be all in the day's work. He gives us an example when an ancient sacristan ventures in to banish the unholy intruders from the monastery, adding in astonishment that he has found in the basement the bodies of freshly murdered men. Kharis rather casually adds him to the number.

It is the following day, and we are treated to the film's one striking shot. A bulldozer is clearing the swamp. We close in on the fine soil left in its wake, and see a shrivelled hand break through the dirt. An old crone, white-haired and hag-like, her withered skin thick with grime, rises slowly and painfully to her feet, staggers towards a convenient lake, and immerses herself in the centre of it. Literally a few seconds of screen time later, we find her transformed, wandering along a road on the far side of the water. Her dress is still tattered, yet oddly presentable. Her hair, black as jet, is neatly styled in a page-boy bob. Her face is immaculately made up. She is rescued by Cajun Joe, who takes her for an amnesiac, since all she can say is 'Kharis'. News of her is received at the monastery, and Kharis is sent out to get her; yet when he arrives, she screams and runs away, so he makes do instead with strangling Tante Berthe who had been looking after her. ('What's the funny marks on her throat?' – 'Looks like mould.') Now Halsey picks up the strange girl, who when she recovers from one of her faints speaks quite logically and in perfect English: 'What's happened to me? I woke up and everything is so strange. Who are you? I can't remember who I am or what I'm doing here.'

Let us pause to examine the situation's curious logic, or lack thereof. The page-boy bob and the make-up are absurd either way, but the fact that a resurrected princess of ancient Egypt speaks perfect English might not be if one has seen the previous film, where it was made clear that Ananka crumbled into dust and the girl carried into the swamp by Kharis was only the unfortunate Amina, possessed by Ananka's soul. But if she is now to all intents and purposes Ananka, why is she afraid of Kharis? And how can she speak modern English? If however she is Amina, how did she survive twenty-five years in the swamp, and how at the end of this film can she crumble into dust like a mummy?

The questions are unanswerable unless she is also Dr Jekyll and Mistress Hyde, and we are, after all, talking about films conceived on the level of comic strips. This one luckily doesn't have far to go. We next find Amina/Ananka (AA for short) helping Dr Halsey with his research, and assuring him that she can never get too much sun. (Not too sure of the exact point of that.) Through his microscope, by examining the supposed mummy wrappings, she is able to assure him, because of the number of strands per square inch, that 'this fabric was woven during the dynasty of King Amenophis – and worn by Kharis, a prince of the royal house.' When asked how she can possibly know this, she shakes her pretty head in typical Universal vagueness when detail is required: 'There's really no way to explain. Sometimes I feel as though it's all part of a strange dream.'

Meanwhile the impatient Kharis makes another bid for his loved one. ('Hurry now while the moon is full,' hisses Ilzor, having got his monster slightly confused with the Wolf Man.) 'He's coming for me!' declares AA in one of her trance-like moods; but when the mummy stumbles into her tent and is momentarily delayed by having to strangle a hovering doctor, she runs away again. Halsey half-persuades the doubters that a mummy could be responsible for the killings, and the posse starts to search the swamp. Cajun Joe gets his comeuppance from the mummy when he tries to help AA, who rushes into the tent of the film's nominal and very boring heroine Betty, who clearly *isn't* going to finish up strangled; but she can't stop Kharis from carrying off his intended. It remains only for Halsey (with the help of an editor and some cuts from *Frankenstein*) to point the guys with the flaming torches in the right direction; but Betty isn't out of the wood yet. Ragheb has cast an amorous eye on her, and persuades her to accompany him to the monastery, where Ilzor is beside himself in admiration of the mummy's work:

Our prayers to the mighty Amon-Ra have been answered, Kharis. The Princess Ananka shall be lifted from her mortal state and, sealed in this case, shall be returned with you to Egypt, there to be embraced by the sands of the past.

But Ilzor's joy is shortlived. Betty's presence forces him to reveal himself as the High Priest of Arkam, and he threatens Ragheb with the curse of Amon-Ra:

ILZOR: Your tongue shall be torn from your mouth for the vows you have sworn to falsely!
RAGHEB: Master, I am but flesh and blood . . .
ILZOR: The vultures will pick your flesh from your bones – after Kharis learns of your treachery!

Impetuously Ragheb stabs Ilzor, which is his undoing, for when Kharis finds his grandmaster dead he goes berserk despite Ragheb's cry of logic: 'No, Kharis, no! If you destroy me, the secret of the tana leaves will die . . .'

Ragheb locks himself in an old cell, but a mere door can hardly hope to stop an enraged mummy. Unfortunately he collapses a whole wing in his anger, and is buried under it along with Ragheb. Meanwhile AA, placed for safety in a mummy case, has very suitably if inexplicably turned back into a decrepit old hag, leaving only Halsey and Betty alive for the closing clinch. We wonder, however, whether they will live happily ever after, for Halsey doesn't seem to know when to let well alone. 'I'll set a crew of men to work,' he says, 'digging Kharis out of the rubble. Then send both of them back to the Scripps Museum!'

It doesn't sound like the end of the series which it proved to be. Perhaps Universal was just leaving the door open for a sequel that never came. What did come, ten years later, was *Abbott and Costello Meet the Mummy*, a rather sad parody filled with reprises of half-baked vaudeville routines such as 'the disappearing body' and 'look out, he's behind you!' When the mummy finally makes his unfrightening appearance it is in perfunctory garb, a sort of turn-of-the-century one-piece bathing suit with facial wrappings amounting to little more than a yashmak, behind which the healthy features of stuntman Eddie Parker shine cheerfully. There is such a teddy bear aspect to this mummy that it seems a pity he has to be blown up in the finale. For Abbott and Costello there was only one more film to go: the mummy comedy had been their last chance, and they (and their scriptwriters) muffed it.

ABBOTT AND COSTELLO MEET THE MUMMY (1955). Chaney's stunt man Eddie Parker takes over in his own right as a rather cuddly mummy. Costello and Richard Deacon are speechless.

'In *The Mummy*,' said Christopher Lee in 1959, 'I only kill three people, and not in
a ghastly way. I just break their necks.' Hammer's master of horror was
constantly apologizing for his horror roles, hoping to find the great dramatic
character he thought he deserved; but like Karloff before him he had been typed
by accepting the role of the Frankenstein monster, and when he played Dracula
after that, there was only one way he could go: the same way. *The Mummy* was
inevitable. It showed rather more technical certainty than anything which had
previously come out of Bray, but it turned out to be a pretty dull film, not helped
by unimaginative sets or garish colour. Only its title related to the Karloff version;
it played in fact more like *The Mummy's Hand*, and although set in the 1890s its
plot was a reprise of the Caernarvon expedition of 1922, with mysterious
retribution meeting members of the expedition which dared to invade the sanctity
of the ancient tomb. The only genuinely chilling moment comes when the

THE MUMMY (1959). A starker kind of horror returns as Christopher Lee rebels against the instructions of his custodian, George Pastell.

mummy is sent to destroy one of them who has been put away in an asylum: it breaks in on the terrified victim through the iron grille of his padded cell, from which there is clearly no escape.

By way of exposition, *The Mummy* segues into a long and boring flashback to ancient Egypt, with a few shocks but no surprises except that the tomb seems spectacularly well lit. The main action, possibly for economy's sake, is set largely at night around a country house in Victorian Britain. Mummy custodian George

Pastell (an exceedingly disappointing substitute for George Zucco) easily imports his bandaged avenger but keeps him rather mysteriously in a nearby bog, a motif borrowed perhaps from *The Mummy's Curse*. At least there is no reincarnation this time, just a great deal of savage killing by a muddy, expressionless creature which moves rather faster than usual, stalks round country lanes without meeting even the village bobby, and survives not only bullets but a harpoon through the chest. Whimsically, the script carries forward the name of Banning for the archaeologically inclined family of which Peter Cushing is eventually the sole survivor, his wife being the nominal heroine to be put into danger. ('Just stay here, Mrs Banning, I'm going round the front to check up.') But the ever-gallant Kharis refrains as usual from harming a woman. 'Tell him to put you down,' cries Cushing in his firmest Van Helsing tones. 'Put me down,' she says. And Kharis does.

One might claim for the film that the character actors killed off by the monster seem of a higher calibre than usual: Raymond Huntley, Felix Aylmer, Eddie Byrne. Right: but once they are eliminated the film fizzles to a flat, dark ending, with an obvious cyclorama behind the bog, and colour so thick that one would like to scrape off some of it with a palette knife. Even the ancient sayings lack the

THE MUMMY (1959). The bog into which the mummy sinks at the end is revealed by this still to be a small puddle in an artificial studio set. Yvonne Furneaux, Peter Cushing, Eddie Byrne, Christopher Lee.

THE CURSE OF THE MUMMY'S TOMB (1964). Producer Michael Carreras and stunt man/mummy Dickie Owen relax on the set. Only the third party takes things seriously.

usual declamatory style: 'He who defiles the graves of Egypt dies', is about as inspired as they get; though it may have lost something in the translation from HAL YISIRK MIN KABRA MISR ETWAPA. The scroll of Thoth has for some reason become the scroll of life; and it isn't the mummy who has a gammy leg on this outing, it's poor old Cushing, who got it from neglecting a broken bone during the dig. But little changes can't disguise the fact that the first mummy adventure in colour is a film deliberately composed from scraps of other films, a stodgy shocker about which there is almost nothing to say.

Five years later, Hammer tried again. They ought to have realized after *Dracula Prince of Darkness* that CinemaScope is the wrong shape for horror: it limits the possibilities for shock editing and for shadowy suspense. But they misguidedly used it again for *The Curse of the Mummy's Tomb*, which like its successor could not rise above the lower half of a double bill. Writer Henry Younger (a pseudonym for producer Michael Carreras, who didn't like to seem to be doing everything) also cramped his own style by inventing a plot in which the mummy remains dormant until half an hour from the end, and is then activated by a medallion (shades of *The Golem*) rather than tana leaves. Even then, his bandages are of too pristine a whiteness to be either convincing or frightening; this monster looks as though he would make an acceptable teddy bear. The year is 1900, and yet another Anglo-Egyptian expedition is coming to grief after opening a tomb. What they found there among other things is the mummy of a Pharaoh called Ra Antef. One of the leaders is promptly attacked and killed by savage nomads, who cut off his hand in the process, but this is an irrelevant piece of mayhem intended only to fix our attention until something supernatural happens three-quarters of an hour later. The members of the expedition are divided among themselves, especially about their brash American financier. King is a showman with a clear relationshp to Barnum: he sees the possibility of making millions by exhibiting the mummy all over the world, and refuses to sell it to the Cairo Museum. 'For the good of mankind,' expostulates Sir Giles Dalrymple. 'Who's in a better position to do 'em good, you or me?' rasps King. 'You'd let the whole lot go into some stuffy museum in a one-camel town where no one would see it except a few tourists on a wet afternoon. I can show it to the world. If folk want to be educated, I'll educate them – at ten cents a time.'

King of course is the first to go, in the back streets of London after his first, aborted, public performance, when the mummy is found to have disappeared from its sarcophagus. It turns up to confront King on his way home, making a startling appearance at the top of some ill-lit steps which he is ascending, and tosses him over a convenient bridge. (This is a *strong* mummy.) By now we have been introduced, on board ship and at somewhat boring length, to a handsome and refined but extremely mysterious gentleman of leisure called Adam Beauchamp, who rather fancies the daughter of the first archaeologist to be killed, and invites her to stay at his luxurious home overlooking Regent's Park. It turns out that Mr Younger, in an attempt to freshen up the mummy legend, has added an element of the Wandering Jew, who failed to help Christ at Calvary and was thereupon damned to live through the centuries until he did a good deed. We learn with mingled incredulity and delight at the writer's nerve that Adam, played by the perennially boyish Terence Morgan, is in fact 3,700 years old, the royal brother of the mummified Ra Antef; the unlikely explanation for his longevity is that he murdered his brother and was condemned by the gods to live forever unless Ra Antef could be revived to slay him in his turn.

The Egyptian in the fez, again dully played by George Pastell, is only a red herring this time, given to such flat pronouncements as: 'There are forces at work which even the most highly developed scientific minds at work in this country could not hope to comprehend.'

After a few more indiscriminate killings, everything comes to a head in the cellar of Adam's house, which has a unique basement passage leading to the London sewers. Ra Antef stalks into the latter holding our heroine above the swirling waters and giving Adam what he wants (i.e. death) almost as an afterthought. He then abandons Annette to the hitherto nominal hero and, as the police burst in with their useless firearms, stretches Samson-like for the roof beams and brings most of the house down upon himself, apparently (but not necessarily) expiring in a chaos of masonry, dust and dirty water. This somewhat arbitrary climax does not induce audience benevolence towards what has been a distinctly tedious adventure.

The Mummy's Shroud, which in 1966 shared a bill with *Frankenstein Created Woman*, had the distinction of being heralded by what must surely qualify as the world's most banal publicity tagline:

Beware the beat of the cloth-wrapped feet!

THE CURSE OF THE MUMMY'S TOMB (1964). The mummy looks much more frightening in this scene from the movie.

THE MUMMY'S SHROUD (1966). The mummy wrappings this time are supposedly authentic but Maggie Kimberley's look of terror could have been more convincing.

In every sense, the film lived up to the promise of its publicity, offering little more than a sensational rehash of the Tutankhamun curse stories. Members of an Egyptian archaeological expedition have failed to enjoy their success, being strangled in rapid succession by one Prem, a mummy once bodyguard to the young pharaoh whose bones they have recklessly uncovered. As in the Universal series, the mummy has guardians, in this case two of them, an obvious villain called Hasmid (who lets loose a few splendid Egyptian curses and makes one of the most threatening words sound like 'rissoles') and a toothless old crone called Haiti, the latter living at Number 8 in the Alley of the House of Mukhtar and played with more relish than sense by Catherine Lacey, once the elegant nun of *The Lady Vanishes*. It's crude stuff with only a few sudden shocks to commend it, and there aren't even any performances to enjoy after André Morell is bumped off early on. The lighting is flat, the actors cast shadows across the desert blackcloths and look pathetically unused to their costumes, and it takes 50 minutes for the mummy to come to life. Even when he does, every shot seems twice the length it should be: Universal would have got through this much plot in two reels. On the plus side there is a genuinely startling (if fake) shot of the mummy's eyes literally cracking open and, at the end, undone by the reading of the magic words, he literally tears himself into dusty pieces until only the hands are left.

There isn't a single convincing moment in this sad little film: certainly not the dialogue, which drones on in the following vein:

> – I had the feeling that if I spoke the words I might animate some horrible thing that would be uncontrollable.
> – At this stage I think we ought to remind ourselves that we're living in the twentieth century.

As usual, the mummy stalks around town without being seen, except through a crystal ball by those who command it, and after each murder retires obediently to its sarcophagus in a museum which seems woefully lax in security.

In 1971 Hammer made a genuine attempt to bring some uplift to the mummy theme by filming for the first time Bram Stoker's curious post-Dracula novel *Jewel of the Seven Stars*. This postulated what we now regard as the usual death-dealing to members of an expedition who are considered by the ancient gods to be guilty of sacrilege, but in this pre-Caernarvon case the vengeance is extracted many years later by the daughter of the leader of the expedition. Into her soul, it seems, has passed the vengeful spirit of the female mummy, which remains snug and inert in its sarcophagus while the mayhem takes place. The reincarnation theme, though quite unEgyptian in origin, had served Universal well enough, but in order to spin out this film to feature length it had to be repeatedly suggested rather than stated, and wrapped in much mumbo jumbo. *Blood from the Mummy's Tomb* seemed in any case an unlucky film: Seth Holt died while directing it, and his sometimes subtle touch was replaced by the heavy hand of Michael Carreras. Commercially it failed to attract and was consigned to the lower third of a double bill with *Dr Jekyll and Sister Hyde*. Perhaps not surprisingly, the punters resented laying down cash for an apparent horror film with so much high-faluting talk and so little mummy (strictly speaking, none at all). The movie did have a few critical adherents: Tony Rayns declared that it made the genre seem like new. The majority, however, would have concurred with John Coleman in the *New Statesman* when he called it 'not even funny peculiar'.

Astonishingly, this failure was remade nine years later, as an Anglo-American co-production with a far more generous budget. *The Awakening* at 105 minutes may be the longest horror film on record, and is almost certainly the dullest except when it is being actively unpleasant. Here Charlton Heston is the archaeologist taking much longer than the audience to realize whose spirit is killing his colleagues and whose daughter the evil is working through; Susannah York as his toothsome assistant is messily killed off at the halfway point. The final suggestion that the spirit of the unseen mummy may now bend the whole of London to its evil will was too absurd to be chilling, and at least three critics concluded their remarks with the suggestion that the project had really needed more sleep before being awakened.*

The mummy theme, limited as it was, led to fewer imitations by independent (i.e. hard-up) producers than either Frankenstein or Dracula. In 1936 there had been a Wheeler and Wolsey comedy called *Mummy's Boys*, but although the comedians played half-baked archaeologists they encountered no supernatural problems. The Universal mummy movies attracted no rip-offs until Abbott and Costello had had their way with the somewhat worn-out monster. Then in 1957 there appeared on the throwaway half of the non-circuit double bills something called *Pharaoh's Curse*, followed in 1958 by *Curse of the Faceless Man*. Though the latter postulated a monster lava-dried by the Vesuvius eruption which obliterated Pompeii, in all essential respects these were re-runs of *The Mummy's Hand*. Also in 1957, the Mexicans got into the act with *The Aztec Mummy*, and although few experiences are more horrifying than sitting through a Mexican copy of an American exploitation movie, this was followed by *The Curse of the Aztec Mummy* (1958), *Robot versus the Aztec Mummy* (1959), *The Mummy versus the Robot*** (1963), *The Attack of the Mayan Mummy* (1963) and (believe it or not) *Wrestling Women versus the Aztec Mummy* (1965). Later on, the Spaniards had a go with *The Mummy's Revenge* (1973), but luckily for the sanity of the world this provoked no sequels.

The seventies were a thin time for marauding mummies. London was briefly treated to an Egyptian film called *The Night of Counting the Years*, but though much of it took place in dark pyramids, its terrors were of the mind rather than the mummy case. *Sphinx* was a much-vaunted movie version of the best-selling thriller, but despite its authentic Egyptian settings and a few post-*Omen* shocks, it was disappointingly unsupernatural. The critics derided it, and the public passed by on the other side. Then in the early eighties a few *aficionados* managed to see an oddity called *Time Walker*, independently made for the American hinterlands on the lowest of budgets. With a tighter script, more attention to detail and a little thought for the restless audience it could have been reasonably memorable; as

---

* In fact the best dramatization of *Jewel of the Seven Stars* was made in 1971 by Thames Television. *Curse of the Mummy* was its title, and Isobel Black as the monster/victim had a splendidly haunted look.

** This may have been a disguised reissue.

things were it barely explored its quite ingenious theme, which according to the synopsis was that a mummy recovered from the Valley of the Kings actually contains a creature from another planet which had inhabited the body of an ancient Egyptian and had thus been forced to lie inside his corpse for four thousand years. Now released in an American campus, the monster briskly murders a few guests at a fancy dress 'mummy party', before assuming its original form, murmuring a few words of peace, and vanishing into the unknown along with the hero of the piece who has been fatally shot. The plagiarism from *E.T.*, even to the touching of outstretched fingers, has to be seen to be believed, and the final legend 'TO BE CONTINUED . . .' has so far proved a false prediction.

Television has dipped only an occasional finger in these waters. Harlech in 1979 got co-production finance for what started off as a drama documentary of the Caernarvon expedition, with commendable attention to period detail. The mid-Atlantic monstrosity which finally emerged, and is usually known as *The Curse of King Tut's Tomb*, was fatally compromised by the insertion of sub-plot villainy concerning Raymond Burr in brown make-up and a burnous, and a few interesting moments are all it can claim. Mad mummies have occasionally turned up in fantasy series like *The Night Stalker* and *The Outer Limits*. My own favourite among these was the episode of *Voyage to the Bottom of the Sea* in which the occupant of a sarcophagus, being transported by *Nautilus* across the Atlantic as a favour, rises in the night, strangles a few seamen, and causes those famous electronic dashboards to flash in a wide variety of colours. When the monster is finally lured back to its stone bed, and screwed down, we are offered a coda in which Captain David Hedison speaks to Admiral Richard Basehart as follows:

> CAPTAIN: But sir, why do you suppose after 3,000 years that creature suddenly came to life and started killing people?
> ADMIRAL *(sucking at pipe)*: I think, Jim . . . that there are some questions better left unasked.

Connoisseurs of sheer gall need surely seek no further.

Chapter 4

A NOTE ON ZOMBIES

And the Assorted Undead

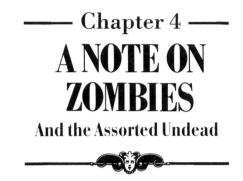

In one of their unremembered comedies of the early forties, the three Ritz Brothers ambled up to a bar in search of sustenance. 'Three zombies,' said Harry in the middle, nodding from side to side. 'I can see that,' replied the barman, 'but what'll you have to drink?'

One can scarcely forgo, in a book about the walking dead, some account of that striking if basically undramatic figure, the zombie. The word seems lately to have passed into the language with the meaning of any kind of mindless slave, but more specifically it refers to dead people who are revived, more or less intact, to serve the purposes of the living; Frankenstein monsters created not by science but by black magic. Both word and practice derive from Haiti, and throughout the twenties there were occasional references in travellers' tales to voodoo ceremonies performed in that country by the light of the moon. One series of articles by William Seabrook commanded international interest because he claimed actually to have seen the dead revived, and although the resultant flurry was somewhat less than that caused a few years earlier by the curse of Tutankhamun, there did result a play called *Zombie* which took the attention of Hollywood to the extent that in 1932, in the wake of *Dracula*, Bela Lugosi was engaged by the Halperin Brothers, two independent film-makers with almost nothing to their credit, to star in a film called *White Zombie* which was to be shot in six weeks on the Universal backlot. The fee was derisory, but Lugosi, having foolishly turned down the role of the *Frankenstein* monster, had already learned to take whatever he could get. The rock-bottom-budgeter was a box-office favourite which astonished the film world by recouping many times its own cost. Not that it had much to do with zombies in the original sense of black slaves revived to work in the sugar mills. The blacks are there, but only as a chorus, probably because the Halperins realized that the black zombie is a sombre but rather boring figure. His actions are like those of a black mummy, but he doesn't have behind him the thrill of Egyptian romance, nor is he obsessed by the urge to kill or the love of a departed dear one. He merely does what he is told. Even Lugosi's white zombies, pirates and bearded scholars, form no more than an inner cabinet obedient to Lugosi's every word. He plays Murder Legendre, a sorcerer who apart from controlling this supernatural work force is employed by a fellow with evil designs on the heroine's fortune to hypnotize her away from her intended suitor. He goes rather far, putting her into a zombie-like trance and even having her buried, presumably as a final sign to the suitor that the romance is over; but when the forces of good finally prevail, she quickly recovers and seems to be none the worse for her experience. *White Zombie* subsequently became a cult movie because of its dream-like atmosphere, which may simply have been due to slack editing, bad acting, and an insufficiency of plot. Visually nothing very frightening happens, but atmospherically the movie has something, though one is never quite sure what. Clearly its makers were not sure either, for they were unable to repeat the dose. Paramount hired them, but let them go after a rather miserable little film called *Supernatural* with an immature Carole Lombard; and their 1936 follow-up *Revolt of the Zombies* was pitiful indeed, with its strained story of a whole regiment of dead soldiers revived to fight again for their country.

The most memorable zombie with the shortest screen time is undoubtedly the nameless one which menaced Bob Hope in *The Ghost Breakers* (1940). Played with a true sense of terror by Noble Johnson, he provided a totally unexpected savoury course for a film which had been a feast of wisecracks. (Momentarily petrified by rolls of thunder and flashes of lightning, Hope recovers with: 'Basil Rathbone must be throwing a party.') The heroine, Paulette Goddard, insists on travelling alone and by night to the spooky Cuban castle she has inherited. She finds its moonlit corridors full of coffins (one containing a freshly dead friend) and organs which play themselves, not to mention a genuine ectoplasmic ghost; but of course Mr Hope is not far behind, nervously accompanied by his black valet Willie Best.

WHITE ZOMBIE (1932). Bela Lugosi, as the splendidly named Murder Legendre, has at his command a whole roomful of zombies, including the heroine.

('I'm going upstairs to look round,' Hope tells him. 'If two fellows come hurrying down, let the first one go. That'll be me.') What none of them know is that the castle has a giant black undead guard, posted to repel strangers. He is revived by a witchlike old woman in a shack by the water's edge, and within seconds he is lurching, with vague malevolence, up the castle walk. His role is brief indeed – after causing a shriek and a shudder he is disarmed before he can do any damage – but as photographed by Charles Lang he presents a few images guaranteed to give nightmares to schoolboys. When the story was remade for Martin and Lewis as *Scared Stiff*, the zombie did not have the same frisson.

Then there was *I Walked with a Zombie* (1943). At the time the title seemed outlandish, though it had been used for a series of up-market magazine articles. Producer Val Lewton called his story 'Jane Eyre in the tropics', but it played on the thin side, with its timid nurse-companion going out to the West Indies to look after the ailing wife of a remote plantation-owner. It is the invalid who, after hypnotic treatment, has been reduced to a zombie-like state, without speech or much sensibility; yet of course she is not technically a zombie at all, never having been dead in the first place. Most of the film's chills come not from horror itself but from the apparent imminence of it, with lowering skies, shadows in the night, and curtains blowing in the wind. Then there is the walk taken by the two women on their way to a voodoo ceremony which the nurse has been told may help her

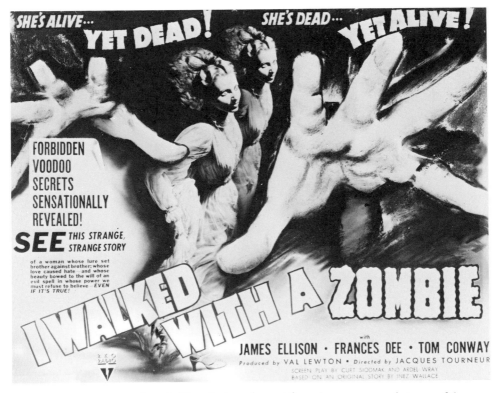

I WALKED WITH A ZOMBIE (1943). The ad, though great fun, gives no sense whatever of the style of the film.

patient's condition: they are stopped by encounters with ritual artefacts, and (at last) with a real zombie. For all its style, though, *I Walked with a Zombie* doesn't add up to a great deal, and its images do not linger in the mind as do those of the similarly dreamy *Vampyr*, which may well have inspired it.

The major American studios tended to leave zombies well alone. Even Universal never touched them, and that can hardly have been a matter of taste. Warners did star Karloff himself, in 1936, in a smoothly made movie called *The Walking Dead*, all impressionist shadows in the best Michael Curtiz manner. Karloff himself was the 'zombie', a pianist electrically brought back to life, or a shuffling semblance of it, after unjust electrocution for murder. Edmund Gwenn, of all people, was the 'mad' scientist in charge. Karloff looked picturesque, with his taut face and grey-streaked hair, but apart from scaring to death those who framed him he found no reason to live again, and gladly returned to his own grave by the expedient of being shot to death by police. For the next twenty years, with the exception of the Lewton film, native zombies figured only in the cheapest of potboilers such as *Valley of the Zombies* and *The Zombies of Mora Tau*, neither of which has lingered in the memory of film buffs. The theme was of course adapted for general use. *Back from the Dead* (1957) had a tropical zombie cult reincarnating a man's first wife in the body of his second. But by then modernization was afoot. *The Creature with the Atom Brain* (1956) imagined the dead being returned to life by atomic radiation, to be controlled by the familiar mad scientist. (This plot was virtually reprised in a 1974 telemovie called *The Dead Don't Die*, with Ray Milland; it seemed quite old-fashioned by then.) Possibly the last of the old-style zombies to emanate from Hollywood were those teased by Boris Karloff in *The Incredible Dr Markesan* (1962), one of television's *Thriller* series: he revived a number of the colleagues who in life had reviled him as a madman, and forced them to parade by night, weary and rotting, around his derelict house. At the time it seemed so macabre that British censors cut out all the close-ups before transmission.*

The British had no truck with zombies until the sixties. Then in 1964 director Terence Fisher, on leave from Hammer, directed a second feature called *The Earth Dies Screaming*, about a world of the future controlled by robots who raise people from the dead to be their slaves. It didn't work at all, but may have given an idea or two to the Hammer folk themselves, who in 1966, ten years after *The Curse of Frankenstein*, released *Plague of the Zombies*, directed (and written) not by Fisher but by John Gilling. A very good, and very frightening, piece of work it was, and it may well have influenced the revival of the zombie theme in the seventies. Gilling went back to basics, in that his zombies were revived as cheap labour, but they were British corpses, required for work in a Cornish tin mine. (Their master, played by John Carson, was said to have learned the trick in the West Indies.) The

---

* Karloff had of course appeared in several 'mad doctor' shockers in which he brought himself or others back from the dead, including *The Man Who Changed His Mind* (1936), *The Man They Could Not Hang* (1939), and *The Man with Nine Lives* (1940). The last-named concerned frozen therapy, which later re-emerged as crionics, i.e. freezing the terminally ill and bringing them back to life when a cure has been found. This development of the sixties and seventies has sparked off nothing but TV movies, including *Live Again, Die Again* and *Chiller*.

THE WALKING DEAD (1936). Boris Karloff obviously has cause to regret being brought back to life.

scene in which the half-rotted undead scrabble their way out of graves in an English churchyard is still talked of in hushed whispers by connoisseurs of the genre. Meanwhile in 1965 Roger Corman, at the tag-end of his Edgar Allan Poe cycle, produced in *The Tomb of Ligeia* the story of the spirit of Vincent Price's first wife taking over and reanimating the dead body of his second; and the complications didn't stop there.

Within a very few years the lunacy grew even wilder. The trouble with zombies had always been that they had little character of their own and shambled around at the will of other people. George A. Romero changed all that. In *Night of the Living Dead* (1969) his zombies definitely have their own strength and will to harm. Opening the cinema floodgates to admit every conceivable kind of cinematic nastiness, he created a whole army of recently buried dead men (and women) roaming around the countryside in search of human flesh as food. Later on, the same director rather overdid his effects in *Zombies: Dawn of the Dead* (1979) in which his decomposing army shambles in colour for most of the film round a shopping mall. (Zombies, according to the new creed, always return to the locations where they spent much time in life; and incidentally they can be disposed of only by having their heads removed or exploded.) By now zombies were back with a vengeance; in mostly inferior films, it is true, but then that had always been the case. *Twice Told Tales* (1963) included Nathaniel Hawthorne's story of a magic flute which restores life to the dead. There were *Astro Zombies* (1969), though their story on examination proved closer to Frankenstein than to Legendre. In *Tales from the Crypt* (1972) Peter Cushing, or what was left of him after several months underground, came back from the grave on Valentine's Day to give his wife an unexpected present. *Psychomania* in the following year brought

TALES FROM THE CRYPT (1972). Peter Cushing returns for vengeance after some months underground. Some audiences wished he had phoned in his message.

back echoes of our starting point, 'The Monkey's Paw', with its story of a distraught mother who makes a pact with Satan to bring back her son, killed and mutilated in a motor-cycle accident: the end result is a horde of undead motor-cyclists terrorizing the country. A few months later America contributed another variant on the W. W. Jacobs story: *Dead of Night* concerned a Vietnam veteran, posted missing, who returns to his home town amid scenes of great celebration . . . until the family begins to notice his peculiar habits. *The Manchurian Candidate* (1962) had already brought the theme into politics by postulating a brainwashed veteran programmed by the communists into eliminating far-right candidates for the American presidency; in *The Resurrection of Zachary Wheeler* (1972) a synthetic body was created for a presidential candidate badly injured in a car crash. In *Shanks* (1974) Marcel Marceau played a mad puppeteer who extended his talents to the control of the dead. In *Don't Open the Window* (1974) a sound machine designed to eliminate insects in the soil accidentally stimulated a cemeteryful of dead, who thereafter prowled the countryside as carnivorous zombies. In a Spanish produc-tion of the same year, *Beyond the Living Dead*, yet another mad doctor program-med yet another batch of long-dead to murder his rivals. 1974 was a big year for zombies, for it also produced *Neither the Sea nor the Sand*, an abject curiosity in which Susan Hampshire falls for Michael Petrovitch without realizing that he's really dead . . . and decomposing. And let's not forget Hammer's *The Legend of the Seven Golden Vampires*, in which Dracula went to China and found at every crisis that he needed the help of an army of the local undead! A lull then prevailed until 1980, when John Carpenter in *The Fog* presented an evil band of long-drowned fishermen who returned in a sinister fog bank and laid waste to their old home town; and within a year or two, stimulated by the generally accepted new permissiveness in the horror genre, we were being offered all the nastiness the depraved brain might imagine. *Dead and Buried* (1981) was comparatively discreet in its account of a village all of whose inhabitants are zombies killed and revived by the undertaker; but *The Evil Dead* (1982) encountered a great deal of censor trouble for its adolescent excesses tacked on to a thin script about savage zombies brought to unpleasant life when a holidaymaker reads from an ancient Sumerian manuscript.

It was long rumoured, from the middle sixties, that a film existed under the title *The Incredibly Strange Creatures who Stopped Living and Became Mixed-Up Zombies*, but although it figures in a good many trade lists, I have met nobody who can claim actually to have seen it. If it is a spoof title with no movie behind it, as seems likely, we should perhaps accept it as a signal that zombie films had nowhere to go, having already been numbered among the poorest of Hollywood's poor; even the senior Lon Chaney had derived neither pleasure nor profit from reviving the dead in his 1925 comedy-thriller *The Monster*. They keep on coming all the same, and one can even feel quite affectionate towards such items as the ghoulish *City of the Dead*, with its ruthless sacrifice of the heroine and its abundance of white graveyard fog. In 1985 even the highbrow critics seemed quite charitably disposed towards *A Nightmare on Elm Street*, an outright shocker devoted to inspiring unpleasant dreams; and it is worth recalling that a celebrated classic of 1919, *The Cabinet of Dr Caligari*, concerned a white-faced so-called somnambulist who all too clearly, for those with eyes to see, was nothing more nor less than a zombie.

Nor was burial alive a popular theme, though by definition it featured in all the mummy films. The threat of it was the mainstay in 1931 of a rather tawdry little mystery called *Murder by the Clock*, which was banned by the British censor after two days' exposure at the Plaza Cinema in Regent Street; there had been public outcry at its morbid theme of an old lady who builds herself a tomb equipped with alarm systems, all of which are mysteriously activated after her entombment, and at Irving Pichel's too-vivid depiction of a skulking moron. Four years later in *The Crime of Dr Crespi*, Erich Von Stroheim, borrowing an idea from Poe, gave his rival in love a paralysing drug which caused him to be buried alive; luckily for the victim, this foul deed was discovered in the very nick of time. Many years later, in 1962, Roger Corman filmed *The Premature Burial* not only at full force but with added plot complications; Ray Milland was the man with the tomb full of modern conveniences, but he was prey to plots from greedy relatives and rivals. A less frantic and more efficient treatment of the theme had been used in Val Lewton's *Isle of the Dead* (1945), in which, on a Greek island riddled with plague, a woman prone to cataleptic trances is pronounced dead after a series of tests, and duly buried. Later, the camera tracks in through darkness to her coffin, as water drips on the sound track; and scratching, first faint and then desperate, is heard from inside the coffin lid. The sequence is at least as terrifying as David Gray's dream of being buried alive in *Vampyr*.

Premature burial was of course an obsession with Poe. It turns up in the films of *The Oblong Box*, *Morella* (in *Tales of Terror*), *The Black Cat*, and above all in *The Fall of the House of Usher*, with its theme of a rotten aristocratic family in a rotten unstable house, which to Poe doubtless symbolized the world in which we all find ourselves. None of the film versions so far has been able to convey the horror of the climax to the original story, which may be left to speak for itself. The unhappy visitor to the House of Usher is reading to his host, after the crypt burial of the latter's cataleptic sister, from Sir Launcelot Canning's *Mad Trist*:

> I had arrived at that well-known portion of the story where Ethelred, the hero of the Trist, having sought in vain for peaceable admission into the dwelling of the hermit, proceeds to make good an entrance by force. Here, it will be remembered, the words of the narrative run thus:–
>
> 'And Ethelred, who was by nature of a doughty heart, and who was now mighty withal, on account of the powerfulness of the wine which he had drunken, waited no longer to hold parley with the hermit, who, in sooth, was of an obstinate and maliceful turn, but, feeling the rain upon his shoulders, and fearing the rising of the tempest, uplifted his mace outright, and, with blows, made quickly room in the plankings of the door for his gauntleted hand; and now pulling therewith sturdily, he so cracked, and ripped, and tore all asunder, that the noise of the dry and hollow-sounding wood alarummed and reverberated throughout the forest.'
>
> At the termination of this sentence I started, and for a moment paused; for it appeared to me (although I at once concluded that my excited fancy had deceived me) – it appeared to me that, from some very remote portion of the mansion, there came, indistinctly, to my ears, what might have been, in its exact similarity of character, the echo (but a stifled and dull one certainly) of the very cracking and ripping sound which Sir Launcelot had so particularly described. It was, beyond doubt, the coincidence alone which had arrested my attention; for, amid the rattling of the sashes

of the casements, and the ordinary commingled noises of the still increasing storm, the sound, in itself, had nothing, surely, which should have interested or disturbed me. I continued the story:–

'But the good champion Ethelred, now entering within the door, was sore enraged and amazed to perceive no signal of the maliceful hermit; but, in the stead thereof, a dragon of a scaly and prodigious demeanour, and of a fiery tongue, which sate in guard before a palace of gold, with a floor of silver; and upon the wall there hung a shield of shining brass with this legend enwritten:–

> Who entereth herein, a conqueror hath bin;
> Who slayeth the dragon, the shield he shall win.

And Ethelred uplifted his mace, and struck upon the head of the dragon, which fell before him, and gave up his pesty breath, with a shriek so horrid and harsh, and withal so piercing, that Ethelred had fain to close his ears with his hands against the dreadful noise of it, the like whereof was never before heard.'

Here again I paused abruptly, and now with a feeling of wild amazement – for there could be no doubt whatever that, in this instance, I did actually hear (although from what direction it proceeded I found it impossible to say) a low and apparently distant, but harsh, protracted, and most unusual screaming or grating sound – the exact counterpart of what my fancy had already conjured up for the dragon's unnatural shriek as described by the romancer.

Oppressed as I certainly was, upon the occurrence of this second and most extraordinary coincidence, by a thousand conflicting sensations, in which wonder and extreme terror were predominant, I still retained sufficient presence of mind to avoid exciting, by any observation, the sensitive nervousness of my companion. I was by no means certain that he had noticed the sound in question; although, assuredly, a strange alteration had, during the last few minutes, taken place in his demeanour. From a position fronting my own, he had gradually brought round his chair, so as to sit with his face to the door of the chamber; and thus I could but partially perceive his features, although I saw that his lips trembled as if he were murmuring inaudibly. His head had dropped upon his breast – yet I knew that he was not asleep, from the wide and rigid opening of the eye as I caught a glance of it in profile. The motion of his body, too, was at variance with this idea – for he rocked from side to side with a gentle yet constant and uniform sway. Having rapidly taken notice of all this, I resumed the narrative of Sir Launcelot, which thus proceeded:–

'And now, the champion, having escaped from the terrible fury of the dragon, bethinking himself of the brazen shield, and of the breaking up of the enchantment which was upon it, removed the carcass from out of the way before him, and approached valorously over the silver pavement of the castle to where the shield was upon the wall; which in sooth tarried not for his full coming, but fell down at his feet upon the silver floor, with a mighty great and terrible ringing sound.'

No sooner had these syllables passed my lips, than – as if a shield of brass had indeed, at the moment, fallen heavily upon a floor of silver – I became aware of a distinct, hollow, metallic, and clangorous, yet apparently muffled reverberation. Completely unnerved, I leaped to my feet; but the measured rocking movement of Usher was undisturbed. I rushed to the chair in which he sat. His eyes were bent fixedly before him, and throughout his whole countenance there reigned a stony rigidity. But, as I placed my hand upon his shoulder, there came a strong shudder over his whole person; a sickly smile quivered on his lips; and I saw that he spoke in a low, hurried, and gibbering murmur, as if unconscious of my presence. Bending closely over him, I at length drank in the hideous import of his words.

'Not hear it? – yes, I hear it, and *have* heard it. Long – long – long – many minutes, many hours, many days, have I heard it – yet I dared not – oh, pity me, miserable wretch that I am! – I dared not – I *dared* not speak! *We have put her living in the tomb!* Said I not that my senses were acute? I *now* tell you that I heard her first feeble movements in the hollow coffin. I heard them – many, many days ago – yet I dared not – *I dared not speak!* And now – to-night – Ethelred – ha! ha! – the breaking of the hermit's door, and the death-cry of the dragon, and the clangour of the shield! – say, rather, the rending of her coffin, and the grating of the iron hinges of her prison, and her struggles within the coppered archway of the vault! Oh, whither shall I fly? Will she not be here anon? Is she not hurrying to upbraid me for my haste? Have I not heard her footstep on the stair? Do I not distinguish that heavy and horrible beating of her heart? Madman!' – here he sprang furiously to his feet, and shrieked out his syllables, as if in the effort he were giving up his soul – '*Madman! I tell you that she now stands without the door!*'

As if in the superhuman energy of his utterance there had been found the potency of a spell – the huge antique panels to which the speaker pointed threw slowly back, upon the instant, their ponderous and ebony jaws. It was the work of the rushing gust – but then without those doors there *did* stand the lofty and enshrouded figure of the Lady Madeline of Usher. There was blood upon her white robes, and the evidence of some bitter struggle upon every portion of her emaciated frame. For a moment she remained trembling and reeling to and fro upon the threshold – then, with a low moaning cry, fell heavily inward upon the person of her brother, and in her violent and now final death-agonies, bore him to the floor a corpse, and a victim to the terrors he had anticipated.

From that chamber, and from that mansion, I fled aghast. The storm was still abroad in all its wrath as I found myself crossing the old causeway. Suddenly there shot along the path a wild light, and I turned to see whence a gleam so unusual could have issued; for the vast house and its shadows were alone behind me. The radiance was that of the full, setting, and blood-red moon, which now shone vividly through that once barely-discernible fissure, of which I have before spoken as extending from the roof of the building, in a zigzag direction, to the base. While I gazed, this fissure rapidly widened – there came a fierce breath of the whirlwind – the entire orb of the satellite burst at once upon my sight – my brain reeled as I saw the mighty walls rushing asunder – there was a long tumultuous shouting sound like a voice of a thousand waters – and the deep and dank tarn at my feet closed sullenly and silently over the fragments of the 'House of Usher'.

Finally, one should mention the handful of somewhat necrophiliac movies in which obsessed gentlemen kept the bodies of their dead wives in handy caskets, but *failed* to revive them. Karloff was thus unlucky with Lugosi's wife in *The Black Cat* (1934), and with his own in *The Climax* (1944). Lugosi was no more fortunate, even by infusing his dead spouses with virgins' blood, in either *The Corpse Vanishes* (1942) or *Voodoo Man* (1944). As for Vincent Price, in Corman's 1963 remake of *The Raven* he has already given up the attempt when the picture starts, and on admitting Peter Lorre through the front door feels the need to apologize for the imposing glass catafalque which impedes their progress.

'I keep my wife in the hall,' he explains.
Lorre shrugs. 'Where else?' he asks.

A CHRONOLOGY OF THE WALKING DEAD

THE COUNT
at **Universal:**

DRACULA (1930): Bela Lugosi, Edward Van Sloan, Dwight Frye. Writer:
  Garrett Fort, from the play by Hamilton Deane and the novel by Bram
  Stoker. Director: Tod Browning. Photographer: Karl Freund. Art director:
  Charles D. Hall. Music: Tchaikovsky.

DRACULA'S DAUGHTER (1936): Edward Van Sloan, with Gloria Holden,
  Otto Kruger. Writer: Garrett Fort. Director: Lambert Hillyer. Photographer:
  George Robinson. Music: Heinz Roemheld. Art director: Albert S.
  D'Agostino.

SON OF DRACULA (1943): Lon Chaney Jnr, with J. Edward Bromberg.
  Writer: Eric Taylor. Director: Robert Siodmak. Photographer: George
  Robinson. Music: Hans Salter. Art directors: John Goodman, Martin Obzina.

HOUSE OF FRANKENSTEIN (1944): John Carradine, with Boris Karloff,
  J. Carrol Naish. Writers: Edward T. Lowe, Curt Siodmak. Director: Erle C.
  Kenton. Photographer: George Robinson. Music: Hans Salter. Art directors:
  John Goodman, Martin Obzina.

HOUSE OF DRACULA (1945): John Carradine, with Onslow Stevens.
  Writer: Edward T. Lowe. Director: Erle C. Kenton. Photographer: George
  Robinson. Music: Edgar Fairchild. Art directors: John Goodman, Martin
  Obzina.

ABBOTT AND COSTELLO MEET FRANKENSTEIN (1948): Bela Lugosi,
  with Lenore Aubert. Writers: Robert Lees, Frederic I. Rinaldo, John Grant.
  Director: Charles Barton. Photographer: Charles Van Enger. Music: Frank
  Skinner. Art directors: Bernard Herzbrun, Hilyard Brown.

at **Hammer:**

DRACULA (HORROR OF DRACULA) (1958): Christopher Lee, Peter
  Cushing, with John Van Eyssen. Writer: James Sangster. Director: Terence
  Fisher. Photographer: Jack Asher. Music: James Bernard. Art director:
  Bernard Robinson.

THE BRIDES OF DRACULA (1960): David Peel, with Martita Hunt, Peter
 Cushing. Writers: James Sangster, Peter Bryan, Edward Percy. Director:
 Terence Fisher. Photographer: Jack Asher. Music: Malcolm Williamson.

KISS OF THE VAMPIRE (1962): Noel Willman, with Clifford Evans. Writer:
 John Elder (Anthony Hinds). Director: Don Sharp. Photographer: Alan
 Hume. Music: James Bernard.

DRACULA, PRINCE OF DARKNESS (1965): Christopher Lee, with Philip
 Latham, Andrew Keir. Writer: John Sansom. Director: Terence Fisher.
 Photographer: Michael Reed. Music: James Bernard.

DRACULA HAS RISEN FROM THE GRAVE (1968): Christopher Lee, with
 Rupert Davies. Writer: John Elder (Anthony Hinds). Director: Freddie
 Francis. Photographer: Arthur Grant. Music: James Bernard.

TASTE THE BLOOD OF DRACULA (1969): Christopher Lee, with Geoffrey
 Keen, Peter Sallis, John Carson, Ralph Bates. Writer: John Elder (Anthony
 Hinds). Director: Peter Sasdy. Photographer: Arthur Grant. Music: James
 Bernard.

SCARS OF DRACULA (1970): Christopher Lee, with Dennis Waterman,
 Patrick Troughton. Writer: John Elder (Anthony Hinds). Director: Roy Ward
 Baker. Photographer: Moray Grant. Music: James Bernard.

DRACULA A.D. 1972 (1972): Christopher Lee, Peter Cushing. Writer: Don
 Houghton. Director: Alan Gibson. Photographer: Richard Bush. Music:
 Michael Vickers.

THE SATANIC RITES OF DRACULA (1973): Christopher Lee, Peter
 Cushing. Writer: Don Houghton. Director: Alan Gibson. Photographer:
 Brian Probyn. Music: John Cacavas.

THE LEGEND OF THE SEVEN GOLDEN VAMPIRES (1974): John Forbes
 Robertson, Peter Cushing. Writer: Don Houghton. Director: Roy Ward
 Baker. Photographers: John Wilcox, Roy Ford. Music: James Bernard.

Hammer's distaff side:

THE VAMPIRE LOVERS (1970): Ingrid Pitt, Peter Cushing. Writers: Tudor
 Gates, Harry Fine, Michael Styles. Director: Roy Ward Baker.
 Photographer: Moray Grant. Music: Harry Robinson.

LUST FOR A VAMPIRE (1970): Suzanna Leigh, Yutta Stensgard, Mike Raven
 with Ralph Bates. Writer: Tudor Gates. Director: James Sangster.
 Photographer: David Muir. Music: Harry Robinson.

TWINS OF EVIL (1971): Madeleine and Mary Collinson, Peter Cushing.
 Writer: Tudor Gates. Director: John Hough. Photographer: Dick Bush.
 Music: Harry Robinson.

THE MONSTER

at **Universal**

FRANKENSTEIN (1931): Boris Karloff, Colin Clive, Edward Van Sloan, Dwight Frye. Writers: Garrett Fort, Francis Edward Faragoh, John L. Balderston (Robert Florey uncredited). Director: James Whale. Photographer: Arthur Edeson. Music: David Broekman. Art director: Charles D. Hall.

THE BRIDE OF FRANKENSTEIN (1935): Boris Karloff, Colin Clive, Dwight Frye, with Ernest Thesiger, Elsa Lanchester. Writers: John L. Balderston, William Hurlbut. Director: James Whale. Photographer: John Mescall. Music: Franz Waxman. Art director: Charles D. Hall.

SON OF FRANKENSTEIN (1939): Boris Karloff, Bela Lugosi, Basil Rathbone, Lionel Atwill. Writer: Willis Cooper. Director: Rowland V. Lee. Photographer: George Robinson. Music: Frank Skinner. Art director: Jack Otterson.

THE GHOST OF FRANKENSTEIN (1942): Lon Chaney Jnr, Bela Lugosi, Lionel Atwill, with Cedric Hardwicke. Writers: W. Scott Darling, Eric Taylor. Director: Erle C. Kenton. Photographers: Milton Krasner, Woody Bredell. Music: Charles Previn.

FRANKENSTEIN MEETS THE WOLF MAN (1943): Bela Lugosi, Lionel Atwill, Dwight Frye, with Lon Chaney Jnr as the wolf man. Writer: Curt Siodmak. Director: Roy William Neill. Photographer: George Robinson. Music: Hans Salter. Art directors: John Goodman, Martin Obzina.

HOUSE OF FRANKENSTEIN (1944): Glenn Strange, Boris Karloff, Lionel Atwill, with Lon Chaney as the wolf man. Writers: Edward T. Lowe, Curt Siodmak. Director: Erle C. Kenton. Photographer: George Robinson. Music: Hans Salter. Art directors: John Goodman, Martin Obzina.

HOUSE OF DRACULA (1945): Glenn Strange, Lionel Atwill, with Onslow Stevens and Lon Chaney Jnr as the wolf man. Writer: Edward T. Lowe. Director: Erle C. Kenton. Photographer: George Robinson. Music: Edgar Fairchild. Art directors: John Goodman, Martin Obzina.

ABBOTT AND COSTELLO MEET FRANKENSTEIN (1948): Glenn Strange, with Bela Lugosi as Dracula and Lon Chaney Jnr as the wolf man. Writers: Robert Lees, Frederic I. Rinaldo, John Grant. Director: Charles Barton. Photographer: Charles Van Enger. Music: Frank Skinner.

at **Hammer:**

THE CURSE OF FRANKENSTEIN (1956): Christopher Lee, Peter Cushing, with Robert Urquhart. Writer: James Sangster. Director: Terence Fisher. Photographer: Jack Asher. Music: James Bernard. Art director: Ted Marshall.

THE REVENGE OF FRANKENSTEIN (1958): Michael Gwynn, Peter Cushing, with Oscar Quitak. Writers: James Sangster, Hurford Janes. Director: Terence Fisher. Photographer: Jack Asher. Music: Leonard Salzedo.

THE EVIL OF FRANKENSTEIN (1964): Kiwi Kingston, Peter Cushing, with
Peter Woodthorpe. Writer: John Elder (Anthony Hinds). Director: Freddie
Francis. Photographer: John Wilcox. Music: Don Banks.

FRANKENSTEIN CREATED WOMAN (1966): Susan Denberg, Peter
Cushing. Writer: John Elder (Anthony Hinds). Director: Terence Fisher.
Photographer: Arthur Grant. Music: James Bernard. Art director: Don
Mingaye.

FRANKENSTEIN MUST BE DESTROYED (1969): Freddie Jones, Peter
Cushing. Writer: Bert Batt. Director: Terence Fisher. Photographer: Arthur
Grant. Music: James Bernard. Art director: Bernard Robinson.

THE HORROR OF FRANKENSTEIN (1970): Dave Prowse, Ralph Bates.
Writers: James Sangster, Jeremy Burnham. Director: James Sangster.
Photographer: Moray Grant. Music: James Bernard. Art director: Scott
McGregor.

FRANKENSTEIN AND THE MONSTER FROM HELL (1973): Dave
Prowse, Peter Cushing, Shane Briant. Writer: John Elder (Anthony Hinds).
Director: Terence Fisher. Photographer: Brian Probyn. Music: James
Bernard. Art director: Scott McGregor.

THE EGYPTIAN
at **Universal**

THE MUMMY (1932): Boris Karloff, Edward Van Sloan. Writer: John
Balderston. Director: Karl Freund. Photographer: Charles Stumar. Music:
uncredited. Art director: Charles D. Hall.

THE MUMMY'S HAND (1940): Tom Tyler, George Zucco. Writers: Griffin
Jay, Maxwell Shane. Director: Christy Cabanne. Photographer: Woody
Bredell. Music: uncredited. Art director: Jack Otterson.

THE MUMMY'S TOMB (1942): Lon Chaney Jnr/Eddie Parker, Turhan Bey,
George Zucco. Writers: Griffin Jay, Henry Sucher. Director: Harold Young.
Photographer: George Robinson. Music: Hans Salter. Art director: Jack
Otterson.

THE MUMMY'S GHOST (1944): Lon Chaney Jnr/Eddie Parker, John
Carradine. Writers: Griffin Jay, Henry Sucher, Brenda Weisberg. Director:
Reginald LeBorg. Photographer: William Sickner. Music: Hans Salter. Art
directors: John and Abraham Grossman.

THE MUMMY'S CURSE (1944): Lon Chaney Jnr/Eddie Parker, Peter Coe,
Martin Kosleck. Writer: Bernard Schubert. Director: Leslie Goodwins.
Photographer: Virgin Miller. Music: Paul Sawtell. Art director: John
Goodman, Martin Obzina.

ABBOTT AND COSTELLO MEET THE MUMMY (1955): Eddie Parker,
Michael Ansara, Kurt Katch. Writer: John Grant. Director: Charles Lamont.
Photographer: Charles Van Enger. Music: Joseph Gershenson.

at **Hammer:**

THE MUMMY (1959): Christopher Lee, George Pastell, with Peter Cushing. Writer: James Sangster. Director: Terence Fisher. Photographer: Jack Asher. Music: Frank Reizenstein. Art director: Bernard Robinson.

CURSE OF THE MUMMY'S TOMB (1964): Dickie Owen, Terence Morgan. Writer: Henry Younger (Michael Carreras). Director: Michael Carreras. Photographer: Otto Heller. Music: Carlo Martelli. Art director: Bernard Robinson.

THE MUMMY'S SHROUD (1966): Dickie Owen, Catherine Lacey, Roger Delgado. Writer/director: John Gilling. Photographer: Arthur Grant. Music. Don Banks.

BLOOD FROM THE MUMMY'S TOMB (1971): Valerie Leon. Writer: Christopher Wicking. Directors: Seth Holt, Michael Carreras. Photographer: Arthur Grant. Music: Tristan Cary.

INDEX

NB. Only principal references, with comments, are given. Bold numbers indicate illustrations. Titles of films are in small capitals, books in italics.

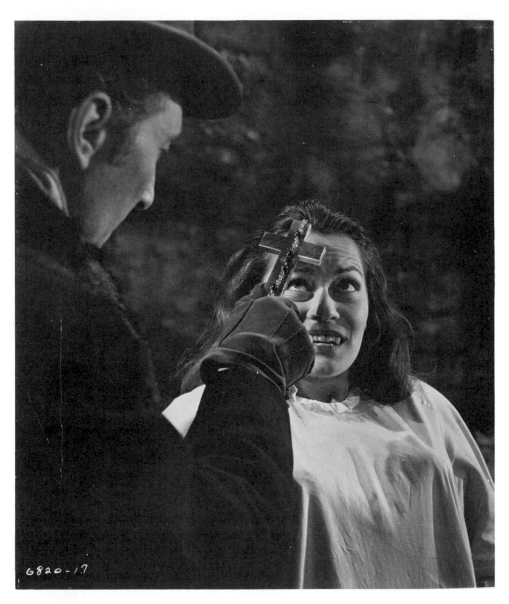

6820-17

Peter Cushing as Van Helsing was always firm with vampires. In this scene from *Dracula* (1958) he knows the surest way to deal with Carol Marsh, who has returned from the dead in her shroud to put the bite on her former friends.